Paul on Mazursky

Paul on Mazursky

SAM WASSON

WESLEYAN UNIVERSITY PRESS

Middletown, Connecticut

Wesleyan University Press

Middletown, CT 06459

www.wesleyan.edu/wespress

© 2011 Sam Wasson

All rights reserved

Manufactured in the United States of America

All photos courtesy of Paul Mazursky.

Wesleyan University Press is a member of the
Green Press Initiative. The paper used in this book
meets their minimum requirement for recycled paper.

Library of Congress Cataloging-in-Publication
Data appear on the last printed page of this book.

5 4 3 2 1

For Carly & Katie & Molly & Tommy

The most difficult thing to do

is laugh with compassion.

—Paul Mazursky

Contents

Acknowledgements

It was my parents who introduced me, through *An Unmarried Woman* and *Blume in Love*, to Paul Mazursky. Mom was—and still is—furious that Erica Benton (Jill Clayburgh) didn't go off with Saul Kaplan (Alan Bates), and I clearly remember where I was when Dad told me that *Blume* was a *real* grown-up love story, and one day, when I had suffered a bit more, I would see what he meant. Well, I've suffered. Years later, my friend David Freeman introduced me to Mazursky himself and in no time I realized that if I was truly going to know Mazursky, Mazursky would have to introduce me to Alan Ladd Jr. and Mel Brooks. He did. And then I started getting ideas. I loved Mazursky's people, and the more I met, the more I got hooked on loving them. So I called Alex Horwitz, who introduced me to Jill Clayburgh and Albert Wolsky; and I called Dick Pearce and Lynzee Klingman, who introduced me to Donn Cambern and Fred Murphy; and I called David Freeman (again), who called Josh Greenfeld, and also, Elaine Kagan to see if she would introduce me to Gena Rowlands (she did); and somewhere in there I spoke with Lynn Povich, who told me just how to get in touch with Juliet Taylor, which I did, and we met (it was snowing). Wait, have I mentioned the Market? I have to mention the Market. In the unwritten musical of Mazursky's life, they are the chorus. Weekday mornings, between 9:00 a.m. and 10:00 a.m. you'll find them—Charlie Bragg, Freeman, Jeff Garlin, Greg Pritikin, George Segal, Ronnie Schell, and a few others—presiding over the most hilarious breakfast table in Los Angeles. They're so funny that—take my advice—if you want to put in an appearance, you really should hit at least three or four other tables in advance just to try out your material. I am not exaggerating.

And in the middle of all of this, there's my *mishpacha*, watching Mazursky's movies, talking about them, thinking about them, loving them, liking them, getting angry, feeling good, feeling *anything*, and then letting me in on that feeling, or that thought, so I could bounce it off mine, or Paul's, or the movie itself, to see if, and how, it bounced back. They are Genevieve Angelson, Gary Copeland, Pablo Davanzo, Maria Diaz, Bob Dolman, Jack Dolman, Joe Dolman, Kate Eickmeyer, Amalia Ellison, Rachel Fleischer, Judy Gingold, Max Goldblatt, Mark and Ann Goldblatt, Nathan Lane, Lynne

Littman, Cory Madley, Patrick McGilligan, Andrea Martin, Nicky Martin, Jocelyn Medawar, Lisa Petrazzollo, Sarah Shepard, Steve Shepard, Holland Sutton, and Sophie Wasson. I want to give my fondest thanks also to Joanna Ney, who curated the definitive Mazursky retrospective at Lincoln Center ("The Magic of Paul Mazursky," May 4–11, 2007); Maryte Kavaliauskas, who shared with me her own work on Mazursky; and Jeff Kanew, who drew me into a dark corner and told me just what happened between him and Paul that magical night at Rage.

At Wesleyan University Press, Stephanie Elliott, Parker Smathers, Leslie Starr, and Suzanna Tamminen should have their hands shaken (by me and amongst themselves). In the thornier groves of academe, this funny book might have been taken for a weed. It's to their credit that it wasn't. Jeanine Basinger, Lisa Dombrowski, and Eric Levy, you were always, always there, and more than once. I broke down, but you put me back.

To my agent David Halpern, Kathy Robbins, Rachelle Bergstein, Ian King, Arielle Asher, and Michael Gillespie, and everyone else at The Robbins Office: I don't know if this is the right venue to bring this up, but I've given it some serious thought and I think we should live together.

Before I go, I want to thank—sincerely thank—the Mazurskys. Betsy, Jill, Meg, Carly, Katie, Tommy, Molly, Steve, and John, you didn't have to let me in, but you did. I really, really hope you love this book. And Paul . . . Paul! You are my Richard Brooks.

Mazursky!

The Jewish Foreword Mel on Mazursky

On the phone.

MEL BROOKS: You're really writing a book about Paul Mazursky?

SAM WASSON: Yes.

MB: I will do everything in my power to stop you from writing this book. Are we recording?

SW: Yes.

MB: You want to test it first?

SW: Sure. [*Beat*] Okay, testing.

MB: Yo, yo, yo! Hey, hey, hey! Go, go, go!

Playback works.

SW: Got it.

MB: Now ask me anything about Paul Mazursky.

SW: When did you meet Paul Mazursky?

MB: I don't remember. Next question.

SW: Where did you meet Paul Mazursky?

MB: We both had offices opposite each other on the third floor of the Executive Building at Fox. I was doing . . . I can't remember exactly what film I was doing . . . In seventy . . . [*Thinks*] Let me go through my entire career while you wait . . . In '68 I did *The Producers*, in '70 I released a movie called *The Twelve Chairs* . . .

SW: This was in the mid-seventies, right?

MB: Yeah. Yeah.

SW: *Blazing Saddles?*

MB: Oh! [*Beat*] No, after . . . after . . . Then I did *Young Frankenstein* right on top of that . . .

SW: So you're either in *Silent Movie* or *High Anxiety*.

MB: Wait a minute. [*Beat*] Yeah, it must have been. That's it. Yes. So what would that be . . . '76?

SW: '76.

MB: So we're talking about '77 or '78. When I did *High Anxiety*.

SW: That makes sense because your next movie was *History of the World: Part I*, and you gave Paul a little part in it.

MB: [*Laughs*] He was a Roman solider who queried the populace on what the punishment would be for some offense. But we met before he was on that movie because he would run across the hall with problems. What was Paul doing then in '78?

SW: I can't remember exactly . . . let me go through his career . . .

MB: Okay . . .

SW: In '76 he did *Next Stop, Greenwich Village* . . .

MB: Right, it wasn't that . . .

SW: In '78 he did *An Unmarried Woman* . . .

MB: That was it. Anyway, he was an incredibly good neighbor because he would spill his troubles and worries to me and I would spill all my doubts and fears to him. We would buoy each other up with false statements and lies. [*Laughs*] He would just walk into my office and, you know, sit down on my desk and say things like, "So what's it all about?" Worldly, like that. And I'd say, "Don't be meshugge." [*Laughs*] We'd talk about each other's work, and I'd read him things from scripts I was working on, and he'd read to me from his stuff. We worked together like that, and saw each other all the time, but not for lunch. Paul ate sandwiches at his desk. But not me. I was at the commissary almost every day for appointments. But Paul was pretty diligent when he was working on scripts. He wouldn't leave his office. When he was writing, he really didn't like to get away from the page. He stayed with the script until it was finished. [*Beat*] My take on Paul's writing is that there was probably a long and complicated gestation period of thought, but once he started it was a long burst of creative energy until it was spent. Later he would come out of his stupor and say, "What is this? What have I done here?" He was a natural.

SW: That's one of his great strengths. Naturalness.

MB: Dialogue in *Bob & Carol & Ted & Alice* flows so naturally. It's incredible. The great thing about Paul's movies is that they never seem to be made up. They seem to spring from life. You believe everything! You just believe those things are happening when you watch his movies. You know? That's the most important thing about Paul. Everybody thought it was just kind of a documentary. [*Beat*] In watching his movies, you see that he never sacrifices intelligence or truth for an angle or a shot. He wasn't camera crazy. He doesn't shove the "Art" down your throat. Like a Ridley Scott—who is a very good filmmaker—will let you know it's being directed by Ridley Scott. [*Beat*] But I'll tell you something else about Paul: He's a very meticulous editor. A lot of filmmakers just ask for a rough cut and come back when it's done to watch it and give notes and then go away again. Not Paul. He never phoned it in. He was with the editor on every frame. [*Beat*] "The American Renoir." That's what I once called him.

SW: Tell me what you mean by that.

MB: Yes, because Renoir is the great naturalist. You just believed every minute. It was like the camera wasn't there.

SW: How would you describe Paul's sense of humor?

MB: It's very much like Paul himself. It's a weird combination of worldly sophistication and kind of a Jewish provinciality. It's an amazing combination, really. He's so worldly, but he knows the bottom line is: "I met a girl who's so skinny, I took her into a restaurant and the waiters looked at us and said, 'Check your umbrella.'" [*Laughs*] He knows the cheap joke works because he knows what people amount to. Worldly is a part of that, but Paul also knows what's beneath it.

SW: One more thing: You've known Paul for thirty years. What do you love most about him?

MB: I'll tell you. It boils down to his pursed lips that are starting to smile that I know will break into helpless, uncontrollable, insane laughter. He's always on the edge of losing it. It's hard not to go along with that. [*Beat*] Now I've got to go—I'm a busy man, you know—but I will say one last thing. Paul and I have lunch every Friday and I always pay. And he's the only one that always orders dessert. He gets a fruit plate and it's not cheap. I think you should know that.

Paul on Mazursky

Introduction On *Paul on Mazursky*

I was in a used bookstore in Hollywood when I found a slim hardback called *Afterglow: A Last Conversation with Pauline Kael*. For eight dollars and change, there was no resisting. *Afterglow* was coming home with me.

That night I read the whole book. In two conversations with her fan and friend, the jazz critic Francis Davis, Kael riffed on her old favorites—*Last Tango in Paris*, *Pennies from Heaven*, *Casualties of War*—discoursed on some of her newer ones—"Sex and the City," David O. Russell, and *Death to Smoochy* (what?)—but her largest statement, which I privately rewarded myself for having said many times in the past, was dedicated to the writer/director of a movie called *Next Stop, Greenwich Village*. "Paul Mazursky," she said, "hasn't been given his due. *Enemies, A Love Story* is one of my favorite movies of all time, and most people haven't even seen it." It's true—on both counts—but why? How could the filmmaker responsible for one of Pauline Kael's favorites go largely uncelebrated by the critical collective?

I jumped backed into his movies, eager to find out. What I saw was the work of an auteur, specifically, a great American humanist, one with the old-fashioned open heart of Frank Capra, but with a contemporary satirical squint. Like Jean Renoir, another great humanist, Mazursky never let jokes get between him and the hard truths of his characters; and like any of the Italian neorealists, his pictures were explicitly, almost aggressively, enmeshed in the here and now (or from the vantage of decades passed, the then and there). Remember the psychedelic brownies? The suburban orgies? Remember the gurus, the shrinks, and the Rodeo Drive fetishists? They're all there. Chronicling these shifts in the cultural ethos, Mazursky has preserved the changing passions of the American middle class in a kind of comic formaldehyde. Adapting to the climate of each era, Mazursky has seen us through a half-century-long history of love and turmoil, from the post-war anxieties of the 1940s (in *Enemies, A Love Story*), to the awkward fifties (*Next Stop, Greenwich Village*), the rebellious sixties (*I Love You, Alice B. Toklas!*), the neurotic seventies (*Bob & Carol & Ted & Alice*, *Alex in Wonderland*, *Blume in Love*, *An Unmarried Woman*), the wild eighties (*Down and Out in Beverly Hills*), and the jaded nineties (*Scenes from a Mall*).

I bought Mazursky's 1999 autobiography, *Show Me the Magic*. Reading the book, I got a feel for Mazursky, personally and professionally. He started out a New York actor before getting his big break in Hollywood—a small part in *Blackboard Jungle*—in 1954. From there, Mazursky went back in New York, returned to the theater, and started doing a little stand-up before deciding, late in the fifties, to move back to Hollywood. That's where the work was. In L.A., Mazursky reconnected with Larry Tucker, an old comedy acquaintance from New York, and they started writing together, first for *The Danny Kaye Show*, and then left television to try to break into movies. Their script, *I Love You, Alice B. Toklas!*, about an uptight Jewish lawyer who falls in love with a hippie, was filmed in 1967, and brought Mazursky and Tucker a considerable amount of attention. Dissatisfied with director Hy Averback's work on *Toklas*, Mazursky decided his next script—*Bob & Carol & Ted & Alice*, written with Tucker—was going to be a Paul Mazursky picture. With the support of agent Freddie Fields and producer Mike Frankovich, Mazursky made *Bob & Carol* his way, on his terms, and became an instant hit.

For the next two decades, he went on to make some of Hollywood's most passionate comedies. From *Blume in Love* to *An Unmarried Woman*, and *Down and Out in Beverly Hills* to *Enemies, A Love Story*, his pictures were prescient, honest, and always hilarious. In those days, Mazursky was untouchable; both the popular and critical consensus deemed him so. But the tides turned in the early nineties. *The Pickle* was panned, and Mazursky's subsequent efforts, though intermittently wonderful, have not lived up to his work of the seventies and eighties, his golden age.

Show Me the Magic satisfied everything but the critic in me. It was candid, casual, and funny—everything, in other words, that made Mazursky's movies what they are—and it added a poignant autobiographical layer to my understanding of his films. But I still hungered for more insight into his process. How, I wondered, did Mazursky actually make these movies? How did he think about them? How did he manage to portray, with startling consistency, some of the most robust characters in recent Hollywood? Upon completing the book, it became clear to me that there was no other Hollywood writer/director with Paul Mazursky's generous admiration of human foible, no other American auteur so shrewdly attuned to the cockeyed truths of how we love. How could such an accomplished filmmaker have slipped by?

I threw myself into the critical writing on Mazursky. In a 2001 *New York Times* article, "Doing Justice to Mazursky, Long Bypassed," Elvis Mitchell wrote, "Maybe part of the reason Mr. Mazursky's work has been ignored is that he's hardest to imitate." It's a good point. Consider his contemporaries. Scorsese, for one, has been recognized for his attitude, flourish, and technical extravagance. He is, like Coppola, a bombastic stylist, full of opera and amped-up sensationalism, and with a Wellesian ambition that's easy to lionize. Then there's Altman, who, with his fifty-some movies, is unforgettable for his scope alone. Lucas and Spielberg have their terrific toys (not to mention box office), and Cassavetes, the hard-core independent, has been justly celebrated for doing it his way and no one else's. These filmmakers—all brilliant in their own way—are easy to exalt because they are easy to define, and as icons of the seventies—a decade renowned for its countercultural ambition—that makes them even sexier. But flipping through the index in Peter Biskind's *Easy Riders, Raging Bulls*, a book consumed with the rampage of sex, drugs, and revolution in the Hollywood seventies, one discovers "Mazursky, Paul" has only two page numbers after it (Scorsese alone takes up six lines). Nearly forty at the time of his directorial debut (*Bob & Carol & Ted & Alice*, 1969), Mazursky was just above the average age of a fresh batch of younger iconoclast directors,[1] a fact that understandably clashed with the then-popular notion of director-as-rebel. Mazursky, by comparison, was old-fashioned. He had the romantic ethics of a classicist. James Monaco:

> Mazursky's films are noticeably traditional. Not only because they
> avoid cinematic pyrotechnics to focus more intently on characters and
> story, but more important, because they echo the American satiric
> sensibility that stretches back to Will Rogers, Chaplin, and even Mark
> Twain. Not to put too fine a point on it, but if Cassavetes is the Ameri-
> can Bergman (an invidious comparison, but not inaccurate), then
> Mazursky is our Fellini. I've often thought, only half jokingly, that the
> main problem with Bergman's characters was their environment—if
> only they'd take a vacation, go visit Fellini's people. Likewise, there are
> very few characters of American films of the seventies, from Travis
> Bickle [*Taxi Driver*] to Nick and Mabel Longhetti [*A Woman Under the
> Influence*], who wouldn't benefit greatly from a visit to a Mazursky
> movie. At the very least, they'd learn to take themselves considerably
> less seriously. My point is that it's relatively easy for a filmmaker to por-

1. Bogdanovich (b. 1939), Cimino (b. 1939), Coppola (b. 1939), De Palma (b. 1940), Friedkin (b. 1935), Lucas (b. 1944), Nichols (b. 1931), Polanski (b. 1933), Schrader (b. 1946), Scorsese (b. 1942), and Spielberg (b. 1946) are all younger than Mazursky (b. 1930). Altman (b. 1925), Ashby (b. 1929), Cassavetes (b. 1929), and Lumet (b. 1924) were older.

tray the death force rampant—it's so overwhelmingly present in our lives; all the evidence points to its imminent triumph. It's much harder to suggest convincingly that the life force still exists—harder and also more accurate.

Part hippie and part father, Mazursky had what most filmmakers of the New Hollywood didn't—perspective. "Mr. Mazursky was not like them," Mitchell wrote, "he was a cultural anthropologist, tagging love and following the damage left in the name of amorous misadventure. There was probably no writer and director more in love with love and its power to heal and disrupt since the heyday of the screwball comedy."

Andrew Sarris, I discovered, was also a Mazurskyite. On the occasion of the Film Society of Lincoln Center's 2007 eleven-film retrospective, he wrote, "Mr. Mazursky is a testament to the sheer depth of American mainstream movies way back (it now seems) in the days when directors—and Mr. Mazursky in particular—knew how to be funny and adult at the same time." Back then (way back), in the American cinema's most formidable post-war decade, Richard Corliss had a sense of what would come. He wrote, "Paul Mazursky is likely to be remembered as *the* filmmaker of the seventies. No screenwriter has probed so deep under the pampered skin of this fascinating, maligned decade; no director has so successfully mined it for home-truth human revelations. . . . Mazursky has created a body of work unmatched in contemporary American cinema for its originality and cohesiveness." But, as always, it was Kael who said it best: "Mazursky is a comic poet."

Not everyone saw the poetry so clearly. Surely, in this era of cinematic rebellion, differences of opinion were apt to arise, but a discrepancy of this magnitude was downright alarming. Was Corliss too generous? Was Biskind too flip? The old material was sending me in circles—for every argument there was a counterargument and for every counterargument an equally compelling response.

Part of the problem, I realized, was Mazursky's tenuous relationship to the medium itself. In the nearly twenty films—from *Bob & Carol & Ted & Alice* through *Yippee*, his final film to date—I saw a casual, seemingly haphazard approach to style. At first glance, I was sure these films were without cinematic definition. The very long wide shots were often undiscerning in their placement and direction, creating an atmosphere of aimlessness, as if the man behind the camera just set it down in the place of least possible resistance and let it run, and run, until the film ran out or someone flubbed their lines. The lighting was largely inconspicuous, mostly flat, designed less, it seemed, for aesthetic than pragmatism. Indeed these films contained few fancy camera movements, or the kind of bravura gestures that would have had me reeling in film school. In other words, in this cursory aesthetic survey, Mazursky's visual presentation was shaping up to be a film analyst's worst nightmare.

But cinema per se is only one part of the cinematic experience. The camera is only a facet of his expression, not, as was the case with the great craftsmen, its touchstone. Unfortunately, certain orthodox critics have held that against him. When a writer-director is as competent on the page as he is on the screen, his aesthetic is often deemed inadequate, and he can be dismissed with disparaging euphemisms like "talky" and "actor's director." (This is truer of no one more than of Woody Allen, whose talent on the page has often led the critical collective to underplay his talent with the medium.) The same has been said of Billy Wilder, whose films, Sarris once wrote, "decline in retrospect because of visual and structural deficiencies."[2] But Sarris was off the mark there: *Double Indemnity*, *Some Like it Hot*, *The Apartment*, and *Sunset Blvd.* persist in most forceful opposition. These movies may not be the works of a Hitchcock, von Sternberg, or Scorsese—filmmakers who speak loudest in pictures—but as innumerable best-of lists indicate, they remain among the century's most significant American movies.

When thinking about Mazursky, the work and legacy of George Cukor also comes to mind. Though, unlike Allen and Wilder, he did not write his own pictures, Cukor's contribution, like theirs, was at first criticized for its nondescript aesthetic. Mercifully, Gavin Lambert's *On Cukor* has helped to restore the director's work to the high standing it retains today. "Cukor's work," he wrote, "has been underrated by those who expect an immediate signature on film, and imagine there is no 'personality' behind it unless they can respond to Buñuel-surrealism, Hitchcock-suspense, Fellini grotesquerie, or the Lubitsch touch. Even [Kenneth] Tynan . . . could only come up with the argument that Cukor's films 'epitomize Hollywood at its most stylish.' " Mazursky's films have posed the same problem. "With Mazursky's films," James Monaco wrote, "what you see is what you get, and you either respond to it with admiration, even *con amore*, as I do, or you do not."

But isn't there a middle ground? Can't one respond to Mazursky with

---

2. Sarris later reconsidered, writing that he had "grossly under-rated Billy Wilder, perhaps more so than any other American director."

learned admiration? It's difficult; with film form sidelined, speaking empirically about his movies becomes problematic. There is also the question of genre. In a picture like *Enemies, A Love Story*, for example, tone fluctuates so much that no label seems accurate; "comedy" is reductive, "dark comedy" is too bitter, and "drama" is incomplete. Additionally, the niche appeal of certain Mazursky movies, so heavily rooted in their time and place, can make them seem inaccessible to certain audiences.

These aspersions must be recast. If a Mazursky film feels emotionally unstable, then Mazursky, true to the tenets of human comedy, is doing his job. If a picture like *Alex in Wonderland* seems dated, all the better; it means the director's anthropological comb was fine-toothed enough. If his depictions of bourgeois life are more forgiving than critical, it's because Mazursky's comedies won't tolerate anything harsher than affectionate laughter. "Can the middle class handle all the freedom it's now being offered?" he once asked. "Does anybody really change? My pictures are about a reaction in the United States against and to authority, a re-assessment of social values, of moral values, of how people live."

Mazursky's film form, I saw, was a direct expression of these freedoms. Even tone had the freedom to change. Extending scenes past the point of narrative necessity, Mazursky would keep the camera rolling just to keep the points of views shifting. Think what you're watching is funny? Wait. Think it's sad? Keep waiting, because in the realm of human comedy, where everyone is human and therefore empathic, nothing is funny or unfunny for long, and there is always another side. Consider, for instance, the nearly fifteen-minute-long bedroom scene between Elliott Gould and Dyan Cannon in *Bob & Carol & Ted & Alice*. Or the musical passages sung between George Segal, Susan Anspach, and Kris Kristofferson in *Blume*. These are long stretches of film time, wholly disproportionate to the amount of exposition they exposit, but with them Mazursky creates arenas for different, often conflicting emotional states to coexist. What results is a depth of feeling as comprehensive as it is complex, as eccentric as it is ordinary—and an emotional patina that belongs to all of us in life, but in Hollywood, to Mazursky's films alone.

Because of their length, these sequences undermine, and continually revise, our understanding of character. Just when we think the scene will end, just when we think we have a definitive sense of emotional truth, Mazursky complicates it with a refinement, a coda, a coda on a coda. The final product is as satirical as it is revelatory, and creates a sense of pervasive craziness, the impression that being human is no different than being nutty. "[The character of] Larry is crazy in a sane way," Pauline Kael wrote of *Next Stop, Greenwich Village*. "As a comedian, he puts his craziness to work for him. And that's Paul Mazursky's greatest gift. What made his earlier films so distinctive was the acceptance of bugginess as part of the normal—maybe even the best part of it. In his films, craziness gives life its savor. When Mazursky makes fun of characters, it's not to put them down; quite the reverse—the scattier they are, the more happily he embraces them."

To fully capture craziness in all its destructive/wonderful glory, Mazursky ensures his characters are as free cinematically as they are in their humanity. Scene length, digressive story maneuvers, and contrapuntal tonality all play a part in his aesthetic of freedom, producing a feeling of spontaneity—but only a feeling. Mazursky's films are heavily scripted, and contrary to appearance, are not improvisational, only made to *look* that way.

But what would emotional freedom be without physical freedom? Mazursky's knack for dialogue has been recognized (he's been Oscar-nominated three times for the Best Screenplay and once for Best Adapted Screenplay), but few have celebrated his subtler penchant for physical humor. We see embryonic traces of it in his earliest pictures, and yet not until *Down and Out in Beverly Hills* does the farce full bloom. Amidst the lunacy of California affluence, the excesses of the era are italicized by a refined ordering of physical comedy, one that emerges not from a zany Mel Brooksian world, but from the ever-broadening impulses of the characters. In his book on slapstick, *Comedy is a Man in Trouble*, Alan Dale writes, "Preston Sturges has a literary comic sensibility but works out of deep pockets of impulse with the physical freedom and intensity of the silent comedians, offering the most sophisticated combination of high and low comedy until the movies of Paul Mazursky."

"His directing style is based on the actors intuitively taking off from each other," Kael wrote. "He does something that no other American movie director does: he writes, shapes, and edits the sequences to express the performing rhythm—to keep the actor's pulse. As a result, the audience feels unusually close to the characters—feels protective toward them. Mazursky brings you into a love relationship with his people, and it's all aboveboard."

It is no coincidence the definitive works on Allen, Wilder, Cukor, and Cassavetes are interview books. The movies of certain other filmmakers—those who think better in pictures than words—are more conducive to the kinds of analytic treatments that have been applied to the likes of Godard, Buñuel, and Hitchcock. (For my money, Robin Wood's work on Hitchcock is unquestionably stronger than Truffaut's interview book, *Hitchcock/Truffaut*.) But as directors of actors—moreover, as writers—auteurs like Allen, Wilder, Cassavetes, and Mazurksy are talkers. Talk is how they communicate.

And in a book about their films, talk should be reflected with as much authenticity as possible. In Mazursky's case, it should unfold in the manner of a real conversation, chock-full of all the bumps, misdirections, and interruptions of any other real conversation. For reality—a word Mazursky uses often—is a lynchpin of his work, and Mazursky's golden rule.

Paul on Mazursky, true to its topic, strives for a kind of photo-realism, rooted in the moment, and spontaneously lifelike—a kind of documentary filmed on paper. What can emerge then is a diptych of a great filmmaker and a good guy, Paul Mazursky, man and artist, preserved in his own kind of comic formaldehyde, bottled between March 23rd and November 18th, 2007; a brief span of creative, personal, and political ups and downs, fluctuations in mood and susceptibility, all human and therefore all real, and therefore all pertinent to the portrait of the man whose portraits of his changing world were just as sensitive, and just as open to the joys, losses, and ironies around him. "The detail is what makes it so human," he has said. As a director, Mazursky is a selector of details; as an interviewer, I strove to do the same.

I was at the Beverly Hilton on Wilshire after a really, really long tribute award dinner when I spotted Paul Mazursky on what was easily the longest valet line he or I or anyone had ever waited on. It was late, people were visibly cranky, and in the very back of the line, even Paramount head Brad Grey, sitting on his swag bag with a claim ticket in his mouth, looked like a broken man. One of the biggest honchos in town, and like the rest of us, he was brought down to earth by the great Hollywood leveler: valet parking. How fitting, I thought, that Paul Mazursky, L.A.'s swami of social satire, was here to see it all. The serendipity was too good to pass up, and like a schmuck fan, I introduced myself, thanked Mazursky for his movies, and then offered to run back into the hotel to get his ticket validated (he had forgotten). I returned in time to see Mazursky into his Lexus, thinking Hollywood comedy is on its deathbed, and here's its Mayo Clinic putting on its seatbelt and driving away. He was probably the only guy on line who felt sorry for the valet.

That was two years ago. Now I ask my friend David Freeman, who I discover is a longtime pal of Mazursky's, to make an introduction. He does, and in two days I'm in Mazursky's office, clutching a copy of *On Cukor*, hoping I don't appear to him as nervous as I feel. But so what if I do? This is Paul Mazursky, after all. The man gets feelings.

Boychick Brooklyn, 1930–Los Angeles, 1968

"So you want to write a book on me?"

"Yes, but not really 'on,' it's more 'with.' Like Gavin Lambert's book *On Cukor.*"

Mazursky sits back in his chair and gives his chin a contemplative massage. Rushing, for reasons I can't explain, I open the book on his desk and say, "I kind of think of you like a Cukor, like today's, well, the actor's director, or, you know, I think comedy . . ."—I start stammering—mercifully Mazursky holds out a hand.

"Okay," he says. "Whatever you want."

I try not to smile. "Oh? Okay, well, I think—"

"Whatever you want, kid." There is a pause, a long pause, and the longer it gets, the more nervous I become. Should I not have compared him to Cukor? Did he think I meant "actor's director" as a kind of euphemism? "When do you want to start?" he asks, flipping through the book. I hesitate a moment, and Paul looks up "How about now?"

Now?

SAM WASSON: Okay. You were born in Brooklyn in 1930.

PAUL MAZURSKY: Yes, in Brownsville, Murder Inc.

SW: What are your earliest memories of the movies?

PM: The first movie I saw in a movie theater alone, without my mother, was at the Capitol theater in Brooklyn around the corner on Saratoga Avenue. It was *King Kong,* and I saw it with another kid. We were both six or seven years old. And during the movie, when the kid saw the monster, he threw up on my leg. [*Laughs*] It was disgusting.

SW: Do you remember the kid's name?

PM: Carl Hutt.

SW: As a burgeoning actor, you must have had a close eye on the stars. Any stand out?

PM: I always imitated my favorite movie stars, but actually *in* the theater— much to the chagrin of the rest of the audience—as the movie was playing. I did Bogart, Jimmy Cagney, John Garfield. At nights, I would lie in the bathtub in our small bathroom at home and I would do "To be or not to be . . ." That was the only place I had the freedom to do it.

sw: When did it become serious?

pm: I got serious about acting by the fourth or fifth grade. When I was twelve, thirteen, fourteen, my mother took me to see Walter Huston in something and made me wait at the stage door after the show. When he came out she said, "Mr. Huston! Mr. Huston! This is my son, Irwin." You couldn't have been more embarrassed than I was. To me, he was about eight feet tall. She said, "My son wants to be an actor." Walter Huston looked down at me and said, [*full country baritone*] "Well, that's a very noble profession, son. But what you need is a back-up occupation, teaching or something, because it can be a difficult career." He patted me on the head and walked on. That was it. And then years later, my idea was, if Walter Huston told me to get a job, maybe I should be a speech therapist. I didn't really want to be a teacher, so when I went to Brooklyn College, I studied speech therapy, which meant that I could probably get work. But then when the acting thing began, I right away felt that I was going to make it as an actor. I didn't know how, but I knew that I was going to make it.

sw: Was there a time before you wanted to be an actor that you thought of being something else?

pm: I thought of being an explorer. I used to read those wonderful travel books by Richard Halliburton. I've fulfilled many of those travel dreams, but there are a few more that I want to fulfill while I still can, I mean, physically.

sw: I'm not surprised to hear you say that because travel has always been crucial to your characters. It's often an expression of freedom—or craziness—and it generally results in an opening up.

pm: Sometimes I have a fantasy of giving all this [*motions around the room*] up. Why not just travel? Enjoy the world.

sw: While you were at Brooklyn College, you appeared in a production of *He Who Gets Slapped*.

pm: When I was a senior, I decided with a fellow named Bob Weinstein to produce an off-Broadway play. We found out that for two hundred dollars we could mount a play at the Masters Institute up on Riverside Drive in the nineties. I put up a hundred and he put up a hundred. And we decided to do *He Who Gets Slapped*, a play by Leonid Andreyev. Beyond ambitious. We got students from the college to play in it with us and we

1. Paul Mazursky. New York, winter 1957.

did it for two weekends. And that's when Howard Sackler,[3] who was a young writer living in the Village, saw the play. I didn't know him, but he called me up and he said, "I thought your performance was very good and I think you'd be perfect for a role in this film I've written. You should go see the director and read for him." He gave me the address and got me a copy of the script. So I went to 13th Street where I was going to meet the director, and I was early, so I went into a church just to rest, take it easy, and calm down. Then when it was time to go, I went around the corner and rang the bell and this voice said, [*lifeless*] "Yeah, come on up." And I went up and there was this guy with big, round dark eyes and a lot of dark hair.

SW: Stanley Kubrick.

PM: Yes. He had a wife and a dog. I remember that because I had never met a guy with a wife or a dog. He was just a couple years older than me. There were a lot of cameras sitting around. He said, "I'm Stanley Kubrick. I'm going to read with you." And so we read—the whole script. It took about an hour. Then he said, "Okay, you got the part. We're leaving on Monday

3. Sackler would go on to win the Pulitzer Prize for his play, *The Great White Hope*. The character of Robert, played by Christopher Walken in *Next Stop, Greenwich Village*, is based on Howard Sackler.

for California." I said, "What do you mean, 'California'?" He said, "That's where I'm shooting it." I said, "I'm still in school." He says, "Can't you talk to the dean and get four weeks off?" I said, "I don't know," and he said, "Well, if you can, you got the part." So I went to the dean and I got it. That was 1951. It was the first time I had ever seen a plane.

sw: How did Kubrick's handle himself during the audition?

pm: Very quiet. [*Beat*] So I went off and did the movie. Brooklyn College let me. So I feel indebted to them.

sw: On the set—on *Fear and Desire*—I've read that Kubrick did everything. Is that an exaggeration?

pm: No. He did everything. He set up the shots, operated the camera, moved the lights—everything. He had a Mitchell camera and no dolly. I think he might have had a baby carriage that they used . . .

sw: What about talking to the actors?

pm: He said very little to us. He didn't direct the actors.

sw: No notes?

pm: Not that I remember.

sw: That's one of the great Kubrickian mysteries. We know he's gotten these incredible performances, but we have this understanding of him as someone who doesn't reach out to actors.

pm: It's a very profound question you're asking and I wish I had a profound answer. There are those filmmakers who know only what they want and not how to get it. Stanley may have been one of them. Do you understand? I don't think Stanley got much out of Keir Dullea for instance, but when I see the performances in *A Clockwork Orange, Spartacus* . . . I'm amazed. What Stanley had was confidence, he had balls.

sw: And did you see that as early as *Fear and Desire*?

pm: I saw some of it. I saw a strong will.

sw: Did you keep in touch after the movie?

pm: Well, I spent about a month with him recording dialogue after the shoot. You know, the whole movie is looped. Stanley thought it would be cheaper that way, but it ended up being twice as expensive. When I was in London in 1971, I called him to tell him I was in town. I got him on the phone and said, "I'd love to see you" and he said, "Well, I'm cutting right now. As soon as I'm finished cutting we'll get together." I said, "About how long do you think that will take?" He said, "About a year."

sw: Wow.

pm: It was bullshit. *But*, it also isn't bullshit. He doesn't want any distractions.

SW: So that was the end?

PM: I never saw him again.

SW: But you know that he has a clip of *Blume in Love* in *Eyes Wide*—

PM: Of course I do. The question is, was he using it as an homage to me? I don't know.

SW: I think so. I think Stanley Kubrick, who took ten years to make a movie, who is renowned for his obsessive attention to precision, who brings in NASA equipment to photograph *Barry Lyndon*, intends it to be nothing else. Anyway, the story of *Blume* in many ways matches *Eyes Wide Shut*. It was an appropriate choice.

PM: It's very likely true. But wouldn't it have been wonderful if I got a call even from his assistant saying, "Mr. Kubrick wants you to know, he's using a clip from *Blume in Love*." But listen: He's a genius. He made half a dozen of the most wonderful films ever made.

SW: It's funny. I think of you and Kubrick as opposites. Here you have Stanley, who turns his people into monsters; and here you have Paul, who turns his people into humans. Mazursky looks at *2001* and says, "None of these people are interesting," but that's what Kubrick is getting at.

PM: I appreciate that and I don't condemn him for it. *Lolita* is full of life as anything can possibly be—it comes from Nabokov of course—but Stanley did it. He was brilliant to get James Mason, who is utterly fantastic, to get that girl [Sue Lyon] who is wonderful, and to get Shelley [Winters]! It's brilliant! And then Peter [Sellers]! He's a genius. And *Strangelove*! Everybody talks about Peter as Strangelove, and his performance as the president is a very cute thing and very fun, but the best thing in it is the upper-class Englishman with Sterling Hayden [Lionel Mandrake]. It's subtle, hilarious . . . brilliant beyond belief.

SW: Kubrick publicly disowned *Fear and Desire*. Could you sense his growing dissatisfaction with the project?

PM: That happened much later. After he became Kubrick, he didn't want anyone to see it. I found that weak on his part, as did John Boorman, who had honored Stanley with a retrospective at Telluride and showed the movie. When Stanley found out, he got on the phone with him and said, "Don't do this," and Boorman said, "It belongs to the world now, Stanley."

SW: You married Betsy Purdy in 1953. So you were dating during *Fear and Desire*?

PM: Yeah. And after we finished shooting, when I was working in the Catskills, Kubrick went over and made a pass at her. He knew she was my girlfriend. But she handled it. Betsy's great. She's funny as hell. She called me just now to tell me that she heard about a great doctor and wants to switch. [*Laughs*] I said, "You're calling me now about this? Couldn't it wait until I get home at four o'clock?" [*Laughs again*] But I liked Stanley! I admired him! Here's this young guy, doing all this on his own, getting the money from his uncle, Martin Pervellor, who owned a drugstore—

SW: And then he ran out of money and had to get more . . .

PM: Yeah, after four weeks, me, Stanley, and Frank Silvera—we were high up in the San Gabriel Mountains—drove down the hill back to Kubrick's uncle's house. From the living room, where we waited, we could hear them arguing. Martin was on his little adding machine, "Five thousand dollars? You know how many aspirin I have to sell?" He had a Doberman pinscher that was epileptic, standing out by the pool . . .

Paul rolls his eyes back, sticks out his tongue, and convulses.

It was fucking scary! After the movie was done, Stanley had to loop. His father came up with that money. It was at least another ten grand, maybe twenty. So the movie cost twenty-five plus maybe twenty more— that's forty-five thousand bucks. Well, he never got it back. Joseph Burstyn[4] was a hero in releasing it and seeing his talent, but it did nothing.

SW: And all this time, you're not thinking about wanting to direct a movie, or maybe write . . .

PM: Not at all. All I was thinking was, "I have a shot at the Oscar." [*Laughs*] It's a good part, I rape a girl, I have a mad scene, I sing poetry from *The Tempest* . . . But no, not even a nomination. I thought I was going to make it, going to be a big star, but I was in the toilet. So I went back to Brooklyn and started squeezing juice in a health food store called The Salad Bowl. [*Beat*] That's the Stanley Kubrick story. [*Beat*] So I'm at The Salad Bowl, and I'm squeezing oranges . . .

4. Joseph Burstyn specialized in the distribution of domestic low-budget and foreign films like *Fear and Desire* and Rosselini's *Rome, Open City*. From 1951 to 1953, Burstyn was at the center of *Joseph Burstyn, Inc. v. Wilson*, 343 U.S. 495, which resulted in a landmark Supreme Court ruling that would eventually spell the beginning of the end of motion picture censorship in the United States.

Paul stops.

You see, we're getting into an existential thing here, or maybe that's the wrong word. Karma. Fate. Serendipity. Luck? Or is it, there is talent, and talent will out? I don't know. But there I am, two years after *Fear and Desire*, and Johnny Cassavetes walks into the store and I overhear him talking to this guy Harry Mastrogeorge, an actor, about how he's going to meet a guy from MGM who was casting for *Blackboard Jungle*. He saw that I was interested and asked me to go along so I went. We all go to this casting call together and I walked in there with a look about me, did my tough Brooklyn accent, and I lied to the guy. I said I had done a lot of shows on Broadway and finished a little run of *Mister Roberts*. Well, the guy had me do a screen test and I got the part. But is that luck? What is that? I could still be working at the juice store . . .

SW: It's a scene you would recreate in *Next Stop, Greenwich Village*. Was that the first time you met Cassavetes?

PM: Yeah. He just walked into the store. He didn't know me as an actor, he didn't know me at all.

SW: Okay, so it's 1954, you fly out to L.A. for *Blackboard Jungle*, and you're at MGM, the greatest lot in town.

PM: It was thrilling. We were taken right from the airport to meet Dore Schary, who ran the studio. He was a very liberal guy and had pictures of Franklin and Eleanor Roosevelt all over his office. And there were pipes everywhere—he smoked pipes. He said, "It's a pleasure to have all of you here. I'd like to take you down the hall to meet your director." We go down the hall and there's Richard Brooks: crew cut, pipe, shirt hanging out. He looked like a marine. He later turned out to be a friend of mine. I loved him. I'll tell you more about that later. [*Beat*] So they tell me I'm going to play a kid named Emmanuel Stoker. *Emmanuel Stoker?* Well, who the fuck is Emmanuel Stoker? I read the book and the guy doesn't have a single line! So I go right back and get the script, I'm racing through it, and I see that I have about twenty-five lines. Nothing. So I figure I got to do something. And if you look at the movie, if you look at the classroom scenes, you can see me fighting to get in the shot. I'm always on the edge of the frame leaning in. Anyway, the first day on the set, I go to the men's room—they were outside the soundstage—and as I walk in I see George Sanders taking a piss with tights on. And I have to take a piss next to him. And while I'm pissing, he can see that I'm looking over at him and says, [*silkily*] "Yeeeeeessssss?" And I say, "Mr. Sanders, I can't tell you what a thrill this is . . . I've seen all your movies . . ." He was charmed, zipped up his fly, and walked out.

sw: What about the commissary? You must've seen some incredible faces.

pm: You wouldn't believe it. You wouldn't fucking believe it. Listen to this: As you're casually picking up your salad or whatever it is, there's Errol Flynn. There's Clark Gable. There's Bette Davis. There's Katharine Hepburn. Everyone I ever imitated as a kid. Spencer Tracy. mgm. *Thrilling*. So the shooting continues, all very smooth, I talk to Betsy on the phone about once a week—we're married now—and about a week before we finish, [Richard] Brooks comes up to me and says, "So what are you going to do, kid?" I said, "Well, what do you mean?" He says, "Are you staying out here or are you going back to New York?" I say, "I don't have an agent, so I don't know what to do." The next day an agent shows up. Brooks sent for him.

Mazursky turns to the window.

Yeah. Brooks sent for him.

sw: What was Brooks's directing style like?

pm: Drill sergeant. "Get over there! Stand there! Get your fucking head out of the shot, Mazursky!" After I made *Next Stop, Greenwich Village*, there was a screening of it at the dga. I invited Richard, but I knew he'd never come because he never goes to those things. Well, he shows up. He's alone. He's got the shirt hanging out, the pipe. The picture's over, and he waits until I come out and he cried . . . he cried . . .

Mazursky reaches across his desk for a Kleenex. He's crying.

It was very touching. He was *proud* of me, that he had *seen* something way back then. You understand? From then on, he would come over to my house and bring a bottle of Slivovitz, and he'd tell stories and we'd stay up all night and drink the whole fucking bottle. And he was great. Really. He was *really* a great guy. I got to know him very well. I remember I went to see him just before he died. He was lying in a bed up there in his room. He was in bad shape with cancer. He said, "Don't ever let it happen to you kid. Not this way." And I said good-bye to him. But when he came to the movie I was really surprised. I was nervous to screen what was clearly a very autobiographical movie, but Brooks said, "That's my life." And he was from Philadelphia. It was so touching I can't tell you.

2. Blackboard Jungle *(1955) Paul's on the ladder, Sidney Poitier's on the trashcan.*

sw: And then, after *Blackboard Jungle*, you go back to New York to begin acting classes with Curt Conway?

pm: Yes, briefly. Curt, by the way, was married to Kim Stanley. He was a real nice guy. Before him, I had studied with Paul Mann, and after him, I went to [Lee] Strasberg. [*Beat*] Jesus, there's so much to talk about.

sw: Let's start with Paul Mann, your first teacher. Is that where you learned the Method?

pm: The so-called Method, yes. But be careful, "the Method" is almost generic. It means so many different things now. But basically Mann's way of talking about it was that you had an objective in every scene. For example, in the scene you and I are doing right now, your objective is to find a way to make me tell you as much as possible of the truth— something like that. We learned how to find that. And we'd do scenes that Paul would critique in a way that's a lot like that scene in *Next Stop, Greenwich Village*. He was a very emotional teacher, and loving. He would cry at the drop of the hat when you did a scene. I was with Paul for about two years, but by the time I finished, I realized I didn't always agree with everything that was going on. I began searching for my own answers, so I went to Curt Conway, and I don't remember quite what happened, but finally I went to Strasberg. And by now, Strasberg was a legend. You had to interview with him to get into his private class. And he had a weird sound he'd make when he talked, he went like [*snorting in the back of the throat*], and his whole office was lined with books. In the interview, I told him that I had worked in Kubrick's movie, that I was in *Blackboard Jungle*, and that I was doing a little comedy act, and he said okay. Suddenly, I became his student. With Lee, basically, there was one thing that he said that I loved. That was, "Start every scene as a blank page." Forget actions, objectives—you've read the script, you've read the scene—but you don't know what the other actor is going to do! You have no idea. Just see what happens. Don't start with the objectives, because maybe it's going to be something—

Paul throws his eyeglass case at me.

You didn't know I was going to do that! But if you anticipate it, you'll be sitting there waiting for me to throw it. So I liked that blank page thing. I found it interesting. But in studying with Lee, you didn't get up very often because the class had forty people, and some of them doing their prep would get so involved with sense memory, it would take them ten minutes to even get to the point when they were ready to do the scene! [*Laughs*] You'd be sitting there in the audience—there was no curtain or anything—just watching them prepare with the crying and everything and it reached a point when you're falling asleep before the scene even began! [*Laughs*] Okay, so I was there for six to eight months.

SW: Was it a religious environment? Was Strasberg like a cult figure?

PM: To them he was. He'd say what he thought of the scene and the class would always agree—*always*. So I did a scene with a young actress, a lovely actress, based on a Hemingway short story that took place in the jungle. We do the scene and when it's over Lee says, "I felt no heat! [*snort*] I felt no heat!" I said, "Mr. Strasberg, you mean we didn't have any emotional heat?" "No," he said, "you're in the jungle, where's the heat? It's a hundred degrees! Where's the heat?" Okay, so we come back about two or three weeks later to do the scene again, I pour a bottle of water over my head for sweat, I've got handkerchiefs, and I'm ready to do it again. We got heat. Okay, so we do the scene again, dripping wet, and when it's over Strasberg says, "Too much heat!"

Laughter.

I quit after that. That was it for me. [*Laughs*] But he had a way of finding truths—there was no doubt about it. So after that, I decided to try teaching myself. I took nightclub performers and charged a dollar a person. I had about fifteen people total. My technique was a combination of what I learned from Conway, Paul Mann, Stanislavsky, and what I took from Michael Chekhov's book, *To the Actor*, a wonderful book with great exercises.

SW: Is there one that stands out?

PM: You stand up in front of the audience—Strasberg would do this—standing there self-consciously, but you're trying to be relaxed about it.

Mazursky gets up from behind his desk and stands firm. He lets his shoulders drop.

And Lee would say . . . Well, you stand up now. I'll do it with you. Go ahead.

I stand facing Mazursky, but about a foot away.

Just stand and see if you can *really* relax. And you can look at me if you want.

The phone rings.

Shit.

It rings again. He ignores it.

How much material is between here [*indicates his knee*] and here [*just below the knee*] in your pants? I mean, if you could measure it?

I look down.

SW: About a centimeter. Maybe half an inch.

PM: See how relaxed you are now? You know why? Because you're *doing* something.

He goes back to the desk. I go to my seat.

PM: The minute you start thinking about it, you stop looking like a schmuck standing there. That's a Strasberg thing that I got.

SW: Let's go back to Betsy.

PM: I love that woman.

sw: You picked her up in Washington Square Park, a scene that you recreated in *Willie & Phil.*

pm: The place was packed. She was adorable. She was wearing a purple peasant skirt—gorgeous—Allen Block sandals, a nice blouse, a ponytail—gorgeous—high cheekbones and I gave her *Neurotica.* It was a hip magazine and I was trying to impress her. There were only five hundred copies, I think, in all of New York, but she didn't know what the hell it was. [*Laughs*] After that, I walked her home and she gave me her number. A week later, I took her to the movies. I had tickets to a special screening for *Look* magazine, which I got from one of the guys on Kubrick's crew. When we came back, I tried to kiss her in the doorway, but she shut the door on my nose. [*Laughs*] That was great. I didn't see her again until weeks later when I ran into her at Washington Square Park. In those days, you would hang out in the park. The Village was a village then. It was safe. She said, "Irwin, would you like to come with me on a yacht? My friend Sue's father has a yacht and we're going out at 12:30 this afternoon." I went, of course. I was probably the third guy she asked, but I went, and literally on the boat I fell in love with her. But how do you describe it? How do you describe falling in love? It's the most bizarre thing there is . . .

Mazursky smiles and reaches for his cup of coffee.

"Fell" is a good word for it. I *fell* in love. Yeah. So on the boat, I just held her hand a little bit. I fell in love with her. When we came back we went to the roof of her building and we necked. And that was the most sensual experience I've ever had, in a way. [*Beat*] I wanted to move in with her, but she said, "No one moves in with me unless they marry me. I'm not that kind of girl." I said, "Marry? What are you talking about? I'm only twenty-three . . ." [*Shrugs*] But we did it. We got married at City Hall in Manhattan, and afterwards, everyone came back to our apartment to eat tuna fish sandwiches that my mother had made. When they all left, Betsy and I were alone for the first time. I looked at her and I said, "I think I'm going to go to the movies" and I went to the Loews Sheridan to see a double feature. She probably thought I was never coming back. I thought, "What have I done? Is this my *wife*? I'm twenty-three years old, I love this girl, but I can't do this. I'm not old enough. I'm an *actor.*" When I came home from the movies, which must have been four hours later—I don't remember the movies unfortunately—she says, "Oh my God, I didn't know where you were." "I was at the movies," I told her.

3. *The day Paul fell in love with Betsy. New York, summer 1952.*

[*Chuckles*] She had made a chicken and the chicken was still bleeding when she took it out of the oven. It was bleeding—blood! [*Laughs*] She didn't know how to cook a chicken. I said, "You might want to put it in a little bit more, sweetheart."

SW: Meanwhile, you and Herb Hartig have formed a comedy team called Igor and H. You're on the road, and you're booked at The Gate of Horn in Chicago.

PM: Wow, you know your shit. I was on the bill with the great folk singer Odetta. That's where I met Maya Angelou, who still owes me ten bucks. Anyway, I was a hit. I was a big hit. Okay. So now we're getting into that weird fate thing again. Or I don't know what it is. But in the daytime at The Gate of Horn, there are these actors who are kind of funny who are working on this improvised stuff and they see me and they say, "Why don't you work out with us in the daytime?" So I say okay. Their names were Barbara Harris, Alan Arkin, Severn Darden . . .

sw: The Second City. We'll get back to that in a second.

pm: Yes. So anyway, after I play The Interlude, which was here in L.A., I decided to move to California. I wanted to get more acting work and there was a lot of money to be made in television.

sw: What did you think of L.A.?

pm: Betsy and I arrived at the train station and my good friend André Philippe picked us up, and the sun was shining, and he drove us down Sunset in his Austin-Healey and I was in paradise. We pull up to this gorgeous house on Laramie only to walk in and discover there's no furniture. Nothing. It turns out, André was seeing Nina Foch and when she caught him with another girl, she left and took all the furniture with her. [*Laughs*] "Oh," I thought. "*This* is California." I loved it.

sw: Beginning in 1959, you racked up about two dozen TV appearances.

pm: Yeah, I met a lot of legends in that period. [*Thinking*] "Somebody's Waiting." That's an episode I did of *The Dick Powell Show* with Mickey Rooney. Mickey was reading the paper and I went up to him and I said, "Mr. Rooney, I just wanted to introduce myself—" and Rooney goes [*furiously mimes jerking off*], who the hell knows why . . . Let's see, I did *The World's Greatest Robbery* in 1962, directed by Franklin Schaffner, a very distinguished man who later did *Patton.* In rehearsal, he would just walk by and whisper a word in your ear, a word like [*sly*] "snake" and then disappear. He was a wonderful man and a wonderful director who doesn't quite get the credit he deserves.

sw: In 1963 you write your first episode of television, a show called "The Tinhorn" for the series *The Rifleman.* How did it occur to you to make the transition from acting to writing?

pm: Well, I was already seeing—it's interesting that you ask me this because I never think about it—that I'm not going to become a movie star. I began to think about not knowing where this acting thing was going to lead me. The work was getting, I don't know, it wasn't the *real stuff.* I didn't feel fulfilled. And I had I met a couple of people who were writing sitcoms and they weren't funny. I said, "Jesus, I can do this." It's the early sixties, around 1961 or '62 and The Second City—the group I met in Chicago—comes to L.A. They asked me to fill in the parts that Alan Arkin played, and reconnected me to Larry Tucker, who I had known in New York, who was playing the Severn Darden parts. They told us we could run the company. So we did it. Now Larry and I are around each other every day and we start to improvise new stuff. And our new stuff is *funny*. We are *funny*. Me and Larry, this 350-pound guy. Oh my God he was fat. I'm telling you, he was so fat it's unbelievable.

SW: You made *Last Year at Malibu*, your first film, for these shows.

PM: It was a takeoff of *Last Year at Marienbad*. I wish you could have seen it.

SW: It's gone now?

PM: Gone.

SW: Do you still have the script?

PM: Nothing. But I still remember it. The movie was all done with phony French narration. *"L'année dernier à Malibu . . . merci pour toutes les choses . . . à la merde . . ."* All fake. There was a little bit of piano behind it. And then you see people in tuxedos standing on the beach next to the water. A beautiful-looking woman is trying to light her cigarette, but the wind keeps blowing it out. As she's doing it, a 350-pound guy in a bathing suit is coming out of the water. It's Larry. He's got seaweed all over his body. He crawls up to them and goes under her legs and out of the sand comes two dummy puppets. Then you see me coming down a hill holding a cross. [*Laughs*] I'm so sad we don't have it anymore. After the screening, we'd have a panel of experts on stage discussing it. They'd take questions from the audience. "Well, it's clear from our film, as I'm sure everyone can see, that we're dealing with the Cuban Missile Crisis." Another guy would say, "To me, it's too clear. The body coming out of the water is so obviously representative of Cuba. You've got to give the audience *some* credit." Stuff like that. It was a lot of fun. Larry would say, "I feel you're completely misinterpreting my film. It has nothing to do with Cuba, the film is about food . . ." or whatever. We were free. Freedom gives you a great, great time.

SW: And that's how you got to *The Danny Kaye Show*?

PM: Sort of. One of those nights, the director Perry Lafferty was in the audience. After the show, he came backstage and says, "You know, I'm producing a new show, *The Danny Kaye Show*, and we just lost Larry Gelbart, our head writer. He was brought in just to work on the pilot and now we have an opening. Would you and Mr. Tucker like to try writing for us?" I said, "Yeah!" So Larry and I started writing for Danny Kaye and it lasted for four years.[5]

SW: How did it work? Did you write together?

5. Consult *Show Me the Magic* for Mazursky's Danny Kaye stories.

PM: We'd go off in separate rooms and then once or twice a week we'd all get together in the big room and pitch. "Pitch" meaning coming up with ideas. Sometimes you come up with what sounds like a great idea, but when you finally sit down to write it, you get into one third of it, the idea gets up, walks over to the window, opens the window, and jumps out. It doesn't work. And you have to learn to accept the fact that what you thought was great was just a gag without a completion, which is what you need in a decent sketch. Yeah, so, the *Kaye* experience was a very good one because Larry and I got to try out our ideas on the audience. It was like a test.

SW: Let's talk briefly about *The Monkees* pilot, which you and Larry wrote in 1966, during your last year on *Danny Kaye*. The show has a strong Richard Lester feel.

PM: Right. Bert Schneider and Bob Rafelson, who were the producers, said, "We want to do an American group like The Beatles," and showed us *Help!* and *A Hard Day's Night*. We got the spirit of it. Richard Lester, I think, deserves all the credit—or the blame—for the MTV style of cutting, which is what we tried to bring to America. Well, the pilot got made and Larry and I were supposed to write more, but we got in this dispute over the merchandising. They claimed that they came up with the name *The Monkees*, which was not true. Larry and I came up with that name. But what's the difference? *We* wrote the script, *we* put in all those dissolves and cuts and quick changes from here to there . . . Anyway, that was that. After *The Monkees*, Larry and I had had enough. We didn't want to do any more comedy or variety shows after that. We wanted to be writing movie scripts. Because we had saved enough money—the so-called "fuck you" money—we were able to live good for a couple of years, so we got an office overlooking the Sunset Strip at a time in the Sixties when you'd see hippies walking up and down the street. That right there was inspiration enough for everything that came next.

I Love You, Alice B. Toklas! (1968)

Harold Fine: Am I being a real person?

Mazursky's Tecolote Productions—which feels more like a living room than a place of business—comprises a narrow reception area, a pleasantly unkempt conference room with a television, and Mazursky's office, tucked away in the back. It's a small room furnished without flourish: just a few chairs, a couple of couches around a coffee table, and a desk for Mazursky. With the exception of a single window overlooking Beverly Drive, every inch of wall space is covered with photos from all phases of Mazursky's fifty years in show business, giving one the feeling of having stepped inside a giant zoetrope. (If only the room spun, we could have another Mazursky movie.) Mazursky himself sits on the far side of the room; his desk hidden under a quilt of week-old *Varietys*, half-drunken water bottles, and shots of his family taken, it seems, all over the world. As I pull a chair from the coffee table to Mazursky's desk, I see he's opened the day's *New York Times* to the Arts section, and is reading intently. On the paper sits the better part of a chocolate donut, which Mazursky picks at, carefully breaking off one chunk at a time, without taking his eyes off the page. There are crumbs on his T-shirt.

PM: What can I do for you, sir?

SW: We're going to talk *Toklas*, but first, I wanted to ask about Woody Allen's first film as writer-director, *What's Up, Tiger Lily?* Apparently you wrote some additional dialogue. How did that come about?

PM: When I was a comedian at the Renaissance, which is now the House of Blues on Sunset, the guy who ran it was Ben Shapiro, later Miles Davis's manger. He was the hipster of hipsters. When he had a stroke, I went to see him at Midway Hospital, and he was lying there in bed smoking a joint. *That's* how hip the guy was. He had just had a stroke! So he could only hold the joint in one side of his face. I said, "Benny, you can't go that far!" He was a great guy. Anyway, he knew someone who was involved with Woody's movie, but Woody was off it now, he had moved onto something else, but they needed a few more jokes. So Larry and I came in and wrote a few. The under-the-counter price we were paid was two round-trip tickets to Spain.

sw: Why Spain?

pm: Because I wanted to do research for this idea I had for a script called *H-Bomb Beach Party!*[6] That trip alone was hilarious. First of all, Larry couldn't fit in a normal seat. They had to put him in a seat where they could take the arm out. This was 1965. Larry at this point weighed about four hundred pounds.

sw: He's actually getting fatter.

pm: Oh, yeah. When we did *Alex in Wonderland*, he was actually at five hundred. In Spain, he was so fat the hotels wouldn't take us. They'd take one look at Larry and they'd go, "Gordo." I said, "What the fuck business is it of yours?" They'd say, "We don't have a chair he can sit on or a bed he can lie in." So we go from hotel to hotel and we're turned down everywhere. Remember, this was the Franco era. Finally, we get a hotel that will take us. Well, we go up to the room, Larry decides he wants to take a bath, and so he runs the water and makes his way into this round tub. A few moments later I hear water running onto the floor so I go over. He's stuck in the bathtub! [*Laughs*] He can't get out! At this point, within fifteen minutes, there's screaming and shouting from the people below that the water is dripping down from their ceiling. Soon the management is up in our room, knocking at the door, yelling at us in Spanish. I say, "*Por favor*, help me get this naked fat man out of the tub!" So we go in there to get him out and water's everywhere and we're sliding around and everyone's cursing and laughing. You can't imagine two guys ever having a better time.

sw: But *H-Bomb* doesn't happen, and you're back in L.A., in that office you and Larry rented above Sunset Strip, a picture of Lenny Bruce hanging above your desk. What did that mean to you?

pm: Lenny Bruce meant screw the establishment, let's go counter. That's always intrigued me, and I think you see it in my movies.

sw: Okay, so you and Larry are sitting down to write. How did the process begin for you two?

pm: Well, every one is different, but I remember I would parse out a character the way I used to do when I was studying acting. In those days, I would get one of those notebooks and write out a day in the life of the

6. *H-Bomb Beach Party!*, Mazursky's funniest unmade script, is a broad farce about nuclear disarmament, *Strangelove* meets Mel Brooks. "You know *H-Bomb* almost got made?" Mazursky said. "Hunt Stromberg, Jr. optioned it, Lawrence Harvey read it and said he wanted to do it, and I was going to direct it. We had this fabulous lunch at La Scala—me, Larry Tucker, Hunt, and Lawrence Harvey, who was hot as could be—but then it fell apart."

4. Paul Mazursky and Larry Tucker.

character, not what's in the script, but what I imagine it to be. Like if I was playing you, I might write out, "My name is Sam Wasson, I wake up in the morning and I eat a piece of whole wheat toast—I don't like white bread—I have a glass of orange juice, I get a phone call and don't take it, et cetera." I would write it all down. That helped us so that when we improvised, which we did a lot writing *Bob & Carol*, we had someplace to start. These details make you feel secure. They give you something to believe.

sw: After *H-Bomb Beach Party!*, you began to develop *I Love You, Alice B. Toklas!* Without being hostile, both pictures are about screwing the establishment.

PM: *Toklas* was about the influence of hippie culture on the bourgeoisie. In the past, anyone who was dissatisfied in their life had only a few choices about what to do. One, they accepted their lot even though they were miserable; two, they eased the problem with the bottle; three, they did something drastic. Along came the hippie thing—and Larry and I were right there for it—and people were saying, "Why do I have to live this life? Why do I have to marry this woman? Why do I have to be a lawyer? Why can't I let my hair grow long?" It was a thrilling time, I will say that. I doubt it will ever happen again. As funny as a lot of it now seems to me, we thought we were so hip. It was the opposite of the Beat Generation of *Next Stop, Greenwich Village*. There, in the fifties, we were profoundly interested in the existential realities of "Who are we and why are we here?" In both cases, I was lucky enough to participate, but always as an outsider. I was a hipster, but I wasn't the real thing because I still had a wife and two kids.

SW: It's a very revealing thing you're saying and it sheds light on a general attitude we see across your work. While your films show us the virtues of "being hip"—let's call it that—we always come back to the simpler, domestic pleasures of love and family. That is really the point of view of someone half on the fringe and half in the living room. It gives your satire a gentleness.

PM: At heart, family means more to me than anything. I couldn't abandon that and go to Tasmania.

SW: Harold Fine, the part Peter Sellers plays in *Toklas*, looks like he's going the opposite direction, from family to Tasmania.

PM: The difference is, Harold Fine is a deeply uptight person. I was never that uptight. I had already rebelled against my Jewish mother. But in the end, Harold . . . [*Beat*] How do you see the end for Harold?

SW: It could go either way. He could go back to Joyce [his fiancée] or he could disappear for good.

PM: We don't know what's going to happen. We just know that he's definitely not going to get married *this time*.

SW: You don't come down on either side, but instead leave us with a question. That's what freedom is—a question.

PM: That's exactly where I was in my own life—right in the middle. I went to the love-ins, though, and I took acid, but I had this family. You know, *Toklas* was the first thing that was personal from my point of view. Working for Danny Kaye was just a job.

SW: When you were writing, did you and Larry make a conscious effort to diagnose the public taste? Were you trying to write "now"?

PM: No. I never had that disease. *H-Bomb Beach Party!* came from something that Larry and I saw in the paper. It was in the news—there were two H-bombs lost—but we didn't write it for any reason other than we thought it was funny. *Toklas* came from a thought I had about a middle-class guy dropping out of his own wedding. It was a combination of *Yiddishkeit* and dope. [*Laughs*] That was the kernel of the idea. So Larry and I write *Alice B. Toklas* and we send it to our agent, a guy named Perry Leff. He read it and said, "Look, I like it a lot, but I'm not a movie agent. I'd like to show it to Freddie Fields." At that point, Freddie and David Begelman were the big agents at CMA [Creative Management Associates], which later became ICM. Freddie read it and the very next morning said, "It's the funniest script I've ever read—ever. I couldn't stop laughing. I know who's perfect for it, and I'm going to give it to him today." I asked, "Who?" And he said, "Peter Sellers." What? *Peter Sellers?* Larry and I didn't have any idea it was going to go there. But that's what Freddie did. He put together the concept like that. [*Snaps*] Peter Sellers was their client, Peter Sellers was looking for a movie, and this looked like something Peter Sellers could do. That was all Freddie. If it weren't for him, I don't believe I'd be where I am today. You know about Freddie, right?

Smiles.

Ah, Freddie . . . Freddie . . . Imagine a combination of Frank Sinatra and maybe Ramon Navarro—that's what he looked like. He had such tenacity. He was like a dog holding onto a bone. Anyway, I was excited to hear the name Sellers, but I didn't take it seriously. I didn't think he would do it. But the next day Freddie called me back and said, "Sellers loved it and I think I can make a deal today." This was the *very next day*. I said, "Okay." So Freddie calls again and said, "You got a deal, kid. Two hundred thousand for the script, you guys executive produce—you'll get seventy five thousand each for that—and that's the end of it." Larry and I made more in that one day than in a whole season with Danny Kaye. Sellers loved it, he wanted me to direct it, and I was in heaven—*heaven*. But I got into curious places with Peter before it ever started. I was supposed to direct, but Peter thought I was making a move for his wife, Britt Ekland. Yes, I wish it was true but it wasn't. That's a long story, I've told it many times, but the best version of it is in my book.[7]

7. "Dr. Strangelove," Mazursky's chapter on Sellers in *Show Me the Magic*, tells the story in full color (minus purple). Highly recommended.

SW: Sellers ended up picking Hy Averback, the television director, to direct.

PM: Hy was a very nice man and a very honest man. He knew the whole story of how I got cut. We all talked very openly about everything. He said, "Anything you have to say, tell me. I respect the script so much and I know you could have directed it." I have nothing but praise for him. But a week or so after the movie started shooting, I was summoned to Peter's house—and remember I was still the enemy. Britt answered the door. I think she was in a mini—I thought I'd have a heart attack. And right behind her was Peter. He said, "Come in, Paul. So nice of you to come." I'm saying to myself, "What the hell is going on?" And Peter started tearing up. He said, "Paul, the ship is sinking." He wanted me to take over and get rid of Hy. I said, "No, Peter. It's Hy's movie now. Let me be the first mate." And that's the way it worked out.

SW: You were on the set every day. Were there any points in the filming when you really stuck your neck out?

PM: I rarely changed anything. But there were a couple instances. When Peter started falling for Leigh Taylor-Young, we had reached the point in the script when he was supposed to turn against her character [Nancy] because the hippies had invaded his house, but he played it like he still adored her because in real life he did. So I said to Hy, "Hy, this is wrong." He said, "I know, I can't get him to stop." So I said, "You mind if I try something?" He said, "Be my guest." So I go down to the dressing room and said, "Peter, you're going to win the Oscar, you're brilliant"— all of that shit—"But, I think you're letting your personal feelings for Leigh get in the way." He said, [icy British] "You're giving me very bad vibrations, Paul. Very bad." And I said, "I don't give a shit what kind of vibrations I'm giving you. This is for the movie." And then he kind of flipped. And that was the end of me.

SW: If you had directed Toklas—

PM: I would have had a slightly different tone here and there. Just making the hippies a little realer. You see, I knew the hippie world. Hy didn't. Hy was a well-to-do director living out in Beverly Hills—like I am now—he knew the hippie scene, but it was more superficial. His film was a little sanitized. A little. I would have done it realer.

SW: Let's talk a little about the script. You and Larry seem to have taken great care to make sure the audience was up to speed on certain hipster in-jokes. Like the making of the brownies, for instance, and Harold's long explanation of the fetish, and the walks the hippie-guru takes with his followers . . .

PM: What's your point?

SW: You put a lot of exposition before things today's viewers take for granted. It leads me to think you and Larry *knew* you were heading into tricky territory, maybe even a touch unprecedented.

PM: I know that we were before *Easy Rider* with all the drugs. Remember, that hadn't happened yet. At that point, I had never seen anyone do drugs in a movie before. It was my assumption then that maybe two percent of the audience had ever heard of that stuff.

SW: So it wasn't the studio that came in and insisted these points—the brownie making, the guru, the fetish—be explicated in greater detail?

PM: The studio did nothing except they made us dub the cantors, who were speaking Yiddish, into English. They were nervous about that.

SW: And yet there's Yiddish throughout the whole movie!

PM: Who the hell knows why? I never had trouble with them, though. They were not bothered by ratings, or sexuality—none of that stuff had happened yet.

SW: Do you think the studio liked the movie?

PM: Yes, but they were afraid of it. The posters they made for it were very . . . *tame*. I would have done something more psychedelic, a little hotter. I would have told people to come to this movie stoned. But the studio was a little scared. [*Thinks*] Here's the paradox: They agree to do this movie and give Peter Sellers $750,000, which was a lot of money. They read the script and they know that Peter will play the lead, but that's it. They don't know who is going to direct it. Having done all that, now they're afraid of the Jewish content and the drugs. And the movie's called *I Love You, Alice B. Toklas!* They operate on a level that's . . . I don't know what it is . . . it's almost like, they're not stupid, but they do these weird things. It's bizarre.

SW: That's what I'm getting at. Their sudden fear is indication that you were onto something new. You were ahead of the curve.

PM: What can I tell you? We wrote about stuff we knew. Hippies, Jews . . . Any by the way, we didn't make the wedding scene offensive. We didn't make it *yenta*-like. It was, you know, a Jewish wedding. But look, it wasn't our goal to be daring, it was our goal just to write what we wanted.

SW: *Alice B. Toklas* introduces one of your major themes.

PM: What's that?

SW: Assimilation.

PM: Look, either you're too smart or I'm too lazy, but I don't sit down and think . . . [*Interrupting himself*] You mean about the Jews?

SW: I mean, the Jews, Harry Coombs [*Harry and Tonto*], Stephen Blume [*Blume in Love*] . . . all your characters, in some form of another, deal with the problems of culture clash. It could be accidental, but it's regular. Different types of people mixing, connecting, interacting . . . You find a lot of humor in it. Fish out of water, you know?

PM: Maybe. I'm not saying you're wrong, in fact you might be right. But that's your job. That's for you to decide.

SW: We've talked about the actors that got you interested in acting, but now, with *I Love You, Alice B. Toklas!*, you must have been beginning to think as a filmmaker. Do you remember when you first became aware of the director as an artistic force?

PM: Yes. I was living in Greenwich Village and somewhere in that period I remember going to see Fellini's *I Vitelloni* [1953], a film about four young men in postwar Italy who don't know what to do in their lives. They walk around a lot, they walk around arm in arm, they dream, they play pool, they have girlfriends . . . somehow the movie spoke to me. I remember when I came out of the movie, stepping out into the sunshine— I saw it in the daytime—I could hardly breathe. That got me. I had admired lots of movies, but never from the director's point of view. But Fellini changed that for me. I went ahead and saw more of his movies and then I got into Italian Neo-Realism.

SW: That's an important point. You fell in love with the neorealist side of Fellini, not the Fellini of the dream-life, what we think of as Felliniesque Fellini.

PM: What he had was a kind of anti-slickness, an anti-American combination of pathos and humor. That's what got me. I started thinking about directing, but not that seriously. Then I still wanted to make it as an actor.

SW: How did your experience on *Toklas* change the course of your career?

PM: After *Toklas*, Larry and I became the hottest things in Hollywood. We were all over *Variety* and *The Reporter*. "Mazursky and Tucker Hit It Big!" Headlines like that. *Big*. We were hot. And as Larry I began to write our next script, because of what I saw on *Toklas*, I decided I wasn't going to sell it unless I was going to direct it.

I Love You, Alice B. Toklas! is covered with Mazursky's thumbprints, but none of his touch; a lesson in unfulfilled auteurism. Compare Averback's film to Mazursky's upcoming works and suddenly, Mazursky's directorial resources become clearer. Where Averback underlines his every point with a close-up, a hard-hitting music cue, or an amplified cliché, Mazursky will hold back, using wide shots, silence, and his actor's behavioral whims to create a forgiving atmosphere, one that favors *getmutlich* satire over simple polemics. Fittingly, *I Love You, Alice B. Toklas!* is poised somewhere between the two, a countercultural film with the soul of classical Hollywood.

Before the film devolves into stereotype, it is a punchy Jewish screwball, swarming with Mazursky's dearest preoccupations: bourgeois stiffs, nutty families, the joys of sex, Jewish irony, L.A., marriage and promiscuity, culture clash, quirks of the decade, social awareness, and experimental lifestyles. Taken together in various combinations, these elements gel into Mazursky's signature themes: how we cope—moreover, how we feel—when a change in eras changes our notion of freedom, and ultimately, how we think we should love. All that's in the script of *I Love You, Alice B. Toklas!*, but not much of it made it to the screen. If it had, we might remember it, as we will many of Mazursky's films as a thermometer of its era calibrated by human hearts.

It was Mazursky's next movie, 1969's *Bob & Carol & Ted & Alice*, that brandished its thermometer like a blazing torch.

Bob & Carol & Ted & Alice (1969)

Bob Sanders: How do you feel?

It's Wednesday, 10:00 a.m.—now our regular time. I walk into reception, and Lauren, Mazursky's assistant, greets me with a cup of coffee. She's twenty-one, maybe twenty-two, with a bright face and a bouncy gait. "Paul's in there," she says. "You can go in." So I go in, somewhat shy about discussing a movie I really, really love with the man who made it. Has he heard it all before? Will I talk it to death? Moving quickly, I drag a chair to Mazursky's desk, and Paul looks up from the computer, smiling. He's rubbing his hands together like an eager kid.

PM: Should I tell you how I got the idea or do you know?

SW: You read the Fritz Perls article in *Time*, right?

PM: You got it. I saw this article that had Fritz Perls, the gestalt therapist, sitting in a hot tub with some naked people up at a place called the Esalen Institute. I thought, "Maybe there's something in this." So Betsy and I went up to Esalen for a weekend and it was fabulous. And I knew that it was a movie. But that's all I knew. What I didn't know was that we were the only couple in this marathon encounter. And Betsy and I were the only two there who knew each other. So they picked on us, but especially on me because Betsy would say things like, "He never lets me finish, he never lets me talk," and then she would start to cry and they would say to me, "You're a beast, you're brutal." I was the bad guy. [*Laughs*] So I did what Bob Culp did in the movie. I said, "Well, I'm only up here to make a movie." But they didn't think movie, they thought, *you need help.* When I came home I wrote the first twenty pages of the script—the Esalen pages. And then I showed them to Larry Tucker. He loved it. And then we went to Palm Springs together to finish it. You should have seen it: Larry would lie in the swimming pool, this four-hundred-pound guy, and I would sit with the typewriter or a recorder or something, I think a recorder—like yours—and we'd improvise the parts.

SW: Improvise?

PM: He'd play Bob, I'd play Carol, and vice-versa. And then we'd switch: he'd be Ted, and then I'd be Carol, and then we'd switch again. We wrote about sixty pages like that. It took a week.

sw: So there was no outline? No note cards?

pm: Well, there was. There was an outline, a treatment. I showed it to National General,[8] and tried to get them to give money, but the guy who read it said it was too dirty. So I asked, "What if I get Paul Newman and Joanne Woodward to play one couple?" He said, "Then it would be clean"—which is my favorite line—and I said to Larry, "We better write this on spec." And we did. After that, it only took us a few weeks.

sw: How did you get to direct it?

pm: I said to Larry when we wrote it, "I'll write it with you on one condition: If we like it, we don't sell it unless I direct it and you produce it." He said okay. That's when [producer] Mike Frankovich read it and asked me who I wanted to direct it. I said, "Mr. Frankovich, I have to make it clear to you that if I can't direct the movie, I won't sell it." He said, "Well, what have you done?" I told him that I did a short called *Last Year at Malibu*, I had studied acting, I knew about the camera from observing *Toklas*, I worked at *The Danny Kaye Show*, and I had been studying editing at USC at nights. He said, "Alright, I'll call you tomorrow about noon." The next day he called me and said, "You're on, kid."

sw: Just like that?

pm: Just like that. It was different in those days. People made decisions quicker. [*Thinks*] Anyway, before anyone had been cast, Frankovich suggested we approach Natalie Wood. *Natalie Wood!* Natalie was a big star and he thought we could get her at a reasonable price—she hadn't acted for years and I wasn't sure she could handle satire. So we went off to London to meet her. A day and a half later I'm having lunch with Natalie Wood at Claridges. I'm telling you, the minute I saw her I fell in love with her. You had to. We spent a full day walking and talking. And that was it; she wanted to do it and I wanted her to do it.

sw: What changed? What did you talk about?

pm: We talked about the way I work, about the fact that even though I hadn't directed a feature I knew plenty about it. I told her that we were getting a great cameraman, Charlie [Charles] Lang, who was noted for his great work with women. In those days a lot of women wanted a cameraman who was good to women.[9] Charlie had been nominated for

8. National General Pictures was a film distribution and production company active from the late 1960s to the early 1970s.

9. Lang had already proven himself to Natalie Wood. He had worked with her on *Sex and the Single Girl* and *Inside Daisy Clover*.

sixteen Oscars, and won one [*A Farewell to Arms*, 1932]. He was sixty-seven years old. He wore a shirt and tie everyday. No blue jeans or sneakers. A gentleman. He did a great thing the first day working with me. Before shooting began, I was full of confidence. I had rehearsed for two and a half weeks and before the movie began, I had shown much of it to Charlie and about ten crew members. Since there were no fight scenes or chases they could see seventy or eighty percent of the movie right in front of them. They were on the floor. I knew it was going to work! So, you see, I was very confident when the first day of shooting came around. I had it all in my head. As I hit the set—the interior of Esalen—I saw the entire cast and crew facing me. "Good morning, Paul! Good morning! Hi Chief! Hello Chief! Where do you want to start, Chief?" The whole movie went out of my head. I thought, "I don't know what the fuck to do."

SW: Can you ever tell an actor that you don't know what to do?

PM: Yeah. You can tell them that you're not sure. The older you get, the easier it is to do, though usually I wouldn't say it, but in a certain kind of place, why not?

SW: So, back to the Charles Lang story.

PM: Right. So there I am and everyone's looking at me and I don't know what to do. Charlie says to me, "You know Paul, I think there's a really good shot on top of the crane." I had never been on a crane. I said, "Okay! Let's take it!" And then they tied me into this crane—I don't like heights. He sat down on one seat and I sat down on the other and we went way the hell up, looking down on the set of the interior. Charlie said to me, [*low, gravelly voice*] "There's no shot from up here, Paul. I just thought we could talk about what to do in the scene. Let's start with an establishing shot panning past the crowd and get a few close-ups of our stars and then we'll begin doing twos and threes to cover." I told him I thought that sounded great, and then I shouted out, "Take us down please, we're ready to shoot!" And I got cocky in a minute. And we did it and it works.

SW: What did Lang bring to the look of the movie?

PM: He made the women look beautiful. With Natalie and Dyan [Cannon] it wasn't difficult. [*Chuckles*] I guess I can say this now. [*Chuckles again*] I asked Moss Mabry, the costumer—who I later used as the real estate salesman in *Alex in Wonderland*—if Natalie was built. He was the only man who had seen her naked and I wanted her in a bikini for the film, so I asked him, "How are her breasts?" He looked at me and said [*gay*], "Mine

5. Bob & Carol & Ted & Alice *(1969) Directing is very hard.*

are bigger." [*Laughter*] He used a push-up bra on her and it took care of everything. That was great. I loved Natalie. I actually loved her.

SW: I read in Gavin Lambert's biography *Natasha*—I don't know if you've heard this—that Natalie compared working with you to her best experiences with Nick Ray and Kazan.

PM: Isn't that something?

Paul looks away.

That's . . . Yeah . . . That's very touching . . .

SW: There was one problem with Natalie, though.

PM: We're in the Las Vegas suite—the scene before the orgy. She's in the foreground with Elliott [Gould]—I love these kinds of shots—and they're talking about how there's no reason to be having an orgy. In the background, Dyan and Culp are getting undressed. [*Laughs*] Dyan had on a bra with more lace on it than I had ever seen in my life and Culp has on that suit with the ruffled shirt—he wore his own wardrobe, by the way.

That's when Natalie tells me she isn't going to do the shot. I said, "What are you talking about?" I called cut. She said, "No one's going to be looking at me and Elliott." But that was the point—I told her this—we're seeing the orgy begin, it's actually starting. The point was not cutting to it, but seeing it in one shot.

sw: The contrast is what makes it funny.

pm: Yes. The irony of that, the beauty of it. Well, she wouldn't do it, so I told her I'd get a close-up of her. But no, she still wouldn't do it. Then I said, "If I don't get this shot, Natalie, you're going to need a new director because I'll walk off this movie." Deadly silence. She goes into her dressing room and I call Frankovich and Larry Tucker, and then I called lunch. I went into her dressing room and told her how much I cared for her and how wonderful she was. Still, she wouldn't do the shot. Then I asked her to take a walk. And I told her the story of my life, how I was born in Brooklyn and then did this and that . . . And then I said that I have always operated on the principle that you've got to do what you believe in, otherwise you're nobody. You may as well be a machine. I told her something to that effect and after about fifteen or twenty minutes she agreed to do the shot. And she was great. And she loved it in the movie. That was the only bump she and I had.

sw: Had you planned out the orgy scene?

pm: Not really, but I kept telling them that I had. I wanted it to be a surprise because I wanted them really nervous. I said that once they got there they should all be prepared for anything. At the last minute I said to them, "You go as far as you can and then in the last minute Culp is going to realize that he can't do it." So they went at it. [*Pause*] Culp was really feeling up Dyan. I mean, *really*.

sw: But the characters don't go through with it. Many critics called it a cop-out.

pm: But I didn't think they *could* do it. Not my people. Maybe some other director's, but not mine. Dyan's character was too square. And Natalie's character was vulnerable.

sw: And if they have an orgy, then the movie has to go on.

pm: Of course. There's no question in my mind that I did the right thing. I knew some people wouldn't like it, but it didn't bother me. And then we had that Fellini ending.[10]

10. The outdoor encounter session at the end of *Bob & Carol* looks back to the finale of *8½* when Fellini's company assembles on the set of Guido's unmade movie.

SW: But that wasn't the original ending. In the first draft of the script, after the aborted orgy, they all end up crying in each other's arms. Then they pull themselves together and see Tony Bennett. That was the end.

PM: But I liked the giant encounter in the parking lot. I wanted to indicate that [*sings the song*] "What the world needs now is love, sweet love." The song is what made it. When we cut it together it was okay, but it wasn't working one hundred percent. And then I heard the song on the radio.

SW: Did you want full nudity?

PM: Sure, but Natalie was a major star. They weren't doing that in those days.

SW: When you watch the film today and see Quincy Jones's name on the opening credits, you think it's sure a sign that some kind of great score is to follow. But there is no score. What you get is long stretches of silence.

PM: Quincy just jazzed up "The Messiah." The picture didn't need score. I only wanted source. It's more realistic that way.

SW: One of the interesting things about the script is that we make jumps in time often without any exposition. We find we've leapt ahead only after we've landed in the next scene.

PM: My concern was moving the story forward. What's this movie about? Is it about the fact that they went up there and had an orgy? I wanted to get right there.

SW: One of the things that distinguishes *Bob & Carol* from the comedies of today is that it's not cynical. These people are never criticized or humiliated for the sake of a laugh.

PM: No, no! I love them! I love these people! But I hate to use the word love in a trite way . . . I guess what I mean is, I can *understand* them, and I take them seriously. I couldn't make *Bob & Carol* about Hitler, Goebbels, and Goering and the three women in their lives. I couldn't do it because I'd ridicule them all the time. But with everyone else, I try to be compassionate. I try to laugh with compassion.

SW: When people see the movie, many assume a large part of it is improvised. But it isn't, right?

PM: No. There's no improvisation in it except the scene where Alice goes to the psychiatrist, played by Don Muhich. He was a real therapist—my therapist. I told him to stick with the dialogue in the script, but if something happens in the session he wanted to go with it, go with it. And I told Dyan this. There are a few places in the scene where they go with it. The vagina stuff.

6. Bob & Carol & Ted & Alice *(1969) Paul and Natalie, between setups.*

SW: It may be the best scene of psychotherapy ever shot.

PM: Yes, it's good.

SW: Why do you think people thought it was improvised?

PM: Because that's my style. To make 'em think it.

SW: How do you do that?

PM: I create an atmosphere of familiarity amongst the actors. I make it so they know they can't make a mistake. Not every actor could do it, though. Elliott and Dyan were brilliant at it—and so were Culp and Natalie. And Natalie was the least prepared for that kind of thing.

SW: She was a studio actress from childhood. She grew up with the older generation. A different style of actor.

PM: She was a little apprehensive. A couple of times she was nervous that they were stealing the movie, and sometimes she thought she was stiff. But she was wonderful.

SW: Could you tell the story of Pauline Kael's phone call? You told it to me earlier, but—

PM: The movie opened the New York Film Festival and it was a fantastic evening. They loved the movie. I was exalted. The only tough thing that happened was that my mother came. She called me Irwin in front of Mayor Lindsay and about five thousand other people. Anyway, we were having a great time at the big party afterwards, and about half an hour in—probably nine or ten at night—I saw Jack Atlas, the publicist for Columbia Pictures, walking across the floor. He had a newspaper folded under his arm and a very grim look on his face. I knew right away we were bombed in the *New York Times*. Canby. So I read the review and I felt I'd gone from Mount Olympus into the third ring of hell. The *New York Times* is like your uncle—that's the one review you really want. So I was feeling rotten. The following morning—we were staying at the Sherry Netherland—the phone rang quite early, like 8:00 a.m. or something. "Hello, this is Pauline Kael. You never met me." I said, "I know who you are, Miss Kael." She said, "I just wanted to let you know that . . ."—she said some nasty things about Canby—"he doesn't know what he's talking about, but you're getting a rave review from me, you're getting a rave review from Richard Corliss, and you're getting a rave review from Richard Schickel. You're getting rave reviews. I just didn't want you to feel bad all day." I was very touched. That's how we met—on the phone. She later became a big champion of almost all my movies. I believed in her. But she wanted to get involved a little bit. A few years later, she called and told me she wanted to see the rough cut of *Blume in Love* and I told her that I didn't want any critics to see my movies until they're ready to be seen. But I liked her. She was extremely bright and funny and a real friend. She was a great writer, the best maybe. She's up there with Manny Farber and a few others. She's unique. She was tough on me a couple of times, but she was never mean-spirited.

SW: Psychotherapy is hugely significant in this picture—in most of your pictures.

PM: We're living in a Freudian age. We examine ourselves in great detail before we act. Some day it may disappear and be gone forever. It could turn out to be a fad, but it doesn't look that way. You know, this is the age of anxiety—Auden said that. He said that the twentieth century was the age of anxiety.

SW: There's no question. And *Bob & Carol* is in part about that. But what about your history with therapy? When did you start?

PM: I went to four therapists, starting around when I was twenty-eight. I was having my first child. I decided that I was totally unfit to have a child. I had no idea how I was going to support it. *What was I doing?* So I went to a Russian therapist in New York. He was a Reikian—not as in Wilhelm Reich, but Theodor Reik—which meant that he was more of a PhD therapist, but what he did was dreams. The most profound thing that happened between him and I happened on the street one day after I had been going to him for about a year. He was about forty-five minutes late to our session and when he finally showed up he was drunk. I ran over to him and I said, "You're drunk. You're my therapist and you're drunk." He said, [*Russian accent*] "I am human being." It meant a lot to me.

SW: That's Mazursky.

PM: I understood it. And I kept going to him. And he helped me. Then I went to Don Muhich after I got *The Danny Kaye Show*. I was now making a good living, but instead of being filled with happiness and joy, I was slightly confused, not depressed—I never get depressed—I just didn't know what I was doing. I couldn't figure it all out. So I went to him for about two years. He was helpful.

SW: And you collaborated with him. After *Bob & Carol*, Muhich appears as a shrink in *Blume in Love*, *Willie & Phil*, and as the Whiteman's dog's analyst in *Down and Out and Beverly Hills*. Was he ever involved at the screenwriting level?

PM: No, no. But he's a good actor.

SW: I realize we're jumping a little all over the place here, but I want to go back and talk about the camera. *Bob & Carol* is shot mainly in masters and close-ups.

PM: That style suited me because that's basically the style of some of my heroes. Take a look at William Wyler's movies. Tremendous. *The Little Foxes*. *The Best Years of Our Lives*. There are shots that hold for six or seven minutes and it's not static. You see a whole performance. One character moves out of the frame and another character moves into the same shot. It's got depth of field so you can see back in the other room. A maid! She's cleaning. There's a maid back there! You're showing a *life*. Real life is in the masters, you know what I mean? [*Thinks*] I have scenes in *Bob & Carol* where they're in a certain room and in the background you see the maid walking around. Like in the scene when they're all getting stoned. You just see her feet walk by. That's it. Their little boy's birthday party is also a good example of that.

SW: The children are put on the periphery in much the same way.

PM: Yes, yes. That's part of showing a life.

7. Bob & Carol & Ted & Alice *(1969)* *Making the orgy.*

SW: Also, your long takes can really build tension. They force us to wait and wait and wait. "Is this going to really happen?" we ask.

PM: Yes. In *Bob & Carol* I'd play out entire scenes in one shot where you begin to realize what's going on because you're seeing the interplay of at least two characters in the same shot without cutting to them. Once you make a cut, you're making an emphasis. Without a cut it's actually happening in real time. [*Coughs, reaches for a bottle of water*] Right now, for example, if in this two-shot of you and me, I'm coughing and drinking water and all that, you know it's *really happening at this moment.* As soon as I cut to you looking at me thinking, "Am I alright? Is Mazursky alright?" then you cut back to me, and maybe we took a minute out of the scene. Maybe more. But if we just play it without interruption, you get the thing as it *actually happened*. You get the thing *real*. You know what I mean?

SW: Yes. So would I be correct in saying that Mazursky likes to start with a master and then cuts in only when he must?

PM: That's the way I learned and that's what I did. Not always, but much of the time I'd start with a master. It's very traditional. And off the master, you know your geography. A lot of people don't do that, though. When they want to show a whole room, they'll show a close-up of this tape recorder being put on the table, and then a shot of you as you sit and open your book, a shot of me getting my water, and then cut. You're now in another room listening to what you heard. We've cut the scene down to thirty seconds.

SW: Inserts.

PM: Yeah. When you shoot the thing, you see it one way; you see it real. But when you cut it up, you see the director manipulating it. He's lying to you.

SW: Lying?

PM: It's not true. It's not real.

SW: But the Esalen encounter group scene, which I think is some of the best stuff you've ever shot, is very cutty.

PM: I had a lot of characters. I want to get to meet all of them. And I want to see the interaction between all the people. So when the girl says, "I want to have a better orgasm," I want to see Natalie Wood and Culp make a face. I want reactions. That's why I cut. But, you know, there are no rules.

SW: It's funny you say that because it's what the leader of the encounter group says to everyone. That's how the film begins. That's how your career as director begins. There are no rules.

PM: Yes.

SW: To a certain extent, it's also at the heart of most of your movies. They are about freedom, the fear of it, the love of it.

PM: You start out thinking there are rules, but as life goes on you find out it doesn't work that way.

SW: That's frightening.

PM: And funny. [*Beat*] But I do love long scenes because long scenes allow you to see behavior, the strangeness of it, the wonderfulness of it.

sw: The bedroom exchange between Ted and Alice is ten minutes. It's a full reel.

pm: That kind of length gives you a series of behavioral moments that build on each other, and that's what makes it funnier. In other words, he starts out by jogging, and she's got a headache. She feels rotten—"I never want to see them again!" And then they get into bed and they're arguing about it.

sw: Long scenes afford you more beats. A greater emotional complexity.

pm: It's not just that. It's that you're seeing *real* life. You're seeing a couple in *real* time. She's taking her makeup off and putting her creams on. He's doing his jogging. It's building. If the scene began with the beginning of their argument, it wouldn't be as funny. The length of it makes it funnier. Of course, it wouldn't work if it wasn't well written and beautifully acted. And you're seeing a real performance! Not two actors doing two lines.

sw: Time is good for actors?

pm: Today they shoot a second of film and then break for coffee. Later, another second, and more coffee. My dentist could do it! You know what I mean? With Elliott and Dyan, you're seeing the whole thing.

sw: That's part of why these performances are so great.

pm: Yes, yes! It makes it better. It makes for depth. You'll notice, by the way, in some of Fellini's movies there are long, long scenes. *Nights of Cabiria . . . La Strada . . .* I didn't invent it.

sw: No, no, of course not. But it stands out in part because I think it's gone away.

pm: mtv has ruined it.

sw: Movies today are about precision, but real life is a mess. I remember a professor at film school telling us that a good way for us to ensure we were using only what we needed was to approach a scene like a bad party guest: Come in late and leave early.

pm: Not Mazursky.

sw: You arrive six hours before and stay all night.

pm: The mtv thing works sometimes, but it's of very little interest in terms of believability. Even a picture as well made as *The Departed* has about eight thousand cuts. It's great there, but that's a different thing.

sw: George Cukor always talked about long scenes. He loved them.

pm: He was definitely an influence on me. Once I was in his home for a party for the Oscar nominees in the category of best foreign film. Costa-Gavras was there and so were five young Americans; Mark Rydell was there, Norman Jewison, me, and Mike Nichols. [*Rich, stately voice*] "Cukor talked this way." He said to me on the phone, "It will be a few of my old friends." I was the first to arrive. The old friends were George Stevens, King Vidor, and Willy Wyler. [*Thinks*] Holy shit, can you believe these people? The last one was John Ford. Before he arrived, Cukor pulled me aside and said, "Do you like Jack Ford's work?"—I was the only one there—I said, "Very much, Mr. Cukor, he's one of the greats." Cukor said, "I want you to save his life." "Save his life?" "He's very diabetic, but he also loves the juice. He's going to want to drink a lot of red wine. I want you to cut it with water and switch glasses with him. I'll seat him right next to you." I said, "But he'll catch me." "No he won't," Cukor said, "he wears a patch over one eye." That was the day I saved John Ford's life.[11]

SW: I'm glad you did.

PM: Ford had long scenes, too. So did Truffaut, De Sica, Wilder, Kubrick, and Preston Sturges. These guys are my favorite. *Palm Beach Story* is fabulous. *Sullivan's Travels* is wonderful. The whole opening of that picture, the scene in the executive's office, is one continuous shot.

SW: Sturges offers a nice point of contrast with your work because his pictures are often clogged with bouncing bodies. But you, your spaces are open.

PM: Right. I like them to move around. I like to give you the feeling that they're free to do whatever they want.

No other work evokes the sexual discomfort of the late sixties as comprehensively as *Bob & Carol & Ted & Alice*. Mazursky never deflates his characters' tense situations by moralizing them into submission. He lets their confusions run carefully amok, and allows their emotionally awkward moments—stumbling blocks on the way to new interpersonal territory—to persist, even encouraging them to continue on (and on) long after the conventional Hollywood scene would have ended. The result is hilarious and unsettling, and pushes our understanding of these addled minds to its breaking point. Natalie Wood, Robert Culp, Elliott Gould, and Dyan Cannon all turn out the performances of their careers, imbuing each moment-by-tenuous-moment with the feints and parries of their changing intentions, never once succumbing to the muddle themselves. With dozens of delicious misdirects in every scene, it falls to the actors to make the regres-

11. For the rest of this story, see Mazursky's *Vanity Fair* article "The Day I Saved John Ford's Life" (3/1/04).

sions look like progress, and the bouts of cyclical logic like straight lines. Their work is cut out for them, just listen to the script: Tucker and Mazursky have done to the bourgeoisie's private life what *It Happened One Night* did to Claudette Colbert's upper thigh.

The picture opened the New York Film Festival with a standing ovation. Pauline Kael wrote, "You can feel something new in the comic spirit of this film—in the way Mazursky gets laughs by the rhythm of the clichés, defenses, and little verbal aggressions." That's right: You could—and still can—feel something new, and not just cinematically. Nailing what Tom Wolfe later called "the Me Generation" as early as 1969, *Bob & Carol & Ted & Alice* more than predicted the seventies, it practically invented them. The film was nominated for four Academy Awards (including a Best Screenplay nod for Tucker and Mazursky) and grossed over thirty million dollars.

Mazursky wasn't just on the map, he was the map. Every studio wanted him: Carpets unfurled, lunches went alfresco, and doors flew open all over Hollywood. One door in particular led out to the second-floor balcony of Paul's new house in Hancock Park. The view was beautiful. But from that high up, it would be a long way down.

Alex in Wonderland (1970)

Alex Morrison: I feel confused.

Paul's on the phone, but he waves me in, pointing to a plate of bagels on his desk. I help myself, and a moment later, he's hung up. *"Alex* today?" he asks.

"Yeah."

"Alright," he says, "This is a toughie, but go ahead."

sw: So *Bob & Carol* is a big hit . . .

pm: . . . and we're the kings of Hollywood. But we can't come up with an idea. We're going nuts. What about this? What about that? What about a book?

sw: What about *H-Bomb Beach Party*?

pm: That's a good question. I don't know why. We could've made it.

sw: You could've made anything. That's what *Alex* is about.

pm: Yes, Larry and I could have done anything. Nobody was going to say no to us, but you see, I wanted to do something good—something *profound.* Maybe it was my pretension, I don't know. Then one day, somewhere along the line, I said to Larry, "Why don't we do a movie about a guy who doesn't know what movie to make?" Larry says, "That's *8½.*" I said, "That's not about a guy who has a big hit, that's about a guy who doesn't know what to do."

sw: Your movie is about a guy who is stuck because of *8½?*

pm: He's dreaming in the style of other directors. He doesn't know how to use his own life—not yet—that's the idea. It's a complicated idea because the movie that I made, *Alex in Wonderland, is* using his own life. *That's* the irony. The movie I made is about the relationship between the husband and wife and the two kids. It's about the family.

sw: It's about how to stay real and stay connected to your family in the crazy world of Hollywood.

pm: That was always very important to me.

sw: For all the wild things that go on in the movie, it is the naturalistic scenes that stay with me. Your performance as Hal Stern, the producer trying to woo Alex, is my favorite thing in the picture.

PM: Larry and I improvised that based on experiences we had with a couple of producers. There was a guy named Jay Weston who must have offered me six or seven different movies. You turn one down, they bring you another. He had a huge office. [Producer] Ray Stark offered Larry and I a Mercedes just to take a meeting. I'm not kidding. We turned it down because we felt we'd have to cut the car in half. How would we split it? [*Laughs*] Another time Ray came to my office and wanted to pitch me an idea for a movie. He said, "What are you doing later today?" I said, "Nothing." He said, "Well, I'm going to Israel, come with me and we can talk on the plane." I should've done it just for the experience. [*Thinks*] The office we used in *Alex* was actually a real office at MGM. At some point, it was [Irving] Thalberg's. I liked it because it was huge and I could give my character that long walk back to the desk to keep getting the scripts. He has to get up from the lunch and come back.

SW: You make great use of eating the salad in that scene.

PM: I knew it was going to be funny. A lot of actors like to use eating. It helps you to stop thinking about the lines. The best way to do lines is not to think about the words, but to think about the activity. So if my line is "I never want to see you again!" I can do it this way: [*Shouts directly at me*] "I never want to see you again!" Or I can do it like this: [*Takes a sip of water*] "I never want to see you again." It's making it real.

SW: How do you know when it doesn't work, when an actor's faking?

PM: You don't always know. It's a lot of guesswork, a lot of trial and error. You try it one way and that doesn't work, so you try it another way and another way and another way and then finally you hit it. Or maybe, finally, you throw everything away and say, "Let's forget everything we've talked about and start over again doing just one thing." Let's try it, Sammy. [*Beat*] Just think of yourself as a butterfly.

SW: Me?

PM: Ask me, "Paul, do you think I'm doing a good job with this book?" But do it like a butterfly. Action.

SW: [*Softly, a slight Julie Hagerty quality*] Paul, do you think I'm doing a good job with this book?

PM: Pretty good. See, you weren't thinking about the words. Now, I want you to do the same thing, but like a rat.

SW: A rat?

PM: Do it like a rat.

SW: [*A Bogartish thing, god knows why*] Paul, do you think I'm doing a good job with this book?

PM: Now you're off the lines. It gets you into doing something else that might help you in the end. These things are for rehearsal. Not for performance. For example, tell a guy to sneak into a room and he sneaks in like this.

Mazursky gets up and tiptoes around his desk in broad pantomime.

But it's so obvious. It's a cliché. So you tell the actor, "You've got to cross from here to there, but there are little bits of eggshell on the ground with only small spaces between them. Don't break any egg."

He tiptoes again, but this time he studies specific spots on the floor before he decides where to place his steps.

It's different, isn't it?

It is. It's better.

Now when you're ready to shoot, you might not be thinking about it.

SW: Also, it's real.

PM: You got it.

Mazursky takes his seat.

Go ahead.

SW: A few weeks ago, in our discussion of *I Love You, Alice B. Toklas!*, you said that the fifties, the Beat Generation, was defined by Existentialism; and the sixties was sex and drugs; so what's the seventies?

PM: I can't answer that. I can only answer for Paul Mazursky.

SW: Okay, what were the seventies for you?

PM: I think, for me, the seventies were: You're forty. You're now in your forties. So the seventies, for me, was about getting older and not knowing where to go.

SW: You're talking about Mazursky, but the seventies were, for so many, about fear and confusion.

PM: I just know my thing. I don't want to sound pretentious . . .

SW: No, no. What I'm saying is that you, in your own life, were going through on a minor level what the country was going through as a whole. And that often seems to be the case with your movies. I mean, a synchrony between shifts in your inner life and shifts in America's. Call it good cultural analysis or call it good timing or just dumb luck, but it's what Mazursky does.

PM: Well . . . when I wrote *An Unmarried Woman*, I was aware of the women's movement, which was happening then. But it was happening to me! I wrote it not because it was happening in America, but because I'd see divorce happening around *me*.

SW: Right! But that's what I'm saying. You don't have to be conscious of it to be a sponge of the times.

PM: You're making me think, "What's happening now?" And the answer is, I don't know. Maybe the reason old guys don't get to make movies is that they don't have a handle on *now*. See what I mean? Maybe that's why it's been so hard for me to get the money to make movies, because I don't have a handle on now. Or maybe I do have a handle on it and they don't want it. Because now all the way is remakes and sequels. How are you supposed to get the now when you're doing something that they made already?

SW: And that was most definitely not the case in the seventies.

PM: No. I was getting to that point. If I were trying to break into the movies now, I never would have written a script like *Toklas*. But where were we?

SW: *Alex in Wonderland*.

PM: Okay, so, before it was at MGM, the picture was at Columbia with Mike Frankovich. He made a deal to do the picture, but I could tell he was uncomfortable with the opening scene in which Sutherland takes a bath with his daughter, a little girl. Frankovich thought it was vulgar. I could tell then that we'd have trouble. So I went to Freddie Fields and David Begelman, my agents, and I told them, and they managed to help me get it switched to MGM.

SW: With no hard feelings? No lawsuit?

PM: No. None. It's a funny story, actually. When Freddie and David made the phone call, Freddie pretended to be David and David pretended to be Freddie. I was in their office, I heard it. I said, "Why did you do it that way?" They said, "Just to relax." They wanted to be loose and have some fun. That was their way to have fun. [*Beat*] You know, *Alex* was the last picture made at MGM when it was still MGM. We closed the place down. [*Thinks*] I wish I could get a print of that one. None exists. No one can find it.

SW: It's such an explicitly autobiographical movie, how did your family respond to it?

PM: [*Laughs*] Do you know what my mother said? She said, "You're making fun of me! I'm going to picket." And then she said, "Why couldn't you get Bette Davis to play me?" I was scared! I thought she was going to get a sandwich board that said, "Don't see this movie, my son is making fun of me!" I begged her not to. I really begged her. I'll tell you one other thing—I don't think this has ever been printed—she read for me.

SW: You auditioned your own mother?

PM: Yeah. She didn't get the part. She couldn't do it. She couldn't play herself. [*Laughs*] Boy, she was pissed.

SW: You ended up with Viola Spolin, one of the pioneers of American improv.

PM: She claims. No one discovered it. You think Stanislavski never played with that stuff? I'll tell you a story about that. When Lee J. Cobb was doing *Salesman*, he came to my acting class to talk to us. Someone asked him, "Mr. Cobb, when do you use the Method?" He said, "Only when I have a headache. It's like an aspirin."

SW: What does that mean?

PM: It means, you use your common sense, but when it's not working, when you need more, then you start working in Method. But if you don't need it, you don't use it.

SW: Okay, so under what circumstances would you give line readings?

PM: Only if I'm desperate.

SW: Why?

PM: Because then it's *you*. I want it from *them*.

SW: So what's your first course of action when something's not going right?

PM: I would try to phrase it in a way that made them think about it and might produce the answer, but if I got desperate and wanted to give them some kind of reading, I would be sure to *overdo* it. That way I make the point, but I would do it so big that they would know not to copy it. Then they would then do it their own way.

SW: Ellen Burstyn is brilliant in the movie. She never talks to Alex about their marriage, but she doesn't need to—the whole story is playing across her face. It's superb acting.

PM: The movie is about marriage. It's about having children. It's not about the fantasies.

Mazursky leaps out of his chair . . .

What a bizarre movie!

. . . and sits back down.

You want one of these?

He points to a bag of cherry Ricolas.

SW: Sure.

PM: [*Narrating*] "Mazursky gives him a sugarless Ricola." [*Laughs*] See, those are the touches.

SW: Touches? What do you mean?

PM: If you had this touch in a movie, you'd know it was real. If you write this scene, with you interviewing me, it's just a straight interview. You, then me, then you . . . But if you've got the Ricola and this cold cup of coffee over here, you've got an interesting movie, right?

SW: Right.

PM: You know why?

SW: Details.

PM: That's it. Details and specificity. Okay, back to *Alex*.

SW: You have—

PM: I don't want to tell you what to do, but I think you should think about putting that scene in the book. Back to *Alex*.

SW: You have some massive set pieces in the movie, the biggest and most elaborate of your career. There's the Hollywood Boulevard Vietnam fantasia, the naked dance-orgy on the beach . . .

PM: Shooting that was hilarious. We found some guy in town who handled extras in the African-American community. I said to him, "Can you get me three hundred African-Americans who will be totally naked? We'll pay a little bit more." He said, "Yeah." So we go out to this deserted beach out near Malibu and they start taking their clothes off and they get down to their jockey shorts and brassieres and then I realized that most of them didn't want to do it. I thought, "What the hell's going on? How am I going to do this?" So the guy said, "It's because you're a white director with a white crew and all of you are fully dressed." So I took off all my clothes except for my hat and I got on the crane and I said, "Let's go folks!" and I got some of the crew to take their shirts off, but I went all the way. It was tough—believe me. [*Thinks*] Who knows what that scene means? I don't know what it means. I have no idea. It's just a dream. He was caught in the maelstrom of the Black dilemma. Alex wants to be important, he wants to be good, he wants to make an important movie, and when he tells his daughter, she says—

SW: She says, "Daddy, make a movie about us."

PM: Which is what I ended up making. It's all true. That was my daughter

8. Alex in Wonderland *(1970) Recreating the Vietnam War on Hollywood Boulevard. Mazursky sits behind the camera (in a black hat).*

Meg. When Fellini saw it he said, [*gentle Italian accent*] "Paolino, very sweet, very sweet. I loved the family. But the fantasies I could do without." It was a crushing blow to me in a way.

SW: But that's exactly what the story is. It's about the emptiness of the fantasies.

PM: You know, after seeing *Bob & Carol*, people thought I was limited. They said, "This is very good, but it's so simple, we don't know if he knows much about the camera."

SW: Kael wrote, "Mazursky and Tucker are best when the camera barely moves." She's talking about *Bob & Carol*.

PM: Right. But that's the case in that movie. In the case of *Alex in Wonderland*, the camera's moving all over the joint. It's a different movie.

SW: Were you nervous about it at all?

PM: No, no. We were so excited to go to work every day, but then we were so depressed when we had the first preview. You could tell something was wrong. The audience was baffled and silent. I thought it would be regarded as good work, maybe as an important movie. An art house movie—it only cost two million bucks—not expensive.

sw: Again, like *Bob & Carol*, your story structure is more impressionistic. This is not *Down and Out in Beverly Hills* where one scene births the next scene and that scene births the next scene . . .

pm: No, this is a quilt of scenes. It gives you fragments.

sw: As a result, you don't have a sense of real time.

pm: I wanted to show you the mundane things. He's in the supermarket with his wife talking about Lenny Bruce, he's driving his kid to school, and then the scenes with his mother. There's an accident on the side of the road—mundane things—he doesn't notice them because his mind is in his movie. It's in the surreal.

sw: Was that your experience? One foot in the surreal and one foot in the real?

pm: It's still my experience. Just moments ago I got off the phone with my wife and we were trying to figure out where to have dinner with our kids and our grandkids, who I worship. But I'm still the same guy who took ayahuasca in the jungles of the Amazon. I wouldn't advise everybody to do it, but my curiosity is to experience everything possible.

sw: Characters in your movies keep saying that.

pm: Yes, but when it comes right down to it, I'm happiest when I'm in bed with my wife watching CNN and eating ice cream.

sw: And that's what Alex decides at the end of the movie.

pm: I don't know. I felt that that at the end of the movie his search was still going on.

sw: I think it's a happy ending. He goes to his daughter's performance and sees that she's done the kind of work that he's been trying to get at. It's political, it's surreal, it's a musical—it has all the elements that have been floating around Alex's mind. And it's not a fantasy.

pm: Except he sees all the Fellini stuff in the background of her performance—the giraffe, the clowns. He's still in the fantasy world. When he goes to the house at the end, he's talking to the tree and there's no fantasy. It's a big, beautiful tree with roots. The roots are what make that image. He's rooted. He's grounded now. That's real, but it's not a movie. He's still thinking, you see? He's walking and walking and walking. And that's it. It's whatever you want to make of it.

sw: One of the most memorable things about *Alex*—and this is, I think, a very Mazurskyian quality—is that you have people doing and talking about things that occur all the time in reality but never in movies. The Ricola factor!

pm: Right.

9. Alex in Wonderland
(1970) *Paul and Jeanne
Moreau. The actress
has a brief cameo in*
Alex in Wonderland.

sw: For instance, the movie opens with Sutherland taking a bath with his daughter. Later, a bunch of grown men are walking down the beach talking about masturbation.

pm: I wrote those because things like that happened to me. I figured you've got to put everything in this movie. [*Thinks*] Usually you're trying to deal with clarity. At the end of the movie everything makes sense. "I see it now!" That kind of thing. But it's a giant cliché. I wouldn't do it.

sw: You like the rough edges, scenes that don't propel the narrative, scenes most other American directors would have cut.

pm: I wanted this to be like *Juliet of the Spirits*. Flowing.

Mazursky leans forward in his chair.

[*Whispering*] Have I told you about meeting Fellini?

sw: No, not yet.

He takes a deep breath.

pm: I wrote Fellini into the script. I didn't know him then, but I put him in. Frankovich and I were trying to figure out how to get him, and by the sheerest of coincidences, Anthony Quinn was in the office. He was a very imposing figure and of course he had been in *La Strada*. He heard the conversation and he said that he knew the Maestro very well, but that he didn't think he would do it. He gave us Fellini's address and phone number anyway and said that if we couldn't get him, that he'd do it. So then I sent a telegram to Fellini saying, "My name is Paul Mazursky, I made a movie called *Bob & Carol & Ted & Alice* and I've just written a new movie called *Alex in Wonderland* and you're in it." I told him that I only needed him for one day and that I'd come to Rome. The next day or so he sent me back a telegram that said, "Mazursky, I don't know who you are. I never saw your movie. I'm not an actor. I'm a director. My name is Fellini. P.S. if you ever come to Rome, call me." So Frankovich got me tickets and I flew to Rome the next day with Larry Tucker. When I got there I called Mario Longardi, who is his right-hand guy. Through him I made an appointment to meet Fellini in the lobby of the Grand Hotel at eight o'clock that night. So we're waiting there, Larry and I, and it was as though Nino Rota was playing the music right there: The doors turn, there's Longardi, and standing next to him is the Maestro. Black hat, black coat, everything. And he's big, too. Bigger than I had imagined. He takes one look at us—Larry weighed four hundred and fifty pounds—and he started to laugh. "Which one is Mazursky?" he asked. "Me," I told him. "What do you want?" he asked. I told him that I wanted him to play the part in this movie. And he's speaking English, by the way. We became friendly in ten minutes. He was like a piece of sugar. He kept saying, "You don't want me. Use a puppet. Use a giant. Get a dwarf. You don't need the real Fellini. It's in your *imagination*. It will spoil your movie." I said, "No, I need the real thing." For four days and four nights we hung out with him. At the end, when we were getting ready to leave, he said, "Do you really want me in your movie?" I said, "Yes, Maestro." He embraced me and I had tears in my eyes. I said to him, "I have three days left in Italy. Should I go to Florence or Venice?" He said to me, "Firenze or Venezia? You want marijuana or LSD?" I said, "I'll take LSD." "Venezia." And right there he called the Danieli Hotel and booked me a room. Back in L.A., I'm shooting *Alex* and having a wonderful time and I'm very excited because in about eight weeks I'll be going back to Rome to shoot the scene with Fellini. I get a call at my house the Saturday before I'm supposed to leave for Europe and it's Mario Longardi. The reception was bad, but I knew what he was saying [*frantic Italian*] "Mazursky, Mazursky, it's Longardi! The Maestro . . . he changed his mind . . . he changed his mind . . ." So I hang up and I say to Betsy, "I'm pretty sure he just said Fellini won't do it, but I'm not going to tell anybody." So I get Larry, Sutherland, [cinematographer, Laszlo] Kovacs, [associate producer] Tony Ray and his wife Gloria Grahame, and I don't tell any of them that Fellini *can't* do it. I call Longardi when we land and he says, "What are you doing here? I told you he can't do it!" I said, "Oh my God! I misunderstood! I thought you said—" "I said he can't!" "I thought you said he *can*!" [*Laughs*] And then Longardi said, "If you want to see Fellini, he's at Cesarina's restaurant." So I went. I walk in, I knew Cesarina—Fellini had helped her found the restaurant—and she pointed out the Maestro. I looked across the room and there he was. He was sitting behind a table, twirling spaghetti around his fork. So I go over to the table and say, "Good evening, Maestro!" Well, Fellini looked up at me. He just looked at me for a long time. A long time. And then he said, [*high voice*] "Okay, I do it." The next day I meet him at his editing room at Cinecittà and I see he's brought with him his film, *The Clowns*, and one of his editors. He was all ready. He would say to me, "Excuse me, my director, is it okay if I move a little bit this way?" I'd say, "No! Don't move that way!" [*Laughs*] He would say, "I am going to stand here, is that alright with you? You are a great director, of course."

SW: When did he see *Bob & Carol*?

PM: In Rome, the time before. Larry and I came with big cans—there was no DVD—we showed him the whole movie. When it was over he said, "Very sweet, very beautiful, I like it a lot." I mean it. Otherwise, he wouldn't have done *Alex*.

SW: Where does Guilietta Masina fit into all this?

PM: I'd see her at dinners at Fellini's house. She came to L.A., I saw her in New York. You know she was the female Charlie Chaplin?

SW: Without a doubt.

PM: Genius.

SW: Did he have affairs?

PM: She accepted it. They were meant to be with each other. They had a little apartment in Via Margutta, not far from where I lived. If you go to 110 Via Margutta, right near the Piazza del Popolo.

SW: That was near the Canova Café?

PM: Yes. That's where he used to hang out. He would buy treats for my kids. He didn't know they were mine, but he would look out for them. My daughter Jill, he would call her Guilletta. That's when he said he wanted to show them *The Clowns*, the movie he was working on. So we went and of course Jill fell asleep. She snored throughout he whole picture. When it was done, Fellini said, joking, "How dare you bring a child here to snore through my work!" There was no one like him. He took you into his soul. I miss him a lot.

Alex in Wonderland was released (read: dumped) on December 22nd, 1970. It was preceded by an inadequate promotional campaign. Mazursky said, "It didn't have a rabbi." He means that a film of this kind should have had a studio man on its side, someone on high who got it and, when the

10. Alex in Wonderland *(1970) Fellini embraces Mazursky. The Maestro is holding Paul's hat—and Paul is wearing Fellini's.*

time was right, could have found the appropriate way to deliver it to the public. What *Alex* got instead was bad timing—the Christmas season was no match for an arty niche picture about artistic paralysis.

And yet no rabbi could alter that Mazursky, taking himself as his subject, was making himself intensely vulnerable. Even in the neurotic seventies, the critical consensus agreed self-analysis in the movies was better off when it was done in Europe. Americans like to nail Americans for opening their psyches on film. That said, Fellini was right about the naturalistic scenes; they make the fantasy sequences look labored and do little to illuminate Alex's predicament.

Ellen Burstyn, however, is top-notch, and the film's flagrant disavowal of Hollywood norms makes it a noble miss. The best thing in *Alex* is Mazursky's scene, opposite Donald Sutherland, as studio executive Hal Stern. It is Paul's greatest moment on screen, perhaps the best description of studio bullshit ever filmed, and without question formalizes Mazursky's status, not just as a serious performer, but as that rare breed of triple-hyphenate—director-writer-actor—placing him in a category that includes Woody Allen, John Cassavetes, and Mel Brooks.

Paul has a difficult time talking about *Alex in Wonderland*. I can see it hurts him even today, but forty years ago, in 1971, it opened the door to crisis. Angry at the movie business, disappointed in the American mainstream, and lured, maybe, by the prospect of dropping out a little, Mazursky packed up his family—Betsy, and his daughters Meg and Jill—and moved them to Rome.

Meg on Mazursky

Amy Morrison, *Alex in Wonderland*

Meg's front hallway, like her father's office, is wallpapered with family photographs. It takes us from the front door into the kitchen, where she picks up a plate of cookies ("If you don't eat them," she says, "you're taking them home") and carries them into the living room. In no time I see Meg has her mother's face and her father's knack for candid conversation. We begin talking about our therapists almost immediately, and an hour later, we're so deep into our own lives, it almost feels rude to change the topic.

sw: Did you want to be an actress when your dad gave you the part of Amy in *Alex in Wonderland*?

MEG MAZURSKY: No, not at all. Actually, I was very shy, to tell you the truth. I was not even interested in acting, but because the movie was so autobiographical, my dad starting thinking, "Well, maybe Meg could play Alex's daughter." So he talked to me a little bit about it, and before I knew it I was doing screen tests. The first screen test was actually with Henry Jaglom, who was auditioning for the role of Alex. [*Beat*] But I had terrible stage fright.

sw: So he took a big chance on you. How did he pitch the idea?

MM: I was surprised. I said, "Dad, you really think I can do this?" But it was a time when people were doing that kind of thing in Hollywood.

sw: Did your dad give you notes between takes?

MM: No. He just gave me a lot of freedom to just be me. When something wasn't working, I think my dad probably talked a lot to Donald about getting the performance that he wanted out of me. I think he directed me through him.

sw: I know Paul doesn't improvise very much in his movies, but that scene in bed between you and Sutherland is extremely natural.

MM: That was my big scene. It was all scripted, but as we were rolling, he started asking me some questions that I wasn't prepared for. One of them was, "Are you interested in boys?" and I got red immediately and they kept it in the movie.

sw: The whole movie is really an experiment, the most experimental of Paul's career.

11. *Meg (in flower dress), Betsy (in white), baby Jill (the clown), and Paul Mazursky (in hat) during production of* Alex in Wonderland. *Los Angeles, June 1970.*

MM: He was on the fringe of being the voyeur and the filmmaker, but once in a while he would partake, so I would get very mixed messages.

SW: What do you mean?

MM: For example, people would often bring over huge bricks of hash to the house. At first it frightened me and then a little bit later I would just steal it. I would open the refrigerator and there would be mushrooms and I didn't know if they were edible. It came pretty close a few times. My parents weren't really into that stuff, but they had it around because all these crazy people were around, and yet they didn't function like that. They had very safe middle-class values. We had dinner as a family every night. No matter what my dad was doing, family came first.

SW: *Alex* ends with family prevailing.

MM: And we all moved to Rome after the movie.

SW: Do you remember Fellini?

MM: Oh, yeah. I was in awe of him. I was really nervous around him. He would come by the house to pick up my dad and they would just drive around the streets of Rome at night. In the mornings, Jill and I would be waiting for the school bus, and Fellini would be right there at the café and he would buy us pastries.

sw: As a Mazursky, you have a privileged angle on the relationship between these movies and Paul's real life. In his subsequent films, did you ever see yourself reflected in the roles of the children?

mm: Oh, definitely. I mean, I *was* Lisa Lucas in *An Unmarried Woman*. She was me. And definitely Tracy Nelson in *Down and Out in Beverly Hills*.

sw: Both precocious girls.

mm: Yeah, totally. Tracy Nelson went to Sarah Lawrence and had a rock and roll boyfriend and that was me. [*Beat*] That group of women in *An Unmarried Woman* was all my mom's friends. Completely.

sw: And Susan Anspach in *Blume in Love* looks a lot like Betsy.

mm: Oh, god. Yes. Susan's portrayal of that character was very much like my mother. They're both very sensitive—*very* sensitive. She'd cry a lot. [*Thinks*] And Blume reminds me of my dad, too.

sw: How so?

mm: Oh . . . Both of them are very romantic men. Did my dad tell you that after he had made *Blume*, he bought an apartment at One Fifth Avenue because it was overlooking the park where he met my mother?

Blume in Love (1973)

Stephen Blume: I love Nina.

Today Mazursky and I meet at his beach house in Venice. Venice, California. "Come in," he says at the door. "Maybe you can help me." His TVs are busted. "My grandkids come in here and fuck the whole thing up with Pokémon." I manage to fix the TV in the living room, but I can't do anything with the one in the bedroom. "Forget it," he says, directing us deeper into the house, toward the living room. "The repairman should be here in an hour." There are very few walls chez Mazursky; the place is airy and open, with wraparound windows that make it all seem bigger, as if the room extended all the way out to the ocean. Stepping over his grandkids' Legos, Mazursky leads us to two chairs at the foot of the biggest window in the house and resumes a line of conversation we started days ago.

PM: It seems to me that if I had anything profound to say about myself, even though I've been doing this for forty years—since 1967—I'm still the same guy. I've got the same values, the same hang-ups. I'm more secure only in that I'm less afraid of everything, because what are they going to do to me at this point?

SW: You know, I was thinking, You've never said yes to a movie you didn't want to do.

PM: That's not going to happen. I've never done that. I couldn't do it.

SW: Even Cassavetes took bullshit jobs.

PM: A few, because he needed the money to make his own movies. So did Orson Welles. But I didn't need the money because I made *Bob & Carol*. That movie made me a rich man. After the first picture I directed, I was a millionaire.

SW: Do you think the movies would be better if actors didn't get major gross points?

PM: Well, I think the movies would be better if there was a very different system. Period. The European system is a little different. People work for less money, people work for no money, people say yes on the phone to a friend. That's what they do. When Fellini would say to Marcello, "I need you for September," Marcello's going to do it for him. He's not going to say, "Can I read the script? Can I get a trailer?" He'd be embarrassed to do that. Only here is there all that bullshit. The irony is that the only one who has beaten that nonsense, and does whatever he wants, is Mel Gibson. [*Laughs*] You understand? That's the irony. Mel Gibson said, "Fuck them! I'm going to do one called *The Passion of the Christ*!"

SW: Did you see it?

PM: Yeah.

SW: How was it?

PM: You either die laughing or go with it. When I saw it, people were crying. I think the next movie he's going to make is going to be about the "real" Holocaust. You know what I mean? There was absolutely no Holocaust. There were Jews all over Europe saying, "This isn't a holocaust, this is vacation! Auschwitz isn't so bad. You know, I think I'll take a dip now—but make sure the Germans think everyone's doing a holocaust." It would be a great Monty Python. [*English accent*] "Holocaust? There's no Holocaust! I'm sitting down to a seven-course meal with pâté and then we'll have Pesach at six o'clock and then we're off to a wonderful show! The Germans are wonderful people! The yellow armbands we're wearing are merely passes to get you into the theaters around Auschwitz!" He'll call it *Holocaust? A Comedy by Mel Gibson*, and Woody Allen will play the Jew. It will start with a postcard, "Dear Mom, I'm having a wonderful time . . ." With Mel's money, it could happen. That's how crazy the business is. In a couple of years no one will be able to stop him. He'll own the studio. [*Laughs*] So, are we up to *Blume*?

SW: Yes.

PM: Okay. Okay. So, after *Alex* came out I decided I wanted to live in Rome. I wanted to see what it was like to live in Europe. I was also hurt by the American response to the movie and I wanted to live someplace where the accent wasn't on box office and all that shit.

SW: Were you living la dolce vita?

PM: No, I was still living the family life with Betsy and the kids. In that five- or six-month Roman period, I had already come up with the idea for *Harry and Tonto* and I had gotten some money from John Calley, a very smart executive, and with Josh Greenfeld, I wrote this thing about a man and his cat. Of course, no one wanted to do it. It's about an old man and his cat! Who wanted that? So I had to try to write another script. After I got back from Rome, I got [agent] Jeff Berg to give me an office at ICM, which was then on Beverly Boulevard above Madeo's Restaurant. I would go in every day, five days a week. I would get in at around nine thirty and stay until about two. I would try to write something every day.

Some days I'd write one page, some days I'd write ten pages. So I started with a scene—I didn't know what I was writing—about a guy sitting in Venice talking about love. It was a fantasy about me being caught by my wife, though none if it happened to me. It happened to someone I knew. I won't tell you who, but that was the kernel of the idea. I based it on stuff that I was familiar with, which was the left-wing-leaning liberal of the upper middle class. That's all I knew. I didn't have George Segal in mind. I didn't have anyone in mind. It was just a guy in a café. As for the script, I didn't see all of it in my head when I was writing it. But I saw the end. I saw *forgiveness*. That's all I knew.

SW: This was your first solo script. Why weren't you writing with Larry Tucker?

PM: When I went to Rome to shoot Fellini for *Alex*, I was gone for a week. When I came back, Larry said to me, "I've had an incredible eight or nine days. I had a three-day marathon gestalt encounter with a therapist and I've decided to leave my wife Marlene and to break up with you." I said, "Both in one weekend?" He said, "Yeah. You know I love you, but I want to be on my own." I said, "But Larry, you know you could still be a producer, you can go do a movie yourself, we don't have to do a movie together. Why so extreme?" He said, "I don't know." And then he went off. He probably didn't want to be a part of Mazursky and Tucker. Just Tucker. That's how it happened. He then went on to have a modest career in television, but no more movies.

SW: Did you remain close?

PM: We did, but we never were close socially. I went to see him in the hospital before he died. This was five years ago. It was sad.

Quiet.

The script for *Blume in Love* came out of me in about six weeks.

SW: That's quick.

PM: It's very quick. The only other time I wrote that freely was when I was doing *An Unmarried Woman*. So my general theory is if it doesn't come quick, it ain't gonna work. Go where your subconscious is taking you. Try to end each writing day with the wisp of an idea that will be where you begin the next morning. That way, when you get there, you don't go, "What the fuck am I going to do?" So anyway, after I finished a first draft of *Blume*, I polished it a little bit and gave it to Jeff Berg, and Berg gave it to John Calley, and Calley said yes. Just like that. That's how it worked then.

SW: And that draft—the script you wrote—is almost exactly what the movie is. You cut a few scenes, maybe one or two, but by and large the *Blume* you wrote is the *Blume* that was made. That's remarkable.

PM: I was lucky. There wasn't much interference on anything I wrote. But I hear long stories about guys who get the most ridiculous notes . . . But I never had that. They either bought it or they didn't. [*Thinks*] Did I ever tell you about how I cast Marsha Mason? She was a real piece of luck. The actress who was supposed to play it, Dorothy Tristan, called me up and told me she got a part in *Scarecrow* with Pacino and Hackman and asked me if I could delay the movie. I said, "Honey, you're doing *Scarecrow*." I called Nessa Hyams, the casting director, and I said, "Where's that girl I met in New York?" She said, "You mean, Marsha Mason? She's in my office." And she was. She was sitting right there at Warners. It was a miracle. She came in a read for me and I took one look at her and said, "You got the part." Anyway, Dorothy Tristan was blonde and Susan Anspach was blonde and I didn't want two blondes. After he leaves Susan, Blume goes for another type because he doesn't want to be reminded of her.

SW: What happens when you realize you've made a mistake in casting?

PM: Mistakes in casting are tough because, the way I see it, you can't make somebody do something they can't do. Ninety percent of directing is casting, so if you cast right, you're going to be a good director. If you cast wrong, there's literally nothing you can do. You can help an actor go faster or you can help an actor produce a little more energy. But you can't give an actor a sense of humor. You can't give an actor a sense of intelligence. What you're looking for is a quality and if they don't have that quality then you can't get it out of them—unless they're genius actors.

SW: So what does a casting director do for you?

PM: Ideas. People you don't know. Sometimes they'll mention people you never thought of for the part. Where it's difficult is when you're casting a star, the main part. Generally, they won't read for you. You've seen their movies, so why should they read? That's what they think.

SW: What about rehearsal? What does it give you?

PM: Rehearsal is there to get the actors comfortable with each other so that they feel they can take risks in their work. And it's just as much for me as much as for them. But of course, you don't have to rehearse. I sincerely doubt that Fellini rehearsed. [*Thinks*] Let's put it this way—this may not be a good example, but . . . what's the difference from the first day you came into my office until now?

SW: I'm more at ease.

PM: Right. Well, that's what happens with an actor. They feel comfortable enough to say, "I don't like doing it that way" or "Can I talk to you for a second?" They start opening up. They get to know each other. Let's say they're playing husband and wife and they have no rehearsal. They meet on the set. "Miss Anspach, this is George Segal, you've been married seven years and he's telling you . . ." It's just not the same. But, you know, I didn't have that much rehearsal for *Blume in Love*. I was shooting out of sequence.

SW: Is there such a thing as too much rehearsal?

PM: There are no rules. In other words, some people will say the first take and the second take are the best because you're going to get accidents and instincts. After that, they say, the actors start repeating it. But there are no rules.

SW: So when you write, you're not thinking about act breaks and character arcs?

PM: No, no, no, no. I never think about that stuff. I don't like the word "arc." It should only be used by Noah. It has no business being used by teachers of writing. It's a mundane piece of nonsense. It's bullshit.

SW: But the idea isn't bullshit.

PM: I think it is. I think if you write truly, something will happen to the character. But life is not like the arc of a character. Life is filled with details that don't add up. It's dangerous to start limiting yourself with rules. I'm not for them.

SW: So why do you think they're so popular?

PM: Because people want to believe they're learning from people that are going to help them sell a script. And the studio people who buy scripts, some of them take those classes too, and they like to use phrases like that when they give notes. They can pretend they know what they're talking about. What's the arc of the character in *Bonnie and Clyde*? You're going to see a guy through a lot of ups and downs and then he's going to die. You're even going to get a hint that he is impotent. But that's not arc. What's arc? That's not real.

SW: But what about the movies where people learn something? Where they change?

PM: They're well-made movies.

SW: Do you feel that's true of *Blume*, for instance? Do you feel that he learns?

PM: Blume, in a paradoxical way, learns from Elmo about how to get his wife back. He starts to change even though he's still devious. Elmo's mantra is "Nothin' to it." Blume uses that, but he's still breaking into her house.

SW: He rapes her.

PM: Yes, you're right. He rapes her, but she wants it and she doesn't want it. What I'm saying is that it's complicated. Real life is complicated. Things aren't perfect.

SW: It's such a ballsy break with the tone of the rest of the movie.

PM: I didn't think about that. I thought it was a great scene and that it would be a surprise, a jolt. Feminists were upset by it, so later I wrote *An Unmarried Woman*. [*Laughs*] It's true—partially. So many women got angry at that scene, angry at me, but it's not me, it's Blume, and Blume is not perfect. At the end of the movie, I think he really, really truly loves her and he's thrilled that she's going to have the baby. She says, "You're not my boss, Blume." I thought it was a revolutionary thing to say in a commercial movie. "We're going to live together and have a baby and not be married!"

SW: Yes, and especially on the heels of this awful, unthinkable thing. But like you say, life's details don't always add up.

PM: Whether they do or they don't, it doesn't matter. What matters is that they're there.

SW: How did you get Shelley Winters for *Blume*?

PM: It was easy. She liked *Bob & Carol* and wanted to work with me. She was great, one of my favorites. You know she couldn't cry without hearing "Un bel di" from *Madame Butterfly*? For that crying scene in *Blume*, the cast and crew had to wait while Shelley listened to Puccini on a little tape recorder and then she'd start to cry and then she'd give me the signal. "Shoot already!" she said. So that's when I started shooting. But I only found out once we were on the set. We had to stop shooting so I could send someone to my house and get my cassettes to bring them back to the set. [*Laughs*] You know, everyone's got their own Method method. It comes from what's called "sense memory." There are certain things that trigger certain emotions. So if I have to cry in a scene, I can summon up something—and I could do it right now—something that I've stored away in my subconscious that happened to me in my real life. It could bring me to tears very quickly. For Shelley it was *Butterfly*.

12. Blume in Love *(1973) Shelley and Paul.*

SW: Do you remember which recording?

PM: Jussi Björling. My mother's favorite. I then later used it in *Next Stop, Greenwich Village*. I put that scene in the movie.

SW: Shelley Winters could make the most depressing women hilarious. How do you do that?

PM: Because it's so true. The passion in it is so strong that humor can come out of it.

Mazursky looks down at his cell phone.

Jesus, this guy . . .

SW: What guy?

PM: The guy who was supposed to fix the TV. He said between three and five. [*Beat*] I hate dealing with TVs. [*Beat*] I'm calling him.

Mazursky dials. We wait. Suddenly he says something and then stops short. We wait again.

SW: What's going on? Are you on hold?

PM: I don't know. [*Into the phone*] Hello! You have to help me. The cable doesn't work. I think it's the satellite . . . the service man is coming, isn't—?

Mazursky scowls—and then laughs.

I'm on hold again. Jesus! I'm going to throw out all the fucking TVs. [*Whispering*] I think you should put in the book a scene of me calling the cable guy and telling him that my wife is dying. [*Mischievous laugh*] I say, "If I don't get a TV set today, there's no point. I don't think she's going to live past Friday and it's really important that she sees this show." [*Laughs*] I'll do anything to get a repairman. I've told them, "I'm a para-plegic, I have no legs, and I had to crawl to the phone." Or, "My son is coming back from Iraq . . ." Or I tell them I'm the director of the neorealist masterpiece, *The Matrix Part Two* . . . [*Into the phone*] Hello! Yes . . . I need you to help me. You see, my wife, she's an old, old woman . . . she could be dying . . .

Mazursky stops.

SW: What happened?

PM: I think he put me on hold again! [*Beat*] Enough!

He hangs up the phone, laughing.

Sammy, that scene is worth half a million bucks! Let's say the movie is you interviewing me and we're talking about life and death and sud-denly we put this scene in. Whoa, what is it doing there? It has nothing to do with the arc of the character! It's just a great scene!

SW: You really have both in *Blume*. Arc and non-arc scenes. The arc scenes give the non-arc scenes emotional power, and the non-arc scenes give the arc scenes reality. Does that make sense?

PM: I think so.

SW: In the beginning of the movie, both Blume and Nina have a cold. It's one of those non-arc scenes, and yet, there it is, front and center. You make a big deal about it.

PM: It doesn't move the story forward, if that's what you mean. It's a connection between a married couple. It's hard not to get a cold when the person you're married to has a cold. It's behavior. Maybe if I had been very clever, we would see Blume blowing his nose in the last shots in Venice.

13. Blume in Love *(1973) Susan Anspach and Paul. Piazza San Marco, Venice*.

sw: Tell me if there's something in this: Everybody in the movie cries except for Blume. He's in more pain than anyone, but he never breaks down.

pm: He's a lawyer. Lawyers don't cry.

sw: Interesting. In the original script it says that when Blume first sees Nina and Elmo together through the window he's starts to weep.

pm: It was a mistake. I didn't want him to be sentimental. I wanted him to be jealous, pissed, and angry.

sw: Is he crazy?

pm: He's obsessed. And he loves her.

sw: Both?

pm: Both. He brings her bagels and lox *and* he breaks into her house! Both! I love that stuff. I also love the Elmo stuff. I told him to try and make up a song about a goat. And he did. The scene when he sings it is improvised.

sw: The camera looks like it's making decisions right there on the spot.

pm: It was. I would just tap the cameraman when I wanted him to move. You know, I'm really taking my time in certain scenes in that movie. Today, they wouldn't do that. Real time makes you feel like it's really happening. Like he's *really* making up a song, and Blume's *really* there, and they're *really* enjoying each other. They're handling it. They're wedded.

sw: You love Blume there, but throughout the movie, you're disgusted by some of the things he does. By the end, he becomes a real shit—and you made him the star of a romantic comedy!

pm: Strange, I know. But I liked that. I wanted to play with the conventional love triangle. If Noël Coward had done the same thing, it would have been a different movie—he would have added a few songs, maybe—but it might have been close. But you know, we have songs in *Blume*. So . . . I don't know . . .

sw: I'm shocked. Coward seems the most unlikely . . .

pm: You don't associate me with Noël Coward?

sw: Not at all!

pm: Remember, he was hip and modern too. That's what *Bob & Carol* was when it came out—I mean, I'm not complimenting myself—but that was daring. I wanted *Blume* to be too, like a kind of *Design for Living* thing.

sw: Let's talk about guilt for a moment. People in your movies are always talking about it. Liberal guilt. Sexual guilt. Jewish guilt.

pm: We spend a lot of our lives with guilt. Our society forces it upon us. It starts with the Ten Commandments and you have it for the rest of your life. Your parents, your marriage, your money. It seems to me a bourgeois pattern. The poor have no time for it. The rest of us have time, and the richer you are the more time you have. [*Beat*] Guilt is everywhere.

Paul checks his watch.

That fucking repairman.

He looks out the window to the beach. It's overcast now.

You know, *Blume* is a very romantic movie, a passionate movie. That's why I set it in Venice. That city has an extremely powerful attraction. It pulls you. It's sinking. Everyone talks about that. And Blume's life was sinking. [*Beat*] I am going to Venice in July because I have to go back one more time for sure and see if Betsy cries when she sees the Piazza. She did the first time I brought her there.

Blume in Love wanders through time and place with an emotional capriciousness that does to the romantic comedy what Stephen Blume does to romance—it messes with it. Why? Because in the films of Paul Mazursky, genre and character are as malleable as the human heart.

The film's flashback structure offers Mazursky the perfect means to convey his view of human impulse. Embracing incomprehension and the improbabilities of love, these cuts in time give us only pieces of people. Gestalt is nowhere to be found. "Mazursky's great gift is for the unexpected," went *The Hollywood Reporter*, "for shifts in characterization and plot that seem to come from left field. So, although the movie knows exactly where it's going and gets there with seductive subtlety, it never telegraphs its intentions and retains a fresh feeling of discovery. Since the time structure is loose and the story moves from Venice, Italy to Los Angeles, the first ten minutes or so is disorienting. But then the pace (slow), the rhythm (sometimes disjointed), the observations (often random and far from the line of the story)—all these fall together into something entirely unique in American movies."

Mazursky's drastic shifts in tone allow him to collude modern strife and sweeping romance, making *Blume* a fickle, manic-depressive screwball comedy. Though our ideas of romance and strife may have changed drastically since the days of Carole Lombard and William Powell, *Blume in Love* confirms that the pugnacious and lyrical round-and-round of falling in and out of love is eternal—more than that—it's elemental. There is ecstasy, Mazursky's films say, but there is also everyday life, and trying to reconcile them can be anything but romantic (and so Stephen Blume goes crazy). But when it all works, as Blume says, "It's a miracle." And for Elmo, there's nothin' to it. Just light up a spliff and pour yourself a pot of Yuban.

  Bob & Carol & Ted & Alice, *Alex & Wonderland*, and even *I Love You, Alice B. Toklas!* all give us some sense of Mazursky's struggle between the utopia of pure feeling and the problems of being people. But *Blume* takes the conflict to its farthest extreme. The rape? The ending? Where do they come from? Have they been earned? Yes and no. No, we don't see them coming; yes, sometimes we never do. But irresponsible passion knows no rules. If it did— if logic were a part of desire—Mazursky wouldn't make a movie about it.

Harry and Tonto (1974)

Harry Coombes: For the first time in my life, I'm beginning to feel sorry for myself and I don't like it.

I walk into Paul's office . . .

PM: What are we up to?
SW: *Harry and Tonto.*
PM: Oh god. I'm ready.
SW: Go ahead.
PM: Okay. This one's about my mother. She's very disguised, but my mother had a red cat named Tonto who was a Manx without a tail. She used to walk him on a leash in Greenwich Village. But the idea came to me when I was about forty years old. It was 1970. Josh Greenfeld, who had gone to Brooklyn College right around the time I was there, was now a journalist writing for *Look* magazine. He came out to L.A. to write a big story about *Alex in Wonderland* and while he was doing it, I said to him, "Have you ever thought about what it would be like to be seventy?" We started talking about it and I told him that I'd love to do a movie about an old guy who finds himself all alone and all he has is his cat. Josh and I went back and forth on it, and sometime after that I moved to Rome, where I wrote a small treatment and sent it to [producer] John Calley at Warner Brothers. Calley said yes and sent me twenty-five thousand dollars and I split the money with Josh. Anyway, I came back to Los Angeles after Europe, and Josh and I finished the script. He had written the first half and he had done a wonderful job. Then I picked up with the second half and then we went back and switched, with Josh looking over my half and me looking over his. By the time we finished—the draft was a long script, by the way, maybe 180 pages—Calley wasn't sure about it anymore, so we went out with it, and we got turned down everywhere. Everywhere. Ted Ashley, who was the head of Warners said, "I don't want to see a movie about my father." Old age is hard to sell. By then, I was desperate. I was so desperate I flew to New York on my own money to meet [head of United Artists] David Picker, who said he liked it, but wanted me to do it for half a million. I said that would work if I shot it in Super 8 and played all the

parts. [*Laughs*] So that didn't happen. I had reached a point where it looked like I wasn't going to get it made and I got very depressed.

sw: That's when you wrote *Blume in Love*. In that mindset?

pm: Yes. Then after that, I got a call from my agent, Jeff Berg. He told me that Alan Ladd, Jr.,[12] who had just become a senior executive at Fox, had read it and loved it. So that night I had dinner with Laddie, and he said to me, "Paul, if you can do this movie for about a million dollars, I think we can get it made at Fox." That's when I went out to Jimmy Cagney, who said he loved it, but he was retired. I went to Danny Kaye, who wanted it to be funnier. I went out to Cary Grant, who said he was giving up the business for good. I think I could have had Jimmy Stewart, but something in my gut said don't. I saw Harry as more of a wise guy. I wanted him to be less sentimental. Jimmy wouldn't have been right. So I thought of Art Carney. I had seen him on Broadway in *The Rope Dancers*, and I knew from *The Honeymooners* that he was a comic genius. But Art turned me down! He said, "I'm too young. I'm only fifty-nine years old." And I, in my wonderful naiveté, said, "But you look seventy! You've got a hearing aid, you're balding, you've got a bum leg . . ."

sw: But he did it. And Fox thought he was a good choice?

pm: Fox was happy with it because they thought that if for some reason it didn't work as a movie, they could air it on TV. You understand? Carney's TV following was huge. So I made the movie and I made it with no interference. *Never.* Everything I did in that movie was done the Mazursky way: no interference!

sw: What was the final budget?

pm: Around $980,000. Things were so tight financially we decided not to bring Sparkletts to the office. We wanted to save money on the water for three months.

sw: How did knowing that you had only a million dollars affect the day-to-day of production?

pm: We had to be quick, which meant we had almost no rehearsal. I rehearsed a couple of family scenes in New York and a couple of scenes with Herbert Berghof. That scene with Larry Hagman I rehearsed once or twice on location. That's all. You know, *Harry and Tonto* is beautiful to me because there are no tricks in it. In other words, no fancy cutting,

---

12. Son of actor Alan Ladd, "Laddie" is famous for green-lighting *Star Wars* when no one else would. After Laddie left Warner Brothers in the late seventies, he formed The Ladd Company and went on to produce an impressive string of hits that included *Chariots of Fire*, *Alien*, and *Blade Runner*.

no slow motion, no echoing sound. These are tricks. There was no time for that. We did straightforward shots. That's my style. I don't like the other stuff; it calls attention to itself. It's film school razzle-dazzle.

sw: You treat the cat the same way. You don't give him cute little reaction shots, which is what we expect from movies with animals.

pm: He's not a comedy cat. It's just a cat! He pisses, he licks himself . . .

sw: Carney's not going for laughs either. You once called him the purest actor you've ever known.

pm: Purest meaning no shtick. He really listens. When he responds, he responds with the truth. One of the great examples of it is when Harry has to identify Herbert Berghof's body. It comes up on the little elevator and Harry looks at the body. He's silent for a long time before he speaks. It's filled with a lot of emotion and there's the semblance of tears, but not much. He doesn't embellish with tricks. He makes it appear simple. Real. [*Thinks*] You know the only thing Art had on was a little moustache? There was no makeup. Maybe a little bit around the eyes, but not much else. And it wasn't just that he looked the age, he moved like the age. I didn't direct him. I just placed him.

sw: So what was your job as director if you didn't need to direct him?

pm: I'm sure I said some things to Art, but you're right, there wasn't much I had to say to him. But I did have to say things to almost everybody else. Almost. "Gimme a little bit more here" or something. [*Beat*] As a director, you really have to trust your instincts, and the only way to do that is to come to it fresh. But I never was totally fresh. Since I wrote it, I had in my mind an idea of what I hoped it would be. You could probably have that even if you didn't write it. You have expectations. So you see, it's tricky. I think every director you talk to will give you a slightly different answer, but in my case, you're dealing with the clock, the money—a certain need to get it done. You don't want to be badly influenced by the pressures and settle when you really don't have it. That's when your instincts come into play. You know, it's hard to talk about acting in this way—I know you're looking for answers—but when it's wrong, it's easier to talk about.

sw: Let's talk about the ending of the picture. It reminds me of the endings of the films that preceded *Harry and Tonto*. They're all circles. Bob and Carol and Ted and Alice and everyone else are walking around in a circle. Alex is walking around in a circle outside of his house. And in *Blume in Love*, Nina and Blume seem to start again. Endings are often beginnings in Mazursky.

14. Harry and Tonto *(1974) Paul and Art.*

PM: You know, the girl on the beach is building circles. It's the circle of life, a circle of continuity. The sun has not set, you see, it's *setting*. Harry starts again. He doesn't have to search anymore. I think he's more at peace. The search is over, but that doesn't mean he has to die. It means he can begin to live. [*Beat*] That's my daughter, you know, building the sandcastles. But that's not why I love that scene. I love it because she's building. I'm saying, "I don't really know how long this guy's life is going to go on, but he's going to be okay." [*Beat*] At the end, Harry wears a little hat and ascot. It means he's become a Californian.

SW: Why isn't Harry Jewish?

PM: I didn't want the movie to be thought of as a Yiddishy film. I thought I had done it with *Toklas* very well. I didn't want them to be Jewish in *Bob & Carol*, even though you know that Elliott Gould is probably Jewish. The character in *Alex in Wonderland* is Jewish, but Donald makes him less Jewish. Then came *Blume*, and Blume is a Jew, but he's a Jew like I'm a Jew. A secular Jew. With *Harry and Tonto*, I didn't want religion to get in the way. I didn't want him to have to go to a priest and ask him what he should do. And you've got to be careful in Jewish things that you don't unconsciously deal with cliché because so many great things in the Yiddish culture border on the cliché.

SW: Was there ever a point when you considered having Harry die?

PM: No. I didn't want him to die. I wanted Harry to be on the West Coast with those old guys you see out on the beach playing chess. He's one of those guys now—he lives in Venice.

SW: In the script, when we first go into Harry's apartment, it says, "Not at all depressing." I think that's a good cue for the movie.

PM: Right. I didn't want the people who put together the set to think of him as a tattered old man. He's an elegant guy. He wears bow ties and wears a nice coat. Remember, Harry doesn't want to leave his apartment. That's key to the character. But you know, I don't usually put much description in the scripts. Scripts that are given to me have so much description they give me a headache.

SW: You made four L.A. movies before this. What makes this one a New York story?

PM: When I made *Toklas*, I had been in L.A. for six or seven years. I knew the scene. Nobody had done a movie about the middle class starting to dabble in drugs and all that stuff. It seemed like ripe material. *Harry and Tonto* was a New York story because if you had a guy out here [in L.A.] walking a cat on a leash just walking in Beverly Hills near the grass, it wouldn't be interesting. It wouldn't be funny. But if you have a guy walking down a crowded Manhattan street singing to his cat—*that's* a movie. L.A. is loaded with people who have a front, with nothing underneath. But New York is not as strange. Like all those shots of old people at the beginning of the movie. That's New York. We stole all that, by the way. We didn't have permits. What I did was set up a camera shooting a pretend scene with no film in it and I had another camera, a decoy, hidden, grabbing shots of these people sitting on the bench or in the park. I said, "Grab that, grab that, grab that."

SW: Your New York pictures aren't as funny. There's something about New York that even you take very, very seriously.

PM: But I love L.A. If you do it right, living in L.A. can be like you're living in the French Riviera. You can play golf all year long. You have beautiful beaches and beautiful women. You've got Rodeo drive. And if you've got once nice suit and a pretty good car, you can pretend you're a lot of things.

SW: And yet, despite all that, your movies have a very balanced view of Los Angeles. Having lived here my whole life, I really appreciate that you see that other side too.

PM: What side is that?

sw: You know, the Venice side. It's in *Harry and Tonto*, and *Down and Out in Beverly Hills*, and it's in *Toklas* and *Blume*. In your movies, it's where the fringe personalities live, where people are authentic. So, naturally, Harry would end there.

pm: Right. He's in a new world now. He saw his family. He got laid. [*Beat*] We shot the movie chronologically, which I try to do whenever I can, because it can only be good for the actors. And it was great for Art. As Harry changed, he changed.

sw: *Harry and Tonto* has an R rating. How did that happen?

pm: Because Josh Mostel says "cunt." I probably should have taken it out. I went to this fantastic meeting at the mpaa [Motion Picture Association of America] with Alan Ladd, Jr. One of the people on the board was a nun, and the dialogue between us was hilarious. I said, "How can you give this movie an R because of one word when you've given PG-13 ratings to movies with horrible violence?" I brought in a clip from a Don Siegel movie that had a guy getting shot fifteen times in the balls. I said, "How come you show a guy getting his testicles blown apart and I can't say 'cunt'?" She said, "Because 'cunt' is offensive." I said, "Well, you just said it and nothing happened." She said, "Don't get wise with me." Something like that. She wanted me to use "bastard," but I was stubborn. It probably would have made more money if I changed it. And it's not gratuitous. It comes from this kid who didn't speak for the first half of the movie. He's silent when we meet him and now he's calling his aunt a cunt.

sw: Were you thinking about De Sica's film *Umberto D.* when you were working on *Harry and Tonto*?

pm: I never think about that, no. I never say, "In the style of . . ."

sw: But I know it's an important film for you.

pm: Yeah, but I wanted *Harry and Tonto* to be more humorous than *Umberto D.* All those chance encounters. Like with the Indian who cures the bursitis in Harry's shoulder.

Paul massages his shoulder.

[*Sighing*] I think I could use a little bit of Chief Dan George right now. My shoulder's been killing me. My *right* shoulder—same as Harry!

sw: Why? What happened?

pm: I don't know. I'm seeing the doctor today. But no, *Umberto D.* is about a man who's really down on his luck. It's really painful. I didn't want *Harry and Tonto* to be that way.

sw: When you were in Rome after *Alex*, and you were hanging out with Fellini, did you get to spend any time with De Sica?

pm: Yes, actually, I did. I went to a party given by Emi De Sica, Vittorio's daughter. It was her birthday party. Well, Vittorio came. Of course, I idolized him; he asked me what I was working on. I told him that I was working on the treatment for the movie that became *Harry and Tonto*. I said, "I'm making a movie about an old man and a cat." He said, "You know I made a movie about an old man and a dog." I said, "I know. *Umberto D*." I said, "I'm already stealing from you." So he said, "Would you like to see the picture again?" He took me downstairs to the basement where he had a sixteen-millimeter print. At the end, I was in tears. I said, "I think I am going to steal some more from you." He said, "Take what you want." And I later wrote a piece called "Take What You Want" for a celebration of De Sica they had at a church at the Piazza del Popolo ten years after he died.

sw: What was he like, De Sica?

pm: I don't know, I only met him that one day. He was very charming. But look, when you're meeting someone whose work you worship, you're not meeting just the person, you're meeting the work. So you're in the presence of *Bicycle Thief* and *Shoeshine*. The night I met him, De Sica asked me if I had seen *Death in Venice*. I said, "No, it's not out yet." He said, "Well, would you like to see it?" I said, "I would *love* to see it." So he got on the phone, and in Italian, he called Visconti. [*Laughs*] Vittorio De Sica is calling Luchino Visconti and I'm standing right there. He said, [*Italian accent*] "*Luchino, Vittorio. Esta momento . . . Paulo Mazursky . . . Registo Americano . . . si, si . . . possible* Morte a Venezia?" And then he turned to me and said, "How is tomorrow at two o'clock?" I said, "Anytime!" So we set the date. Meanwhile, the party continues and I'm talking to Suso Checci D'Amico, Visconti's writer—a great, great writer—and I say to her, "Have you seen *Death in Venice*?" She said, "No, I haven't seen it, but Vittorio saw it and he *hates* it!"

sw: Did Fellini ever see *Harry and Tonto*?

pm: Yes. He liked the movie. He saw it in Paris. He wrote me a letter, "I saw your film in Paris and I just wanted to tell you how much they loved your movie and so did I." Something like that.

sw: I bet he responded to the music. It has a Nino Rota feeling.

pm: That was Bill Conti. I met Bill Conti in Venice for *Blume*. One of the big scenes in the movie uses the orchestra in the Piazza San Marco and I needed someone who spoke English and Italian to deal with the musicians, so they sent me Bill. That's how we met. He was a piano player and he would play at night at the hotel. A year or so later I was getting ready to make *Harry and Tonto* and he said, "Paul, I'm a composer too." So I gave him an idea for what I wanted the score for *Harry and Tonto* to be like. There's a song that kids play when they're learning to play the piano called, I think, "The Spinning Song." I played it for Bill and he wrote a kind of theme with it. He sent me a tape, and when I was looking at the first couple of weeks' dailies, I played the music over the movie. I loved it and I hired him. It was his first American picture. One of my great memories of Bill Conti was that when I first met him, he was so broke, he wearing shoes that he had made! They were those wooden things with brass nails in them. That's a fact. I enjoyed working with Bill because he has no pretense. But, you know, I use music the way anyone else would—to enhance the scene.

sw: One of my favorite moments in the movie is when Harry's son drops Harry off in front of a building, and Harry walks in, sits down, and we realize that he has to identify the body. You made a very conscious decision there to delay the reveal.

pm: No exposition. I wanted it to be a surprise.

sw: Why?

pm: Because it's more powerful. We know he's going somewhere, but we don't know where.

sw: Does that change him, what happens to his best friend?

pm: I think it's a loss.

sw: But you don't give us a scene that explicates that point. I mean, some kind of aftermath.

pm: No, I don't.

sw: These omissions, from my point of view, are part of what Mazursky is all about it.

pm: You'll have to pardon me if I don't agree or disagree. I don't analyze myself because maybe it will start to change the way I think. Next time I sit down to write something, I don't want to think, "Maybe I'll leave this out because omissions are Mazursky-esque." You've got be careful. You understand?

sw: Yes, I understand. Let me put it another way, then. In the Hollywood version of *Harry and Tonto*, which I pray to God never gets made, they would put in that scene. We would see Harry's life without Herbert Berghof's character. They would pay it off. You don't and it's lovely. We have to do our own story work.

PM: Now that I'm the age I wrote about, I can tell you we caught it pretty good. Because I'm with these guys every morning at the Farmers Market, guys like [writer] David Freeman, and [artist] Charlie Bragg. These guys are all late sixties and early seventies. All our conversations have three motifs. One is shoulders, hips, knees, heart—all the medical stuff. Between the six guys there's always some of that. Two is memory lane. Three is looking at girls like, "I would like to jump her bones right now. I would pay five thousand dollars just for her to sit on me." We say stuff like that. Those are the three parts of Harry. Over the course of the movie, we learn things about Harry, but Josh and I didn't make them plot points.

SW: You don't give us a lot of backstory, either. We know very little about Harry's wife, for instance.

PM: I wanted to give you adventures. Ordinary things, but ones that don't ordinarily happen to old people. You know, for a while I was known as a guy who writes about old people. Once a guy gave me a script about an old woman who escapes from a retirement home. She busts out the window and goes out and does all these ridiculous things. I said to the guy, "You've got a lot of stuff in here I don't believe. These adventures are too fantastic." He said, "But you made *Harry and Tonto*." I said, "But those things that happened to Harry were all ordinary. They were believable."

SW: The movie is filled with unfulfilled expectations. Not just in terms of story, but character. Like when Harry goes to buy a used car, you give us every indication to believe that the guy who's selling it to him is going to be a real shyster. He's got the wig and everything. And then, of course, we see that he's just a good guy. It's just a little moment, but it's very telling.

PM: Yes, he's telling him about how he gets laid. Those kinds of details make him real. I told him, "You're a used car salesman, you do your best to sell and you're a salt of the earth guy." He's getting along in age, too.

Mazursky stops.

As I do this with you, I'm thinking that I've realized my dream. I mean, *I got those movies made.* The thought of trying to get them made today makes me anxious. I couldn't go through it again. That's why I was lucky I had Laddie. He said okay to *Harry and Tonto* and *Next Stop, Greenwich Village.* I owe them to him.

SW: What would have happened to you if working back then was like working in Hollywood today?

15. Harry and Tonto *(1974) Paul and Tonto, Vegas.*

PM: I don't know. I really don't know. I would cut my wrists or I would become a shoe salesman. None of those would do me any good. You know, I would probably be making very low-budget independent movies on HD. That's probably it.

SW: That's the closest you could get to what it was like then.

PM: I'm pretty sure, yes. But I don't like to bemoan the past or the future or the present. It's a waste of time. Onward.

When Josh Greenfeld went out to L.A. to interview Mazursky for *Look* magazine, Mazursky told him this: "It may be a cliché but I think California is where the revolution in lifestyles has really begun. And Hollywood is a mirror of some of it. Not just the movie Hollywood but also the California Hollywood. And that's what *Toklas* and *Bob & Carol* were all about. And that's what *Alex* is all about, too. Only heavier. And I don't think many other people are making movies about our generation, the one in between the gap, trying to make certain kinds of transitions and adjustments all the time between the old and new." That was 1970.

Four years later, only the location had changed. *Harry and Tonto* and *Blume* and *Alex* and *Bob & Carol & Ted* and *Alice B. Toklas* fill out the generation gap, taking trips, either by chemicals or back roads, to sample American freedoms. Yet none is more American than the trip taken by Harry Coombes. Bob and Carol drove north, Alex went south, and Blume was sent east, but it is in Harry's trek west that the Mazurskyian picaresque—what Paul calls the "quilt of scenes"—finds its most elegant expression. The idea of travel is, after all, central to his idea of self-realization; if we are to make any headway in our sedentary lives, Mazursky advises us to hit the road, and *Harry and Tonto* guarantees that we'll find something worthwhile along the way. What it does not promise, though, is meaning. There is no moral here. Harry does not come to greater understanding, nor does he achieve spiritual transcendence or resolve the great crises of consciousness. He just goes across the country. That's it. He loses his apartment and goes.

Mazursky's naturalism has never been more ascetic. Coverage is at its simplest, ambient audio proliferates, and the picture's color palette—somewhere in between a Danish and a cup of coffee—is muted to the point of nonexistence. Even exposition is too baroque for *Harry and Tonto*. Why do we never learn why Norman Coombes starts to talk again? How did Jacob Rivetowski die? Why do we know so little about Harry's wife? Because Mazursky is interested in behavior, not psychology. And if there are imperfections or fissures in the narrative tissue, all the better. That's what makes this story about freedom feel so free—in a film that eschews explanations, anything can happen. We see two old guys talk about fucking, a sixteen-year-old girl take her top off in front of a septuagenarian, and Harry making it with a redheaded hooker.

Molly Haskell wrote, "*Harry and Tonto* is as funny and observant and almost as observant as *Bob & Carol & Ted & Alice* and *Blume in Love*. Although its soft spots are softer and its social consciousness a bit less skeptical than is Mazursky's wont—the influence, no doubt, of Josh Greenfeld as co-scenarist—the new film subtracts in no way from Mazursky's claim, or mine for him, of being possibly the funniest and sharpest writer-director of his generation, a specialist in the anxieties and charms of a certain milieu: an emotionally overstimulated and undernourished middle class, that thrives on the psychodrama of the big cities." Frank Rich wrote, "It gives you a lift which can only come from being in the presence of a talent with a fabulous and understanding heart."

Mazursky and Greenfeld were nominated for an Academy Award for Best Original Screenplay. They lost (to Robert Towne, for *Chinatown*) but

Art Carney won Best Actor. He beat Jack Nicholson, Al Pacino, Dustin Hoffman, and Albert Finney.

Mazursky said, "The picture doesn't have a message." Okay, but it has an intention, the same one as every other great Mazursky movie: to relish in human conduct.

Josh on Mazursky

Co-writer, Harry and Tonto

The writer Josh Greenfeld lives at the end of a high road along the bluffs in the Pacific Palisades. As I step through his front door, Josh, in his favorite sailor's cap, introduces me to Fumiko, his wife, also a writer, and gestures for me to exchange my shoes for house slippers. "You want to write?" Josh asks. "Yes," I say. "Then get out of the movies." He laughs a little, but he means it. "I've always found that people who take the movies seriously aren't serious people," he says. A few moments later we're carrying green tea into the living room and Josh, who must think I'm seriously unserious, is pointing through his window to a bench on the hill. "Once," he says, "when I first moved into this house, I saw King Vidor walking around out there with a sixteen-millimeter camera."

JOSH GREENFELD: I met Paul in summer theater. At the Highfield in Falmouth on the Cape. That was the summer of 1953. Paul was the star of the company. He played Willy Loman in *Death of a Salesman*. He was best twenty-three-year-old Willy Loman I had ever seen. Back in the Village, we both lived on Sullivan Street. So we'd hang out together a little bit. Years went by and around 1970 I came out to here to do the *Look* article while he was shooting *Alex in Wonderland*, a movie I like a lot, a really underrated movie. Paul and I spent a couple of days together and we'd begin to talk. Paul would say, [*speedy*] "What do you want to do? Do you want to do a movie?" And we agreed to do something about an old man.

I pull out the Look *article and hand it to Josh. He looks it over.*

JG: Not a bad lead . . . [*Scanning*] André has a great line in here . . . Somewhere . . . [*Beat*] Here it is! "I think that Paul's at a crossroads between Joe Pasternak and Fellini and Second City. By Joe Pasternak I mean his show business smarts. By Fellini I mean his artistic dreams. And by Second City I mean his basic talent, what really makes him. The Joe Pasternak can destroy him, but I think he's got that under control. But the Fellini can do him in, too, and I'm not so sure he knows how to protect himself from it . . ." That's very perceptive. Now that I think about it, I do think the Fellini did do him in.

sw: What do you mean?

JG: The "high art" Fellini. Think of *Tempest* and all that.

sw: All that what?

JG: Pretension. [*Beat*] You know, Fellini was his god.

sw: When you were writing the *Look* piece, you watched Paul on the set. How would you describe his working style?

JG: Paul likes a captive audience and no one has a captive audience more than a director. He really enjoyed that feeling of power. Larry Gelbart once told me a great line about why he *didn't* want to direct. He said, "Who wants the responsibility of deciding when three hundred people eat lunch?" [*Laughs*] When somebody like Larry says a line like that to you, you never know whether he's used it seven hundred times or not. [*Beat*] During Paul's halcyon days at Fox, I remember Bobby Sherman, who was part of the Laddie triumvirate running the studio, saying to me, "How is it that if you go up to any other director on the lot and talk to them about something commercial, they're interested, but with Paul, he isn't?" All the other directors were working on a million projects, but Paul was generally working on only one thing—his.

sw: Yeah, it seems he never compromised. Especially in *Harry and Tonto*, which was turned down everywhere.

JG: We used to call it *Easy Lear*. [*Laughs*] No one at the studio knew what it was about. Mike Medavoy, Paul's agent, called me once and asked, "I have a deal, but refresh me: What is this thing about?" I said, "I don't know. An old man?" Paul and I barely knew! We just had this story about an old guy crossing the country. Either he's got to have someone to talk to or you're going to have to have narration over it. We didn't want that. So who is he going to talk to? We could have gone with the dog like in *Umberto D.* or *Travels with Charley*, but we didn't want to do that. So we went with a cat.

sw: You're saying it was a device.

JG: Yes, and later, at the end of the movie, we used it for a surrogate death. Harry didn't really have enough character weight to die. So we made California represent the opposite, a resurrection. Here comes the sun and all that.

sw: You were two middle-aged guys writing about a seventy-four year old. I know you've seen it recently,[13] so I have to ask, now that all this time has passed, do you think you've made any mistakes?

13. I ran into Josh and Fumiko at a screening of *Harry and Tonto* at the Billy Wilder Theater in Westwood.

JG: Yeah, for one thing, you don't just get up once a night to piss. If you do, you're doing okay. That's a *good* night. What's more likely is three, four, or five times a night. [*Laughs*] One of the things I wanted was to tell Harry's story through the kind of transportation he used. First, you start with the plane; then it was supposed to be a train that he gets on, not a bus. But we changed it because to shoot at Penn Station would cost too much. And then we were going to go to a bus, and then a car, and then at the end we were going to have Harry riding a horse. You see? The modes of transportation were going down, down, down. Finally, Harry is hitch-hiking. Then he's walking around Venice.

SW: That's Harry's story. He's being stripped of everything.

JG: Yes. It was in the design of the script. Paul and I talked about that. At first it scares him and then he learns to be at peace with it. [*Beat*] You know, we gave the script to Jimmy Cagney, but Cagney told Paul the script was dirty? I don't know what he was thinking. Maybe because of the word "cunt." I told you, that line was the biggest laugh we had at the screenings. I wish it hadn't been changed to "bitch." "Cunt" was more powerful and funnier.

SW: Were there any creative disagreements between you and Paul?

JG: I don't consider movies that creative for a writer.

SW: One of the unique qualities of Harry, as far as character writing is concerned, is that he doesn't have a very strong want.

JG: No. That was deliberate. Because that's life. It's a journey. It's picaresque.

SW: Was that a word that was thrown around?

JG: Yes, absolutely. Also, when we go on trips, the best things you and I experience are the things that weren't planned. The accidents. I mean, one of the things that's fun about taking a journey is the unexpected. You want that to happen. You want it to feel free.

SW: So why wasn't there another Mazursky/Greenfeld collaboration?

JG: That's a long story. [*Beat*] So what are you writing? Some kind of hagiography?

The back of my edition of Greenfeld's novel, *The Return of Mr. Holly-wood*, describes its character as "a Hollywood director-screenwriter whose Brooklyn past collides with his Beverly Hills present." If there was any doubt about the real-life basis for this man, it's squelched in the novel's first lines, spoken by Mr. Hollywood himself. "It's very tricky being an artist in the system," he says. "Especially if you're a personal filmmaker like me. I want to be successful. But I don't want to be successful if it means doing what they want me to do and not having any control. I'm an artist and I can't work that way. A film has to be about something I know and care about with very human people—funny and lovable and even a little crazy but still real. I deal with real reality."

Next Stop, Greenwich Village (1976)

Sarah Roth: I'm not your prisoner.

There's a floor-to-ceiling bookshelf directly across from Lauren's desk and some of the shelves are actually sagging. No organizational pattern has survived, but if you look closely, you can see that at one point there might have been some sort of plan. Either the organizer gave up in the middle or time has just separated the subjects. Among the books is *Hollywood's Image of the Jew* by Lester Friedman, *Kubrick* by Michel Ciment, *Baby and Childcare* by Benjamin Spock, *For Keeps* by Pauline Kael, a big book about David Hockney, *Playland* by John Gregory Dunne, *The Satanic Verses* by Salman Rushdie, *As Thousands Cheer: The Life of Irving Berlin* by Laurence Bergreen, *Orlando* by Virginia Woolf, *Einstein: A Life* by Denis Brian, *John Donne: The Complete English Poems*, *Georgia O'Keefe* by Roxana Robinson, *Swifty* by Irving Lazar, *Rationale of the Dirty Joke* by G. Legman, *Heart of a Dog* by Mikhail Bulgakov, *Old Times* by Harold Pinter, *Irving Berlin* by Mary Ellin Barrett, *If Not Now, When?* by Primo Levi . . .

PM: [*from inside his office*] Sammy, come on in.

> *I grab a seat. (Paul—on the phone—is wearing a T-shirt with the Superman logo in a Star of David.) As I wait, I survey the CDs shelved within Mazursky's reach. There's Sinatra's* Point of No Return, La Bohème *(with Victoria de los Angeles), the* Dr. Zhivago *soundtrack,* The Keith Jarrett Anthology, Handel's Messiah, The Best of Ennio Morricone, A Bronx Tale *soundtrack,* The Player *soundtrack,* Live at Stubbs *by Matisyahu,* The Best of Arlo Guthrie, Fandango *by ZZ Top,* Madame Butterfly *(Barbirolli), the original 1955 cast recording of* Call Me Madam, The Best of Louis Prima . . . *Paul hangs up the phone. He's laughing.*

PM: You know this one? This couple, Max and Sadie—they're in their condo in Florida—they're retired, they're having dinner. It's three o'clock in the afternoon. Now it's after dinner and they're watching TV. Max says, "Oh, that was a good meal. I'm going to get up and go into the kitchenette and get myself some vanilla ice cream." Sadie says, "What are you going to get it for? I'll get it for you!" He says, "You've got a bad memory. You're going to forget." "I won't forget," she says. "You'll forget." "I won't forget!" He says, "Alright. Get me a bowl of vanilla ice cream," so she gets up and goes into the kitchenette and calls out, "You want a bowl of vanilla ice cream?" He says, "Yeah, and put on it some whip cream." She says, "Okay," and he says, "And a maraschino cherry, too!" She says, "A bowl of vanilla . . . whip cream . . . cherry . . ." He says, "Don't forget!" "I won't forget!" she says. She comes back five minutes later and she gives him two fried eggs. He says, "I told you you'd forget!" She says, "What did I forget?" He says, "My toast!"

Laughter.

sw: Okay, okay. So Max and Sadie sit out by the beach every day overlooking the water. They talk, they remember the old times, they open up a little picnic lunch, and all the while, Sadie holds Max's penis. She just grips it in her hand while they talk and eat. And every day they meet like this. Beach, lunch, conversation, and Sadie cradles the penis in her hand. This is their life. One day, Sadie goes out to the beach to meet Max when she finds him sitting with Sarah, another woman. Well, Sadie's devastated, she's wrecked. And so she goes up to Max and says, "Max, oh my God, what does she have that I don't?" and he turns to her and says, "Parkinson's."

Laughter.

pm: Does it work if they're not Jewish?
sw: I really don't think so.
pm: So the two of them are in bed and she finds his hand down by her back underneath the nightgown, you know? She says, "Max, what are you doing?" His hand goes down to the middle of her back and she says, "Max, you're getting me excited . . ." and his hand goes down to her ass and she says, "I'm wet!" and he stops. She says, "Why did you stop?" and he says, "I found the remote."

Laughter.

sw: Paul, we're going to talk about *Next Stop, Greenwich Village*, so let's talk about your mother.
pm: Go ahead.
sw: Have you made peace with her? I mean, can you?
pm: I made peace only after she died. Then I felt strangely relieved, but as the years have gone on, I find that I've missed her. I miss her in an odd way.

sw: Do you think you would have been able to make *Next Stop* if she was alive?

pm: No, I don't think so. I wouldn't have had the courage. Look, she threatened to sue me after *Alex in Wonderland*, so I can't imagine what she would have done if she saw *Next Stop*. She would have had me put away. The therapist I went to once said to me, "No matter what you say, your mother loved you. And a lot of mothers don't love their sons."

sw: Yes, but the problem of the Jewish mother isn't about a lack of love. She loves too much. That's the problem.

pm: It's not only that. My mother had an element of paranoia. And she never took to Betsy. She couldn't handle that. But the worst part is that I think she suffered from a bipolar kind of thing. She could have been helped by drugs, but they didn't have that then. Anyway, she wouldn't see a therapist. She had very dark lows. Very dark. As soon as we saw each other, the tension began. When I moved to California, I thought it would end . . . but then the phone would ring. [*Smiles*] But she was fabulous, too . . .

sw: And Shelley Winters never got to meet her?

pm: No. My mother died in 1971. The movie was made in 1975. I told Shelley things about her, but I didn't tell her everything. This is amazing: One day Shelley came to me and asked me questions. She asked, "Was your mother a typist? Could she play the piano?" Both were true, and I don't know how she knew to ask those things. They weren't in the script. I mean, in the script it says that she likes opera, but I don't know where she got the typist thing from. I asked her and she said, "I don't know, I just guessed it." Deep down the thing about my mother was that in another time in another place, she might have been one of those fabulous characters like Dorothy Parker or [Robert] Benchley. She was like a Gypsy lady who operated on instinct, but most of the time she had good instincts. You've got to have good instincts if you're a lower-middle-class Jewish lady and you're going to see the movies of Michel Simon and Jean-Louis Barrault. You know, she took me to see *Children of Paradise*? She loved Noël Coward. She used to ask me to cut school to see a double feature with her. I'd say, "But I have school," and she'd say, "Oh, don't worry about it." And then we'd go eat some candy and see movies.

sw: Where was your father in all this?

pm: My father and I were afraid of her.

sw: Wow, Shelley and Mike Kellin [Mr. Lapinsky] really nailed it.

PM: Those who know, I think, give Shelley the credit she deserves—she was a great, great actress—but I don't think a lot of people really know how great she was because she did a lot of junk as well as great movies. Shelley wanted to work. She was tough but something drew you to her. She was kind of a forlorn creature.

SW: She always seems to be playing two things. *Lolita* is a perfect example. Where one actress might just play pathetic, as Charlotte Haze, Shelley begins with pathetic, and then plays against it. She tries to laugh it away, to cover it up. Mrs. Lapinsky is that way too, though she's less successful at the cover-up.

PM: You could talk about technique, you could talk about casting, you could talk about many, many things, but it all adds up to dishwater in the end when you're talking about that unknown thing, that mysterious thing that makes certain people great. They have an instinctive under-standing of what's going on in the role. And they have charisma. Shelley could even be sexy. It's hard to find it sometimes, but it's there. I don't know anybody else who could have played the part as well as she did. She was very demanding about what she wore and props. In that scene when she brings Larry food, Shelley demanded that I use actual Ratner's rye bread. I had given her a loaf of regular commercial rye bread, but she wanted the real thing. She went nuts. The crew was staring at me, wait-ing to see what I was going to do. So I took the bread, opened it, smelled it, and said, "That is a Ratner's rye if I ever smelled one!" and then I said, "Shelley, I find it difficult to believe that you, who studied at the Actors Studio, can't find the right sense memory from your past." That's when she said, "Of course I can!" And away she went.

SW: How do you know when an actor's demands are really genuine? I mean, when they really need something to make their performance better. Is that an actor preparing or an actor demanding?

PM: The only one in the movie who is naked is the actor. You're looking at them, so they have a right to want it to be the best. Maybe there's a line when it goes over because of insecurity. They can push that button to a degree when they make you a little crazy.

SW: But part of the director's job—

PM: I know you're looking for me to define the director's job and I'm being particularly difficult. I compare a director to a conductor. A conductor has a score, his script. Five different conductors will take the same exact piece of music and turn it into five different feelings. The conductor puts something into it that's coming from inside him. It's *interpreta-*

tion. It's hard to put it all into words because then it sounds like the courses these guys give. That stuff may be okay for TV shows—those guys follow certain formulas, certain clichés—but it's not for anything that's going to be better.

SW: When you're handling material as familiar as Jewish archetypes, are you thinking about how to avoid cliché?

PM: I'm thinking that way when I write. I'd be a fool not to. I thought I made it extremely specific and touching when she hears the opera. When she says at the end, "When you see Clark Gable, tell him that your mother loves him." All of that my mother actually said, so I put it in the script, and that took it away from cliché. [*Beat*] Shelley was fearless. One of the great moments in the movie is her dance. I don't think I could have asked the average actress—

SW: She pulls up her skirt!

PM: She never hesitated, never doubted. Not even a second. Look, you see her swimming underwater in *The Poseidon Adventure*. It's one of the great sights in the movies. She looks like a beached whale. But she didn't care. Shelley was for the art. She was also very giving with the rest of the actors. There's no, "Where's my shot? Are you doing the close-up? Are you going to get me later?" She never did anything like that ever. That's a certain kind of professionalism. You know, some actors don't go as deep in the wide shot because they want to save it for the close-up. They're trying to do the director's work for them.

SW: When *do* you use a close-up?

PM: I use the close-up when I want more, when I want to go in deeper. Sometimes I use it when the master stops working and you want to get off it. In those cases you go to the close-up because you need it to get to another shot.

SW: It's practical.

PM: Yeah. Also, you cut in for a close-up if you want to pick up the tempo.

SW: The close-ups of Dori Brenner in *Next Stop* just knock my socks off.

PM: I think she was a version of the Marsha Mason character in *Blume in Love*. The one who never gets the guy really, but she's smart and funny. She caught that wonderfully. The picture is very well cast. I have to give [casting director] Juliet Taylor a big round of applause because she waited until the very last moment—I was starting in a couple of weeks—I still didn't have my Larry Lapinsky, I kept holding off and holding off, and she said, "I saw this kid [Lenny Baker] up at Boston in a play, I think he's right for the part." So they brought him down, he read for me, and I gave him the part. I spent a couple days with him walking around and talking, stuff like that.

SW: What would you talk about?

PM: I asked him questions about himself. I wanted to get out of the casting office. I realized he was very clever and could do imitations.

SW: It's like what you did with Natalie Wood when you met her in London.

PM: Sure, yeah. You get out of the room. I did the same thing with Robin Williams in *Moscow on the Hudson*.

SW: Because it lets you see the person.

PM: It lets you see what's real. The mask goes away. You're just taking a walk.

SW: So that's as important as a person's ability to perform a role?

PM: It has importance. In the end, it may not be anything more than giving the director reassurance that they're going to be smart enough to get what you're talking about. You know, most actors who have achieved fame are pretty smart, but what you can't find out too easily is what they're really like. That's why we often make phone calls: "What's he like to work with?" I don't like to do it too much unless I'm talking to a director I know personally. When a stranger calls me and asks me about a particular actor, I want to say to them, "What kind of actor do you like to work with?" I don't want to give a bad report on somebody because they may not be suited to a particular director. Generally, directors, when they call me, want to know two things: one, if an actor knows his lines, two, is a cameraman fast. But with actors, most of the time you don't know what you're looking for until you see it. You know?

SW: Was that the case with Lenny Baker?

PM: He was the only one who really made me believe he could do it. I knew others who could do it technically, but no one else made me believe they had the whole thing.

SW: Was it difficult because you knew at some level you were casting yourself?

PM: Yeah, I think there was some of that.

SW: People talk about beautiful casting and it's not always clear what they mean. But *Next Stop* truly is beautifully cast. You had Juliet Taylor. She's a major, underappreciated voice in the movies.

PM: She worked with Marion Dougherty. Marion was the queen of casting directors. She cast *Harry and Tonto*. In *Next Stop, Greenwich Village*, Juliet Taylor was vital. We were doing it all in New York, just me and her. It was a pleasure. She's very smart, and not pushy, but strong. She would not have trouble saying, "I don't think he's right." That's what you want in a casting director. They go to lots of trouble to look around for the next thing in acting. They ask you, "What are you looking for? What do you want?" The casting director has to be really smart and have a good sense of what's exciting. When they bring in people that aren't very well known, they're taking a risk. That's when I tell the casting director not to be afraid of making a mistake. I tell them to bring in anybody they think might be right. Even if you don't like the person, you're only seeing them for fifteen minutes and then you say, "Thank you very much." When I read them, sometimes I'll look up from the script and say something like "Is that what you're going to do in the part?" I would do something to try to catch them. You understand? I would try to find a real moment in the context of what we were doing so it wasn't just the lines. If they got thrown so bad that they couldn't recover, I would get nervous about casting them. One of the great things about Molly Ringwald, who I cast in *Tempest*, was that she had no fear of me. She was fourteen years old. I tried to play with her and she said, "You don't have to mess with me, just tell me what you want." I was so impressed. Remember, you've never seen her play anything before. You don't know who she is. Who is she?

sw: With the exception of Shelley, you cast all unknowns.

pm: One of the things we all like a lot in certain foreign films is that we have no idea who the actors are so we think they're real people. We think that the director got together this group of people and made a documentary. In *Next Stop*, you're not distracted. I wanted you to think that these are people you actually saw in the Village. Now you know who some of the actors are—Chris Walken, Jeff Goldblum—so when you see them, they have a lot of baggage.

sw: And the studio didn't give you a hard time about not casting stars?

pm: None whatsoever.

sw: Does working with non-stars free you as a director?

pm: It's certainly easier to be the boss, in a way. You don't have to worry about ego. But then you run up against other problems. Can they do it? Will it work? No one had ever seen a gay black character in the movies. I'm talking about Antonio Fargas. If I had hired a famous black actor, people would have thought it was a stunt. Now it looks like I just pulled this guy off the street.

sw: Are New York actors different than Hollywood actors?

pm: First of all, New York actors are all happy to read for you. Or if they don't want to read, they'll certainly meet with you. But they will be there.

16. Next Stop, Greenwich Village (1976) Dori Brenner, Christopher Walken, Ellen Greene, Antonio Fargas, and Lenny Baker.

sw: Does the presence of the theater have anything to do with that?

pm: It probably does, but don't forget, we're talking about another period when it was possible to get to actors. Back then, actors didn't have CAA and managers and press people and agents and points agents. Now they're surrounded by bodyguards who are there to say, "I'll get you more money" or "Don't do this part." It's very hard. It's nonsense.

sw: What do you do when an actor resists direction?

pm: Well, there are two kinds of resist. There's the temporary, weak resist which needs a little [*kisses the air*] tickling, kidding, coddling, and petting, and then you're good; and there's the real resist. In that case, I clear everyone off the set and try to take a break. I sit the actor down and talk to them and try to get them to tell me what's bothering them. "Is it someone's breath? Do you hate the script? Do you hate me? Do you hate those shoes? What is it?"

sw: What if they want to rewrite what's bothering them?

pm: Sure, if it isn't ridiculous and it will help them do it. I've done that. If you clear the air, if you give the actor permission to speak honestly, you're going to break through it. All you want is the actor to be comfortable. An uncomfortable actor is going to give a bad performance. That's what I'm doing, just trying to make them feel comfortable.

SW: *Next Stop, Greenwich Village* looks different than what's come before it. It's a very dark movie, visually I mean. A lot of shadows.

PM: That's [cinematographer] Arthur Ornitz. I hired him because he really knew the Village. But yes, there's a lot of darkness. Those coffeehouses look like Caravaggios. The sunniest scenes in the movie are the exteriors after the abortion doctor when they're jumping through Gramercy Park. Instead of doing the clichéd thing of making it dark after they see the abortionist, I go to a nice, clean, grassy place. [*Thinks*] The trickiest scene I did in the movie, which could go either way, bordered on too much, was when Shelley and the father show up.

SW: It's very theatrical . . . and after three surprise visits . . .

PM: Let's just call it an amazing coincidence.

SW: Also, *Next Stop* has more dolly and track than we've seen from you up to this point. You have it in *Alex*, but they're in the dream sequences. Here you're starting to integrate them into the main part of the film.

PM: I think I was concerned that too much of it was going to be people talking in small rooms. I wanted to find ways to get some movement in there. So I had them do a lot of running and jumping, through the park, across Sheridan Square. Those took a lot of work to set up because I had to make it ready for the period. Every detail had to be put in place. Parking meters had to be torn down. Those exterior shots had to be very carefully devised.

SW: All wide shots.

PM: I don't believe them when they're long-lens close-ups.

SW: The entire film is shot on location with the exception of Larry's apartment.

PM: I built Larry's apartment because I had that big party in it and I could never get fifty people into a real apartment and shoot. So we built a little set in some cockamamie studio.

SW: Were you ever using two cameras at once?

PM: No, just a lot of coverage. You use two cameras when you can afford it. Sometimes it saves you a lot of trouble. One camera goes right next to the other camera, generally to get a wide shot and a tighter shot at the same time. Kurosawa did that a lot. He even used them for magnificent tracking shots. They're side by side following racing horses and he'll intercut them. They cut together like butter.

sw: Do you think that moving the camera more in *Next Stop* has to do with an increase in confidence?

pm: Well, *Harry and Tonto* was shot on the run, so we didn't have time to lay a lot of track. However, *Next Stop* was all done in one place and wherever I could move, I move. But yeah, I was gaining more confidence.

sw: I'm thinking of the shot in the rain, right as Larry and Sarah [Ellen Greene] turn left to go back to their apartment to have sex. You make just a little drift right and suddenly a whole a street opens up.

pm: I like shots like that. I like simple shots that you throw away with a simple move that reveals a whole hidden world back there. The great Polish director Andrzej Wajda does that very well. But he does shots where you'll see two people walking down a very narrow, cobblestone street—a long tracking shot—and then as they turn the corner, behind them you see about five hundred guys going to work in a huge factory. It's only a few moments. He throws it away.

sw: How did you come to pick Paul Desmond for the soundtrack?

pm: Brubeck meant a lot to me. I listened to Brubeck when I was in the Village. He was one of my heroes. It was hip music. I didn't know much about music until I got into the Village. That's were I got my education. The irony is that my mentor, in a way, was Howard Sackler, the guy who later cuckolded me, but he was very smart, he was a poet.

sw: We have a scene between Larry and Robert [Christopher Walken], the Sackler character, where they're in the doctor's waiting room, and Robert asks Larry if he knows Dylan Thomas . . .

pm: He's playing Howard. You know, I told Chris very little. He was wonderful. And you know something? He was marvelously attractive. Now he's a bit bizarre. But he's very gifted. Very gifted.

sw: How were you turned on to him?

pm: Juliet Taylor. When he walked in the office, I said, "That's Howard." A blond, blue-eyed, gorgeous, arrogant wise guy.

sw: Near the end of the movie, after Shelley's just burst in on her son and his girlfriend half-naked and emotionally exposed, Lenny Baker smiles. It's a moment of intense pain for him, but he smiles.

pm: He's got the cosmic joke. The joke is that his mother, his nudge mother, who is the craziest woman in the history of mankind, chooses to walk in at the very moment he's just finished making love to his girlfriend. That's the cosmic joke: If there is a God, he's got irony and a sense of humor.

SW: Was that written in?

PM: I would be lying if I said I knew for sure. I told Lenny something, but I didn't tell him *how*. I just said, "You're in a daze because the ultimate has taken place. She now knows everything and as crazy as it is . . . there's something cosmically insane about it." He knows he's in an insane asylum and he's got to get out. That's the main thing. He's got to get out or he'll go crazy like the rest of them.

SW: At that point, with the pain compounded so many times over, you can either go to the pit of depression—

PM: Or you can laugh at the ridiculousness of it. I did both, but I mostly tried to laugh at it. When I was young in Greenwich Village, I was living in fear that my mother would come, because she usually did, and every weekend. [*Thinks*] You'll be surprised to hear me say this, but it was that movie that made me lose my faith in Hollywood. The powers that be didn't even get it.

SW: You're talking about the critics?

PM: The Academy and people like that. But Pauline [Kael] got it. She tried to wake them up. Anyway, Desmond: I almost used Brubeck to score the whole picture, but I decided that I'd use his music wherever I wanted to, but when I needed a little bit more, I'd have Conti do the rest. I thought that if I had Brubeck working for me, I wouldn't be able to have the other music I wanted in it. I didn't know if he would object. Also, I wanted some music that would blend one scene with another, and so Bill Conti and I had the idea to write some saxophone music with a Brubeckian feeling, so we got Paul Desmond to agree to come out and play it. So he came in and played. Some of it was improvised too. Desmond was not in good shape at that time, but he was a most pleasant person. To sit there in the recording studio and watch Paul Desmond was a great thrill.

SW: When you're handling a sex scene—

PM: I have to handle the breasts of the actresses . . . before I cast them . . . [*Laughs*] . . . to see if they're firm. No, of course you're delicate. In those days we were so desperately afraid of what we were shooting that I had to make it a closed set. There was no one there when I shot it. I don't want a lot of people there.

SW: I want to ask you about the party scene. You're directing something like over fifty people there. What do you do in an environment like that to make sure that you get across what you want?

PM: I try to rely on the assistant director as much as possible, but I talk to the entire group first. The more you communicate with the extras, the better off you are. I don't care if you are shooting a scene with a thousand extras and camels like David Lean, or if you are shooting a bunch of kids in an apartment, but I like to give them the background of what's really happening. I told them about the fifties in New York. I told them about how we used to have rent parties and we'd play games and drink and try to pick up girls. I gave six or seven of the extras what they call a "whammy," which is basically just *a little bit more money*. They'd be in the close-up and I'd actually give them something to do. Generally, those were actors, not extras.

SW: What does it mean when they say the director sets the tone for the set?

PM: It changes for every director. Fellini's sets—I saw this—were very relaxed. They played music. No one was tense. I set the tone by trying to set an atmosphere where the actors have a feeling of each other. There's a very good interview in this month's DGA magazine. It's about Coppola, and I agree with a lot of the things he says. He said that for *Godfather*, he rented a house on a lake and had about ten actors there, and for one full day everyone had to play their character from morning to night. No rehearsal, just being that character from breakfast to dinner.

SW: Have you ever gone that far?

PM: No, but it's a wonderful idea. I think it could be very useful. It depends on the material, of course. Improvisation can also help set the tone. It gives them a sense of place and a sense of thinking about their characters—not the words. I also tell jokes on the set. After a week or so, I do imitations of everyone. I'll do the way the cameraman walks. After Bette Midler left, I'd do her. They like it. It brings people together. But not everybody does that. [*Disparaging*] They're busy setting up a shot.

SW: One last question, something we haven't discussed yet. What do you want in an editor?

PM: You want somebody who gets it, somebody who isn't afraid of you. Hopefully you get somebody with a sense of humor. Stuart Pappé [*Bob & Carol*, *Alex in Wonderland*] had a very good sense of humor. Timing. Richard Halsey [*Harry and Tonto*, *Next Stop*], who worked for Stuart, is not as calm, but still very funny. Donn Cambern had a very good sense of music, lyrical even. You can see it in *Blume in Love*, *Willie & Phil*, and

Tempest. You know, a lot of editors want to be directors deep down, so they can get a little frustrated. The editor learns the trade from top to bottom, because editing teaches you what you need to know about cinema. If you know how to edit, you know everything. You may not know about lenses, but you learn that through cutting, you can establish anything in many, many different ways. A good editor can save you by saying, "Let's cut away here. All you need is one shot, and I can cut from there to this, this, this, and this." So if you're lucky, and the picture can afford it, you can bring the editor down to the set.

sw: Was that true of Halsey on *Next Stop?*

pm: No, he was in California and I was in New York. He did the first cut, I saw it, and then I gave him a lot of notes.

sw: How do you stay fresh watching the material over and over?

pm: You psyche yourself into it. You try to. One of the great things for me now . . .

Paul closes his eyes. His head drifts down.

sw: Paul?

Is this shtick?

sw: [*Whisper*] Paul?

He opens his eyes.

pm: I fell asleep.

sw: Okay. Let's stop for now.

pm: Okay. I've told you everything I know.

sw: Wait, what about the last shot?

pm: Of *Next Stop?*

Paul rubs his eyes.

pm: There's a good story to that, actually. In fact, that was one of the best things to ever happen to me on a movie—or maybe ever. The propman, who was your basic, *hamishe* propman, said to me, "What do you need for the last shot on the street?" I said something about this, that, some chairs, and he said, "Would you like a violinist?" I said, "Oh my God, what a great idea"—because they used to have these violinists who would play in the streets for money—and that's how I end the movie. He gave me my ending.

sw: It's poetry.

pm: Poetry from the propman.

No one is neglected in *Next Stop, Greenwich Village*. Every character gets the full Mazursky treatment. Leads and supporting players are distinguished only by their screen time. But each could fill out an entire movie. The Southern gal at the party ("I love black men!") is complete after one scene—we know why she's there, what she wants, where she's come from, and probably that she won't last—and the character of the abortionist, who goes only by "Doctor" in the script, is complex almost instantly (Mazursky confessed to me that she is one of his favorite things in the movie because, in his mind, she represents great efficiency in character design). First we know her only as a Greenwich Village professional and then, a few scenes later, we see that she's actually a bohemian. Though she never says as much, her interest in abstract expressionism (the painting in her waiting room), coupled with her desire for Robert, speaks her truth loud and clear. "Doctor" may amount to nothing more than another one of the picture's fringe personalities, but in Mazurksy, the fringes define the core.

As Larry's acting teacher says, be specific, be specific, be specific. It's practically Mazursky's motto, and it applies everywhere. What results is a feeling of uninterrupted New York so fully populated, it seems to extend beyond the few scenes we're given—as though the world of the film persists into the wings, independent of where Mazursky chooses to direct our attention. We could be anywhere in Greenwich Village. It just so happens that Paul picks Larry to take us through it.

In the same spirit, there is no difference between foreground and background. Mazursky's master shots privilege everything. People are as important as setting, the audience watching Larry act is as important as the scene itself. Close-ups, as Paul says, are reserved for the little moments that need to be italicized. Otherwise, the camera is democratic, allowing for two freedoms, theirs and ours—as if the biggest crime a director could commit would be if he made our decisions for us.

Juliet on Mazursky

Casting Director, *Next Stop, Greenwich Village, An Unmarried Woman, Willie & Phil, Tempest*

Le Pain Quotidien on 72nd between Central Park West and Columbus. Lunch. Snow.

JULIET TAYLOR: The first time that I met Paul—I was Marion's Dougherty secretary—was on *Bob & Carol & Ted & Alice*, and I remember that Marion's office was in this Victorian brownstone and she had these settees and she just flipped out when Larry Tucker sat down next to her because she thought it was going to break. [*Laughs*] I remember working on *Harry and Tonto* with Marion and it was great fun, but *Next Stop*, which I worked on without Marion, is still one of the films I'm the most proud of and is, I think, one of the most fun things ever because it was just all the bright young New York actors of the time. That was before everyone was in L.A. when there were two different acting communities.[14]

SW: Did you and Paul share the same taste in actors?

JT: Yes. Pretty much. I don't ever remember him saying no to someone I thought he should say yes to or vice versa. That doesn't always happen, you know.

SW: Is there such a thing as a casting style? Is there a Juliet Taylor sensibility versus an Ellen Chenoweth sensibility?

JT: I think that our job is of course to please the director, so it's really the director's style, but I think what you can see with casting directors is attention to detail in the very small parts, done originally and with dimension and sometimes unexpectedly. That's certainly what Marion taught all of us who came after her. She was incredibly specific and every little part had to have a flavor to it, a quality to it, and she was never too obvious. She always added a subtlety to it. I think she was on the ground floor of what was a kind of New York look that was sort of in the period of those seventies New York films. You know, there were so many movies

14. "The first person to ever come to New York for the actors was Norman Lear," Juliet added. "Before that, no one had ever come to New York to get the great stage people to come be in their television shows and movies out in L.A. You wouldn't fly people in from New York the way you do now, unless they were the lead."

being shot on the streets of New York back then—*Shaft* kind of movies, *Panic in Needle Park* kind of movies—that there was just such a chance to draw on the pool of actors that worked here and it just took on kind of a real look. [*Beat*] Marion used to say about the casting directors that worked out in Hollywood, that they worked off of the grocery list of casting.

SW: The usual suspects.

JT: Right. She wanted to bring the city to light with the people who lived and worked here. It was a realistic look.

SW: I think that's how Paul would describe the kinds of movies he makes.

JT: When you think about it, his casting is so much like his personality. It's colorful and lively, always funny and with an interesting twist. [*Beat*] I think one of my big contributions to *An Unmarried Woman* was Alan Bates. You know, we had this great part for a leading guy, but he didn't come into the script until page eighty-one—I still remember that—and no American actor was interested in playing a part that entered so late. I had the idea of giving it to Alan Bates. And the English are of such a different discipline—a good part for them is a good part—and to do an American movie back then was great so he just jumped at it. And it's to Paul's credit too. You know, really good directors like Paul don't get too wedded to how to play a part or who should play the part. Inexperienced directors sometimes get quite literal and small. But better directors usually have enough confidence to use what's in front of them, which is oftentimes what they never expected. Casting is very much that way. It's the process of discovering what the story's about. When you start casting, the characters can take on a new life. They can become something you never thought they were. That's one of the fun things about it. What happens often is a director who says something like, "If only I could get Al Pacino," and you don't get Al Pacino. And then you sort of shift a little to the left and shift a little to the right and you might have to compromise something, but in going through the process of saying yes and no, you get to the essence of the part, and that's the essence of the story.

SW: And you and Paul never had pressure from the studios to cast stars?

JT: Not that I remember. The first time that I really remember fighting with the studio, I mean when fighting with the studio was new to me, was on *Working Girl*. I remember it so distinctively and I thought, "This is so silly. This is taking up so much of my time." Since then I've been very cagey about what I tell the studio. But no, that never happened with me and Paul. But I think there might have been with some of Paul's later movies.[15] [*Thinks*] I was so fortunate to work in a particular period of time. My casting pals in the last few years have done such great stuff, but it's so much harder now. Ellen Chenoweth is not a Marion Dougherty person, but she's like our cousin. [*Beat*] Marion had a groundbreaking approach to casting, which was that she would only call in people for a part who she felt were going to bring in something different from each other. The old way would have been if you had a good part for a cute blonde with an overbite you'd bring in ten cute blondes with an over-bite. And she was very strict with directors who'd say, "I'd like to see more," and she'd say, "I'll bring in more if you're not happy, but I'm not going to bring in a lot of people." She really paved the way because it wasn't always popular to do it that way. She was very brave. It was the best training.

SW: And do you pass down the wisdom of Marion Dougherty to your apprentices?

JT: Sure, yes. Absolutely.

SW: You've worked very closely with Nichols, Lumet, and Woody Allen. How does working with Paul compare?

JT: Woody's meetings are one minute in and out. But that has to do with the fact that he's just supremely uncomfortable. Mike's great with that, though. Some directors now don't even want to meet with actors, they just want to look at tape all the time. But there's nothing like being in the room. *That's* Paul. He wants the connection. He took everybody in. [*Beat*] You know, Woody and I bring up Paul all the time. We always think about him for things. One of those turquoise-wearing guys.

Juliet Taylor's filmography reads like a history of New York film from the mid-seventies to today. She's too modest to admit it, but even if her directors are the ones making the final decisions, the fact is, they're deciding amongst a pool of actors she's delivered them. It's her taste, more often than not, that begets theirs. And through a sensibility passed down to her from Marion Dougherty, an entire generation of filmmakers—their names are mentioned in the conversation above—gave realistic faces to a city previously populated by grocery-listers. That means the guys on the bench,

---

15. Something was in the water. Both *Working Girl* and *Moon Over Parador*, Mazursky's initiation into the world of studio antipathy, were released in 1988.

the girls at the bar, and the old lady at the counter. There's no *Harry and Tonto* or *Next Stop, Greenwich Village* without them.

In other words, to know Mazursky's world is to love its inhabitants, which is why, when he's in wide shot, the art of Juliet Taylor is in close-up.

An Unmarried Woman (1978)

Tanya: It's really okay to feel anything—anger, jealousy, depression. It's really okay to feel.

The lights are out all over Paul's office. Jeff Kanew, who cut *Yippee*, sits beside Mazursky, driving Final Cut Pro. Mazursky watches, arms crossed. "We cut a little bit off *Enemies*," he tells me. Kanew hits the spacebar—playback—and the title "Paul Mazursky, actor" fades up from black. "This is a reel of some of my acting stuff," he explains, "for a retrospective they're having at Lincoln Center." The first clip is from Kubrick's *Fear and Desire*. Paul is twenty-three. "We can't cut this," he says to Kanew. But Kanew says it needs to go and the cut is made. At one point, Mazursky asks for my opinion. "I don't know if you need the hallway shot," I say, and without hesitating, or asking why, Paul tells Kanew to make the cut. Here I see the collaborative atmosphere Paul has talked about. Where everyone has a voice, and there are no mistakes or conditions—everything is worth trying. It feels freeing even to me.

sw: I think *An Unmarried Woman* made you something of a marriage guru to the film-going world.

pm: I never thought of myself as a maven about marriage, about divorce, about anything. Don't forget, I was never divorced, but I had been around a lot of divorced people. I mean, most of the people I knew were divorced. And I never thought about making a movie about the woman who was unmarried, I only thought about making movies about guys who were in stress because of the new awakening of attitudes toward sexuality.

sw: So what started you on the script?

pm: We had a friend named Caroline who had just gotten divorced. She was a lovely woman and very smart. A great gal. One day she came by our house with the deed to her new house in Beverly Hills. Next to her name it said, "an unmarried woman" and that phrase led me to think about . . .

sw: They don't say "unmarried man."

pm: Yeah. It's ridiculous. I never saw "unmarried Jew," either. So I began interviewing a lot of women who were no longer married and I got a lot of information and found certain similarities. I decided to make it New York because to be unmarried in L.A., you'd be jogging along San Vicente, but in New York, you'd be jogging along the East River. I thought New York would be more interesting to throw a woman into an unmarried life. And I put her in therapy because I had had a lot of therapy. I found this wonderful shrink named Penelope Russianoff [Tanya, Erica's therapist], who was about six foot three and conducted her sessions at her home on the floor. I met her at a party and I asked her if she wanted to do the movie and she did. It made her very famous. She wrote books and did therapy cruises.

SW: You had never prepared this way before writing a script.

PM: Let's see . . . with *Toklas*, we were just observing the scene. For *Bob & Carol*, I experienced Esalen for a long weekend. Those were real experiences, not research. *Alex in Wonderland* was right out of my head. And then *Blume*. No interviews. And then *Harry and Tonto*. I didn't interview old people. You're right about that.

SW: And *Next Stop* was all out of your memory.

PM: Right. So now comes this movie, *An Unmarried Woman*, and I'm talking to all these women. I didn't tell them that I had a plot or even a movie. I was just talking to them. I'd say, "I'm just curious. What does it feel like? Are you still angry? Are you sad? Do you wish the marriage wasn't over? Are you looking for another mate?" Stuff like that. I got some wonderful answers. One woman said that when she'd go window-shopping, she'd notice the reflection of a couple behind her. They were holding hands and obviously in love and it saddened her.

SW: So why did you feel compelled to seek outside experience?

PM: Because I'm writing about a woman and I'm not a woman. I didn't want to make her just like Caroline; I wanted to make her a woman whose life had been extremely happy.

SW: Once you said, "One of the most important things about *An Unmarried Woman* is to show that Erica's marriage is not a bad one."

PM: Exactly. I wanted the audience to be surprised. Even though the title was *An Unmarried Woman*, this movie opens and you see this couple jogging and they're cute. They're fun. A few scenes later, she's having lunch with him—and I love to place big scenes in public places—and on the street he stops her and begins to sob. He tells her that he's in love with another woman. I wanted it to be a shock not just to Erica, but to the audience. And I wanted them to be shocked by the specifics of things he was saying, things that are on the verge of comedy. He met her in Bloomingdales!

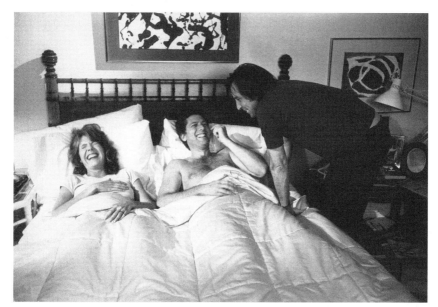

17. An Unmarried Woman *(1978) Jill Clayburgh, Michael Murphy, and Paul.*

SW: Did you rehearse that scene?

PM: No. I just rehearsed their walk. Just for the camera. I told Michael Murphy, "When you hit this wall, back up against it and have a breakdown." I said, "If you cry, fine; if you don't cry, fine. Do what feels right." I told Jill, "Don't look at him as you walk. Just imagine how much fun it's going to be in the Hamptons."

SW: Why couldn't she look?

PM: Because once she looked, she'd see how troubled he is and then the scene would have to change. But no, none of that was rehearsed.

SW: Toward the end of the scene, you have a marvelous 180-degree shot of Erica as she strides away from him—it's the "unmarried woman shot." It looks simple, but in fact, it must have been a very complicated shot in that it opens up a lot of New York sight lines that need to be cleared.

PM: I had that shot planned out in advance and luckily I had a very good A.D., Tony Ray, who assured me that it could be done with a few second A.D.s on walkie-talkies at the end of streets holding the traffic. You hope for the best and we got it.

SW: And then, at the end of the scene, Erica throws up.

PM: One of the women who I interviewed told me that her reaction to the divorce was so visceral she threw up.

sw: It sounds like in telling this story you felt some kind of responsibility to the female experience.

PM: Well, I know that I would get killed by the feminists and other women—that's a funny line—if I misfired. Of course, I didn't know whether I was misfiring or not, so I just decided to try to understand Erica. Erica who was an attractive woman with a really nice husband and doing well with a beautiful apartment with the view of the city and a sixteen-year-old daughter who is as smart as a whip and a wise guy to boot. They've got everything. Of course, some of the criticisms of the movie came from Vincent Canby. He said, "Who cleans their windows?" One of the weirdest critiques I had ever had. He said, "I never saw a maid in this movie." He probably never had an apartment like that. He was jealous because he was living in a fucking closet. Anyway, Canby later liked my movies. He liked *Scenes From a Mall* because he's crazy about Woody Allen.

sw: How did you come to cast Jill Clayburgh?

PM: I cast her easily. I've trusted my instincts many, many times in making movies and most of the time I've been right. I cast the lead in that movie with only having seen *Gable and Lombard* and then a TV movie called *Hustling*, but it was *Gable and Lombard* that sold me. I mean, she played Lombard! She was a daffy, wonderful, sexy, real lady. And that's what came out. A happy lady. I wanted a happy lady. Jill had a goofiness I knew about from *Gable and Lombard*. That was fun because even when she was real down, she'd get a little silly. And she also had great *tendresse*. That's a word I use to describe a certain kind of actor you feel sympathetic toward right away. Alan Bates had it too. I never had a problem with Jill Clayburgh ever, ever, ever.

sw: The people who objected to *An Unmarried Woman* were put off by Erica's class status. They would say that no woman with her privilege could be unhappy.

PM: That was the whole point. It's silly. If you made a movie called *An Unmarried Woman* about a woman who lives in the projects who is working like a dog to support herself, it's a much more tragic story. Are we going to be prejudiced against the upper middle class because they "have it all"? The idea was that they have nothing but misery! She's miserable and he's miserable!

sw: You once said that your heroes are from the upper middle class.

PM: Those are the people that I know and I'm one of them. Everybody makes fun of them. They say that they're spoiled or they're not committed and all they care about is making money or that they don't suffer. But they do. They suffer. They suffer just like anyone else. It doesn't have to be *Macbeth* to be suffering.

SW: At the time you were making *An Unmarried Woman*, did you feel like you had to be defensive about your decisions?

PM: I never thought about it while I was doing it. It was only after it was done that I started to think about it.

SW: And it was a difficult movie to get financed.

PM: I wrote it for Fox, for Laddie, my hero. They said that they liked it but were afraid of making another woman's movie because they had three unreleased woman's pictures ready to come out; Robert Altman's *3 Women*, they were investing in *Julia*, and they had *Turning Point*, and they were afraid of having too many movies about this new thing—the woman. Then I went to Mike Medavoy at United Artists and he turned me down. Medavoy brought in an executive named Marsha Nassatir, who was obviously their brain. She said, "Why doesn't she go off with the guy at the end of the movie? I cannot accept this." I said, "But Marsha, that's the whole point to this movie. This is 1977." I thought that remark was breathtaking. We were then turned down at several other places, and then finally, Stanley Jaffe at Columbia said yes. He said he wanted to be the producer even though he was running the studio— he was a very nice man. I said okay and we were set to make a deal. A week later he was fired. Then David Begelman, who had been my own agent, took over Columbia. But David passed on it. And he was my agent! [*Laughs*] His excuse was something like, "We've got *Close Encounters* and it's costing us too much. We can't take a chance." I was angry, but I never hated him for it. At that point Josh Greenfeld called me up and said, "Did you read the trades today? *The Omen* is a huge hit. Fox is making big money." So I called Laddie and asked him if there was any chance he would reconsider. He said, "Come on down and we'll talk about it." We spoke—they felt the Michael Murphy character could be strengthened. I didn't really know what that meant, but I agreed with them. I said, "Oh yeah, you're right. Strengthened. Sure." I went back and I changed about three or four lines of dialogue, waited a week, changed the date, put a new cover on it, and gave it to them. They read it and said, "Let's make this movie."

SW: Two-point-three million?

PM: About that, yeah. Jill got, I think, $150,000 and Alan Bates got $75,000.

sw: Still, $2.3 million seems low.

pm: I made movies cheaply. I had no padding and I was taking low fees. On *Unmarried* I had points, so I made a great deal of money. I made over a million dollars. It was a big hit.

sw: You're very proud of it.

pm: I am. It seemed to me a step toward proving that I could do stories about a variety of things and still make them my own and real and comic and tragic. All my films are different. And this one was a women's movie, but not directed by a woman. It had something you don't see too much—a lovely woman with a nice sense of humor—and it gets down to the realities of her life. After the divorce, she meets this pain-in-the-ass artist at a bar—brilliantly played by Cliff Gorman—and she decides to go to bed with him. I think that scene really made you feel what it would be like for a woman to go to bed with a stranger for the first time in seventeen years. The scene was pretty bare. He takes her by her nipples and pulls her to him. I don't think I'd seen a scene like that in a movie, where a woman goes to bed with a new guy. In the old days, they would just fade out. I'm all for fading out just because most of the sex scenes you see today are kind of ridiculous.

sw: What do you mean?

pm: You know they're scenes in a movie. They look like actors playing a scene. This scene between Jill and Cliff Gorman didn't look like a scene in a movie; it looked like it actually happened. But this movie had something that made it different from the other movies of the period. It has her meeting this man, Alan Bates, and getting tough about the relationship. That's one of the key things. She's crazy about him, and still she's *tough*. She takes a step that had not been taken before in the movies: "No, I'm not going with you." It's *Dodsworth* in reverse.

sw: Yes!

pm: That's another Wyler movie. I've seen it quite a few times. You can't do better than that. It's *An Unmarried Man*! What a performance by Mary Astor! She played a smart, attractive, decent woman, who really loved him but would never tell him to leave her.

sw: In an early draft of the script, you have a scene in which Erica meets Martin's girlfriend. She actually goes to Erica for advice.

pm: The woman didn't play the part well so I cut it. She read well for me in the audition, but when I did the scene I didn't believe a word of it. I did everything I could, but it didn't work.

sw: Was it a funny scene?

PM: It wasn't funny so much as it was telling. This woman was desperate and she didn't know what to do. Erica says to her, "Don't come to me. I can't help you."

SW: You couldn't have recast it with a different actress?

PM: Had I had the courage . . . I was so nervous about being on budget, about trying to be on budget . . . I should have gotten another actress and tried again. I just didn't do it. I made the edit in my head. After I saw it, I just said, "We don't need it." I talked it over with a few people—don't forget I wrote it, so it was ultimately my choice—but I think I told someone at the studio that I wasn't crazy about it and didn't want to do it again. But I see now that I should have. It would have been interesting. The scene was basically an ironic scene. This woman comes to Erica and says, "Look, I know this is . . . difficult and I know that I'm the woman you must hate and you must have all kind of complicated feelings toward me and I don't blame you and I'm really sorry. But now I don't know what to do. He's driving me crazy." Erica says, "Why the fuck are you coming to me?" In any case, I should've gotten someone who could handle it.

SW: Speaking of script changes, was the part of Saul Kaplan written to be English?

PM: No. After he read the script, Alan said to me, "I'm not Jewish and I'm not American. How could I play Saul?" I said to him, "Saul just became British."

SW: Why is he Jewish?

PM: Because I'm Jewish, *daaaaaarrrrling*. [*Laughs*] Oh, I don't know. He didn't have to be Jewish, but it made him colorful in a certain way. He has a British accent, he's devilishly handsome, he's suave, and he's Jewish. It gives him spice. I'm lucky I didn't get Anthony Hopkins, even though he's a great actor. Hopkins would have made him more elegant . . . also he might have eaten her . . . [*Laughs*] I should make that movie, you know. I should make *Hannibal Lecter Gets Married*. I could pitch it to Dino de Laurentiis and tomorrow morning it will get made. I'm guaranteeing you right now this movie will get made. Hannibal Lecter is now sixty-five, meets a woman and goes crazy for her. She's lovely and understanding and knows about his past. She's very smart—a gestalt therapist. Hannibal's totally reformed now; he doesn't even eat meat. They have their honeymoon in Venice and while they're there he has a slight relapse and eats a gondolier. Dino would buy it in a second. *Mr. and Mrs. Hannibal Lecter*, a Paul Mazursky film.

sw: You offered Saul Kaplan to Hopkins?

PM: Yes, and he turned it down because he doesn't come in until page seventy-four or something like that. I said, "But it's a 125-page movie and he dominates forty-nine pages."

sw: It's an unconventional choice to delay the romantic lead for an hour and twenty minutes.

PM: You don't have to introduce everyone right away.

sw: Erica, like so many of the characters in your movies, travels. She doesn't go far—starting with the stockbroker uptown and ends with the artist downtown—but her journey describes emotional education.

PM: What it tells you is that she's growing. Most of the couples I know use the word "we" to talk about so many things. You'll hear, "We went to a great restaurant Thursday and we both enjoyed the meal." I'd say, "Did you both enjoy the same meal?" We, we, we, we, we, we. I can't believe it.

sw: So "I" was a far-out idea in 1977?

PM: We were beginning to get a sense of that in my Greenwich Village period. The fifties. The Beats.

sw: Erica has none of that.

PM: No, but it's a nice life with a great view. I deliberately picked a place with a view because I wanted them to look over the greatest city in the world. New York is excitement and New York is the place where it happens. Up there, Erica and Martin are on top of the world. I think at the end of the movie, she's at a place that makes you feel *good*. And that's why the movie really worked.

sw: What do you mean?

PM: In other words, it's one of the movies that could end very sad. Maybe she doesn't go off with him and she's left there in despair. That could be her life. It's more Odets. But I didn't want that. I wanted it to be a celebration. Carrying the painting alone in the wind. [*Paul leans in, smiling*] It's my metaphor. I had it with me all along, since the beginning. I knew it would work because the day we shot it, it was windy. A piece of luck. It's not saying she's going to be dancing through life, but she's going to be okay. She's going to be alright. She's going to meet another guy probably.

sw: I always thought Saul was going to come back and they were going to reconnect.

PM: They might. I never made that movie, but I was asked to.

sw: *The Return of Saul*?

PM: They asked me to do a sequel. Every time I came up with something, it would be funny. Like two or three years later, the daughter is on the verge of getting married. Erica, who is now sixty years old, is advising the daughter against it. She's too young. Then Erica meets the guy and she starts to fall for him. Clayburgh falls for her daughter's twenty-eight-year-old boyfriend and the daughter decides to try a lesbian relationship—just try it. [*Laughs*] It's an experiment. She meets a sympathetic woman and the sex is even interesting. She tells her mother, who is disgusted by it. Then we see that Jill Clayburgh is no longer that free woman. Not only that, but her back hurts, you know?

SW: I read that at one point you were thinking of Jane Fonda for the lead.

PM: Yes. I really wanted her. I respected her very much and she turned down the script because she said it wasn't political. I tried to explain to her that it was the most political movie I'd ever written. It was saying, in essence, that a woman who has been discarded by her husband can still operate and be free and have her own life and have affairs and do all the things that men take for granted. But she didn't get it. I said to her, she doesn't go off with Alan Bates in the end!

SW: Okay, this is a practical question—how did you shoot the scenes up in the apartment without getting glare in the windows?

PM: Arthur Ornitz, who shot the movie, had the crew put outside the windows those things painters and window cleaners use and put lights out there like that. Way up high.

SW: Lights were coming in from outside?

PM: Lights or reflectors. It was difficult, but it worked. A New York crew is capable of doing almost anything. I'll get killed if I say this, but for the most part, the New York crew is more involved in the making of the movie than a Los Angeles crew. In L.A. you'll hear a lot of talk about the condos the crew is investing in. That's a generalization of course. The only time I had a not good crew was the brief three weeks I shot in India for *Willie & Phil*. The follow focus guy was not good and the equipment was makeshift and weird. And there was [cinematographer] Sven Nykvist, the master, surrounded by all this bullshit stuff! The Italian crews can do anything and they can do it quick. Remember, they've grown up in the shadow of great art so they are extremely sophisticated about those things and they love art and beauty. They know about stuff.

SW: How would you discuss your aesthetic with Ornitz?

PM: I usually give ideas from paintings I like. Maybe you show a movie or two that has influenced you. With *An Unmarried Woman*, I never showed him any movies, I just told him that I wanted the apartment to be light, airy, and I wanted the artist's studio to have white walls. White everywhere. It's about space, it's about beauty. I wanted the sex scene dark—that was real to me—I didn't want light there. We would talk about it a lot in the scouting. And of course, Arthur had very good taste. I didn't have to tell him too much.

SW: I don't know if this is profound or ridiculous, but dog shit is a big part of this movie.

PM: I was obsessed with shit. At that time New York was constantly complaining about cleaning up after your dog.

SW: It was specific to that moment in New York?

PM: Yeah, people were afraid the city would be drowned in shit. And there was some truth in it. That's when people began with the scoopers. Also, it was a touch of reality. In the middle of the romantic night scene she has with Alan Bates, they're talking about shit. [Costume designer] Albert Wolsky gave her a cape. It's *very* romantic. I thought the cape was fantastic. Jill was a tall woman and the cape had something to do with making her height okay. Also, it was something she could use for these moments outside when she's clearly fallen in love. That's what the scene's about. She just saw this guy get into a fistfight over her. I think if I was a woman and a man got into a fight over me I would think, "This is a pretty good guy."

SW: So that's a part of his heroism? It makes him a romantic hero.

PM: It's a surprise. *An Unmarried Woman* is full of surprises. I've set you up by introducing this wise guy [Cliff Gorman], and the wise guy appears again in the movie and goes to bed with her! And then the wise guy appears again at this art party and turns out to be a son of a bitch and he makes it clear that he's fucked her and Alan Bates jumped him—

SW: Which is also a surprise.

PM: Which is also a surprise, yes, but it's been set up. It made the movie interesting. I had the women learn to ice-skate so I could have a scene with all these women skating freely instead of another scene of endless talk. We had her free. She's flying emotionally. She's up. At the therapist's office, she's down. One of the lines Penelope Russianoff ad-libbed was "discombobulated." I had never written a line like that in my life. That was a therapist's word. By the way, in that scene in the therapist's office, Jill broke down and started to cry *for real.* When the studio tested the movie in San Diego, they showed it after a very dreary Sydney Pollack movie called *Bobby Deerfield.* During the course—

The phone rings.

Let me get this.

Paul hits the speakerphone button.

BETSY MAZURSKY [*speakerphone*]: Hi. Did you hear about the shooting?

PM: What shooting?

BETSY: Fifty people.

PM: Who did it?

BETSY: In Virginia. In a college.

PM: A guy went crazy?

BETSY: I don't know.

PM: A terrorist?

BETSY: I don't know.

PM: Any other good news?

BETSY: No.

PM: Listen honey, I got news. I got news for you. I might as well be honest. There's another woman in my life.

BETSY: Oh yeah?

PM: Her name is Esther.

BETSY: Okay.

PM: She's a younger woman. Sixty-two. Hot as can be . . .

BETSY: Mazel tov.

PM: Thank you, bye-bye.

Paul hangs up, giggling.

PM: Isn't she great? That's why we're married fifty-four years.

SW: I'm going to use that as a segue.

PM: Go ahead.

SW: How did you go about getting Michael Murphy and Jill Clayburgh comfortable with each other?

PM: I would meet with them to talk about the movie. We'd be having lunch and then I would leave, and as I was leaving I would say, "I've got to do something for a couple hours. You guys are on your own. Let's meet again at five o'clock." I made up some excuse to go and for a couple hours they got to know each other. I think it broke the ice.

SW: In the script, after Martin tells her about the other woman, you're very specific about notating behavior, which is rare for you. Generally, you err on the side of less, but here you write, "Erica is not crying." You don't let that be the actor's decision.

PM: I did it because I wanted the throwing up to be the payoff. The throwing up becomes the crying.

SW: Another thing you cut was the chapter titles. Originally, the script was divided into the parts "The Last Days of Erica's Marriage," "The Early Days of Erica's Separation," "Erica Begins to Experiment," and "Erica Falls in Love."

PM: I was imitating Bergman, I think. But you didn't need them. If anything, it was useful to me in thinking about the divisions in the script. The question was, do we want to do this Brechtian thing and announce what's going to happen or do we want them to be surprised and suck them into this ideal marriage. Of course, you know the title of the movie, so you know something's going to happen.

SW: Bergman was on your mind when you wrote it?

PM: No, Bergman was on my mind when I wrote *Scenes from a Mall*. When I wrote *An Unmarried Woman*, I had no idea where it was going. It just came out.

SW: In one of the famous lines from the movie, Erica describes her life as being "part Mary Hartman and part Ingmar Bergman."

PM: I wanted you to be aware of the New York sophisticates. I was writing for them to some degree, but I wanted it to be universal. She's hip enough to realize that her life is now on the verge of being a sitcom *and* a tragedy. She's in both places. "You met her in Bloomingdales? She was looking for a shirt for her father?" That's funny, too.

SW: Does it make you uncomfortable when people call your movies comedies?

PM: No. It's what I call "a human comedy." Like the work of Renoir. "Comedy" doesn't mean broad farce; it doesn't mean sitcom. There are certain comedies you see where I don't for a second believe they're real people. They're amusing—you know, they're Ben Stiller and Cameron Diaz jerking off in the hair—they're very funny, but that's not a human comedy. That's a funny fantasy about young people. It's amusing. I'm into something that has more real soul.

SW: Can you have that real soul and be broad?

PM: I'm trying to think. Do you mean can I or can one?

SW: Can one.

PM: I think it's hard. I certainly don't remember real soul in the Bob Hope movies. Woody Allen has certainly had moments like that. He doesn't have any soul in some of these later comedies, they're just attempts at being funny.

SW: So the idea of broad doesn't turn you off?

PM: No, no. Buñuel's comedy can be very broad.

SW: Right. One of the things that I think makes these comedies so human is that you don't go in for jokes.

PM: I try not to do that. He won't like me for saying this, but he knows that I'm an admirer of his, but Neil Simon, a brilliant craftsman who has written some wonderful plays, finds it difficult to have characters speak in their own voice. Most of them sound like him because they've got jokes. He's a great jokes man, but people don't talk that way.

SW: You allowed Penelope Russianoff a little freedom in terms of dialogue, which is close to how you handled the scenes with Don Muhich [therapist in *Bob & Carol* and *Blume in Love*] and Michael Egan [acting teacher in *Next Stop, Greenwich Village*].

PM: In those cases I knew that these actors—in this case, real therapists and a real teacher—may find the opportunity to say something that's not in the script, and I wanted them to know that it was okay to try it. That's all. Then I would leave it up to them to bring it back to the script. You've got this very good thing working for you, where if it goes on too long you can just cut it out of the movie. I wasn't worried.

SW: How did that change the way you shot the therapy scenes?

PM: I had two cameras on them. I got a wide-ish over-the-shoulder—Jill's shoulder—of Penelope; I wanted a full shot of that room, of them sitting on the floor. And then I got a second camera right next to them getting a medium close-up of Penelope. Then I would do the reverse, and then I would even have an over-the-shoulder of Penelope to Jill so that if Jill broke down, I had it. So I had essentially seven shots to cover a scene that's about seven or eight pages. And you need all the shots because it's a long, long scene—you might want to cut it up. Also, I would communicate with the operator; I'd tap him on the shoulder, and tell him to go in for a good moment. I would whisper, "Swing over to her fingers" and then you'd see her hands—which I didn't plan—going like that. [*Paul rubs his hands*] It's detail. Believe me, it's not a Paul Mazursky trick. The Method, I think, had an influence on that. Brando, you'll notice, in any scene in any movie, has almost always got some of this [*scratches his ear*] or some of this [*picks something out of his teeth*]. Business keeps the actor from playing the lines, as opposed to the style of acting where the acting was emoted, like the cliché of Shakespearean actors declaiming, [*showy English accent*] "Tomorrow and tomorrow and tomorrow creeps in this petty pace from day to day until the last syllable of recorded time!" It's silly. Then there's this thing I call "acting without hands."

sw: What's that?

pm: It's just being there, simply. It's so simple that it's overwhelming. Vanessa Redgrave does it. That version would be [*still, almost dead*] "It is a tale told by an idiot full of sound and fury, signifying nothing." What could be bigger than that, existentially speaking?

Paul takes off his cap and runs his hands through his hair.

I'm getting to the age when I'm starting to think about that *a little bit*. Will I see Tommy, my grandson, graduate? He's only five and a half and he'll graduate high school when he's eighteen—that's twelve more years. I'd be eighty-nine. I'd be a fool to think it was a guarantee.

sw: You never thought about it before?

pm: No. When I wrote *Harry and Tonto* I thought a little about it, but in general I'm day-to-day, minute-by-minute. My cup is full so I don't have a lot of time to think about the other stuff, which is dying.

Paul puts his hat back on.

pm: Next question.

sw: I was surprised to see there are actually a couple of zooms in *An Unmarried Woman*'s therapy scenes.

pm: Yeah, but I don't do much of that. And I hate a rack-focus.

sw: Why? Because it's not real?

pm: It's not just that, it's because when I see a rack-focus in the movies, I don't see the rack-focus, I see the follow-focus guy making the rack. He's actually in my head in the shot. I'm aware of machinery and I don't like it.

sw: Same with the zoom?

pm: Less so because you can have a zoom in a way when you don't know it's happening. Sven Nykvist is a master of that. He makes the zoom so slow that it's only when you're halfway there when you've realized that the shot has changed. Of course, fast zooms are pretty taboo now. We did a lot of that in *The Monkees*.

sw: Watching *An Unmarried Woman*, it's not surprising to me that you've arrived at documentary, in *Yippee*. The way you describe working with Russianoff gets at what I mean.

pm: Yes, all that behavior.

SW: That's like how the piano scene with Clayburgh and Lisa Lucas was originated. You saw it, you liked it, and you put it in. I think I'm beginning to understand what you mean by *real*.

PM: What happened was, between scenes, I saw them playing the piano, so I put it in. It tells you more than all kinds of dialogue.

SW: You don't even link it to the scenes that come before or after it.

PM: No, no. It's just there. One thing happens, and then the next thing happens.

SW: What would you do if an actor was having a hard time finding the right emotional beat?

PM: I would try to find out if they've ever had something like that happen to them in their own lives, or any place period that had nothing to do with what the scene's about but that caused them to have certain feelings. You try it. Try to have them play the scene without the dialogue, but in their own words. Many of them would try that; they would start with a word or two of their own, and then go right to the script. I would say, "No, no, no, no, don't go to the script!" Sometimes they would go off on tangents and that's when it would get good. It would take them other places and those places might get them to the emotional places you wanted for the scene. That's when you say, "You see that? I like that. Now let's do the scene. Keep that in mind what you just did." Then they start to do it and it sometimes works.

SW: At those moments, is your job kind of like a therapist?

PM: No. I'm just trying to mine their—I hate to say their unconscious, because that's what therapists do—I'm trying to get them someplace they're not at. They've been doing a scene in a way that's only comfortably uncomfortable as opposed to *really* uncomfortable. In other words, they're indicating—because they're very good—the *outer* quality of certain moments. A laugh, a maneuver, getting louder; they're superficial. So you get into some kind of improv that might lead you to something better. It may not be in the movie that way, but it could help you.

SW: Let's talk about endings. Your movies tend to end with a question, not really a resolution.

PM: Ending a movie is the hardest thing because you want the audience to feel something and to have something you don't want to be corny and stupid. That's why many movies have five endings. Also, life doesn't really resolve itself. If it resolved itself, we would be dead.

SW: You're mistrustful of endings in that sense.

PM: We don't always know what's going to happen next.

An Unmarried Woman : **125**

Paul shrieks.

PM: You see?

SW: Yes.

PM: Okay.

SW: *An Unmarried Woman* features several paintings by Paul Jenkins, which stand in for the work of Saul. What drew you to Jenkins's work?

PM: When I was in New York, I had to find an artist who could show Alan Bates how to paint and I really wanted to find one who would let us use his loft. The first artist I met was Jules Olitski, who was one of the big abstract expressionists. He didn't want to do it. He didn't want anyone watching him work, so he recommended Jenkins, who was living below him. So I went down there and met Paul. He was a larger-than-life figure and he loved the idea and he let me use his studio.

SW: So it was practical, not aesthetic?

PM: Well, I liked his stuff. It was quite beautiful. He called them "phenomena." I mean, my favorite painters happen to be Velazquez, Rembrandt, and Picasso. I'm not that much of a fan of the abstract expressionists. But Paul and I have become very good friends since. I have about six of his paintings.

SW: It was very important to you to show how a painter paints.

PM: I wanted to do the real thing. I've never liked in movies about painters when you see them with the easels in the foreground and cut to the hand dabbling on the canvas. I never believe it. In this case, I could show the odd and beautiful way of painting with the ivory knife. It's a very free style. He's free when he paints.

SW: Let's talk about Conti's score. For a movie as realistic as this, your choice of music is decidedly romantic, at times even epic. There's some counterpoint working there.

PM: I had the score from *Last Tango* in my head and when I made the first cut of the movie, I used it as temp score to show Bill Conti. When he played me his score I knew it was going to be great. It went from light to dark. I said, "You got it, Bill." [*Beat*] As a side note, I later met Gato Barbieri at a party and he came up to me and said, "Why did you steal my music and not hire me?" I said, "I don't know, Gato." He was right.

SW: We know *An Unmarried Woman* had considerable cultural impact. It's referenced by name in *Private Benjamin*, and it changed the lives of many of the professionals in it.

PM: Jenkins's price went up. Penelope Russianoff's practice grew, she went on couples cruises, and she wrote a book.

SW: And Jill Clayburgh's cape sold many like it.

PM: You know, I've got to give Albert Wolsky credit. He would show me stuff and I would go, "I love it. Jill, are you comfortable?" "Very." I'd say, "Great."

SW: SoHo, too! *An Unmarried Woman* was great publicity for SoHo.

PM: I think I was the first to shoot it. There may have been something that I don't know about, but I can't remember any feature films that did it. The time I was there was the time to buy. *An Unmarried Woman* made it a big deal. People would go to One Fifth Avenue knowing that's where the movie was shot.

He's quiet. I get the feeling it's time to wrap up.

Maybe I shouldn't say this about myself, but I must say, I think I was born to make people laugh. I don't have the need to be a tragedian. Most comedians have that need. Not me.

In *An Unmarried Woman*, Mazursky is as naked as he has ever been and ever will be. Gone are the jokes of *Toklas*, the satire of *Bob & Carol*, and the bombast of *Alex*. Gone is the high romance of *Blume*, the folksiness of *Harry and Tonto*, and the flamboyance of *Next Stop*. There are no filters, only the feeling that *An Unmarried Woman* is life as it appears to those who live it, an anthem to resilience played at the low volume of everydayness.

The film is a high point: For the first time, Mazursky is more concerned with getting it right than giving it spice. He wants only to walk along the street, to sample, as the film's tagline states, from the raw catalogue of "she laughs, she cries, she feels angry, she feels lonely, she feels guilty, she makes breakfast, she makes love, she makes do, she is strong, she is weak, she is brave, she is scared, she is . . . an unmarried woman." American movies had hardly seen naturalism so pure.

The movie was nominated for three Oscars: Best Actress, Best Screenplay, and Best Picture. "*An Unmarried Woman*," Andrew Sarris wrote, "is the best American film I have seen in several years." But was it truly a feminist picture? (Does it matter?) Clearly, Clayburgh and Mazursky's Erica is not a fantasized female; she's no ingénue, gal Friday, kitchen wife, drama queen, or femme fatale. She is none of them because she is all of them—a face for every change of heart—and a history of Hollywood heroines from first to last.

Jill on Mazursky

Erica Benton, *An Unmarried Woman*

On the phone.

SW: Can you tell me about the audition?

JILL CLAYBURGH: Well, just like everything else about the movie, the audition was *so easy.* I didn't even audition really, I just walked in and talked to Paul for fifteen minutes. I didn't even read anything. It was effortless. And that's how Paul wants everything to seem. I mean, I just watched the movie again last night because I didn't remember it that specifically, and he makes everything appear as if it doesn't have a lot of shape or instruction from his hand. It appears effortless. Getting the part was the most casual, casual thing.

SW: Was that what it was like on the set as well?

JC: Totally. Totally. Rewatching the movie, I thought that Paul must have given me direction on every single line, but I don't remember that he ever, ever did. I just remember him being appreciative, funny, you know, cracking people up. Occasionally he'd say, you know, "Why don't you try it like this . . ." He's a very brilliant actor, so he would just sort of say your line off-the-cuff and then you'd go, "Ohhhhhh!" He wasn't, like, [*abrupt*] "Do the line like *this.*" He was like, "When you say the line *duh-duh-duh-duh,* you should just cross over to the coffee." But then you'd hear how he said that line.

SW: So it's not a line reading?

JC: Oh, not at all. He never insisted, but he's clearly there in every line, in every shot, in every look, in every gesture. It didn't *feel* as if I was being directed, and yet when I see it, because the whole tone is of such a piece and because the whole thing has such integrity, you know he was there at every second. It was such a joy. It was *easy.*

SW: You once said that working with Paul, you felt very safe.

JC: [*Hushed*] Yeah.

SW: How did he create that feeling?

Long pause.

JC: Well, it was a very small, intimate crew and we all really kind of knew each other and he was always joking with the crew, so you didn't feel that strange eyes were watching you. That's a part of it, but I would say that's the *least* of it. You just felt that he trusted what you were doing and that he would never abuse the privileges of intimacy, that he would always be there to make your character, you, the story reveal itself in the best way possible.

SW: That must have been especially valuable considering the number of nude scenes and sex scenes you had to do.

JC: Right! I was so shocked last night at how many sex scenes there were. It's so sexual! I didn't really remember that. It was *maturely* sexual. And how it was *mature* in general! Just—I don't know—think of the women and the way they dressed. I mean, you know, when you think of women getting together now in film, and I won't say *what*, but they're all dressed to the nines. Who the hell are they dressed for? They're all so chic! We all looked good, but we weren't done up. We were just . . . wonderfully . . . in our own characters. It just had such a . . . such a . . . I thought, "My god, I wish they made movies like this now." And I wasn't looking at me, I was just looking at a wonderful movie. [*Thinks*] You know, I don't remember how we shot my sex scene with Cliff Gorman. But the fact that I don't remember is really an indication of how intimate everything was. There's a lot of *ease* with the body and with sexuality.

SW: What would happen in rehearsal? Paul said he would leave you and Michael and—

JC: Well, I read that in your chapter and I have to say I don't remember it that way. I guess I do remember one day when he said that. "I have something to do," he said.

SW: And he took off?

JC: I think so. But mostly we just sort of blocked it and went through it and got to know each other. We had the apartment ahead of time so that we could use the actual space. That was very, very helpful. But I think he was concerned, as he should have been, that we appear like two people who are comfortable with each other and are married, and that the physicality and emotional life look right. Those are the only scenes he rehearsed. He didn't rehearse the scenes with Alan. I think he really wanted us to be *physically comfortable*. I remember rehearsing in the bed a lot.

SW: Did you improvise in rehearsal?

JC: No. It was pretty straightforward.

SW: Was the dance blocked?

18. Paul and Jill shooting An Unmarried Woman, *New York 1977.*

JC: Paul told me to do that crazy accent. That's pure Paul. I'm sure he could do it a million times better than I did. I can just see his face doing it right now. I think he told me where to go with the dance, you know, "Go around the table, pull your underpants down . . ." He told me where, but I don't think he told me how.

SW: My favorite scenes in the movie are with Penelope Russianoff. Especially the second one, when you break down. Was the shooting atmosphere of those scenes different than any of the others?

JC: I had to learn these long speeches and I remember the night before learning them. There was incredible freedom within the speech to embellish, let's say. I mean I didn't make up the lines. You know, he just put the camera on. We didn't do very many takes. And they were unrehearsed. [*Beat*] I'm talking about something that happened thirty years ago, so I don't really know if I'm bullshitting or not, but I think I felt that if you rehearsed it, the freshness would go out of it. So I think I said, "Let's just shoot it and see what happens." That's how I remember it.

SW: Did you have any sense that *An Unmarried Woman* was going to be an important, politically significant movie?

JC: To me, Paul had written a story about a woman. This is her personal story and it wasn't emblematic of . . . it was just the kind of talk that the people he knows talk: smart and upper middle class. I was completely shocked by the public's reaction. Not that people loved it, but that it had this political significance. But that makes sense. To me, it just seemed like this wonderful little movie that had a lot of say about humanity, not feminism. Things just collide at certain times.

SW: Paul's movies have that tendency. Collisions.

JC: He's good with the zeitgeisty thing. Feminism was in the air, but it hadn't trickled down. It was a bit rarified. Intellectuals. Left-wingers were feminists. It hadn't reached the entire country. [*Pause*] There was something about Erica that was so interesting because she didn't ask for any of this. That makes her very vulnerable and kind of . . . she looks like someone for whom life is easy.

SW: That was integral to Paul's conceptualization of the character.

JC: She looks like things are fine. Life is good to her. Everything is good. She has a placidity about her. She isn't neurotic. As wonderful as Saul [Alan Bates] is, Erica can still see that he is a domineering, self-involved ego-maniac. Had she gone off with him, she would have been subsumed in his world. [*Beat*] Can I ask you a question? Were there any actors he didn't get along with?

SW: One.

JC: Who?

SW: Cher.

For her performance in *An Unmarried Woman*, Jill Clayburgh received an Oscar nomination, a Golden Globe nomination, and won the Best Actress award at the Cannes Film Festival.

After Mazursky read this interview, he said, "She's captured the way I work better than anything else I've ever read."

Willie & Phil (1980)

Phil D'Amico: Anybody who likes Truffaut ought to be a feeling fella.

We're sitting on couches across from Paul's desk on the other side of his office. On the coffee table between us, there's a signed headshot of Mel Brooks in *Blazing Saddles*. He's wearing Native American regalia. His inscription is in Yiddish.

PM: *Willie & Phil*. That's when the budgets went up. You know, there are people who love that movie. Every now and then someone says, "That's my favorite movie." Usually, they're of the age when they remember the Vietnam War.

SW: I know Spielberg loves it.

PM: He wrote me a letter. He said, "How do you make a movie like this?" I said, "How do you make a movie like *Jaws*?" I told him that anyone can make a movie like *Willie & Phil*, you just have to dig into your own life to do it.

SW: Is that your life?

PM: No, it's not my life, but it was a continuation of what I started with *Bob & Carol*. I'm saying that things are not what they seem to be anymore. They seemed to be out of order. Things weren't *The Best Years of Our Lives* anymore. For a decade after the war, that world went on and then there was this reaction against authority and protests. Nothing was assured anymore. I even have that in *Harry and Tonto*. Don't tell me an old man has to go to an assisted living home. I ain't doing that. You want me to leave my apartment? I don't want to leave my apartment. You want me to put my cat through a machine at the airport? I'm not doing it! [*Beat*] Also, in *Willie & Phil*, I wanted to be right out front and say, "This is not *Jules and Jim*," but this is stealing from *one little notion* that two guys can become the best of friends and still love the same woman. In no other way does the movie resemble *Jules and Jim*—

SW: Well, there is the voice-over.

PM: Yes, stylistically, yes there is *Jules and Jim* in there. Of course, they [the critics] killed me for it.[16] "Who the hell is *he* to do Truffaut?"

16. Not Richard Corliss. He wrote, "The two filmmakers share a critical, but ultimately optimistic, view of life, approached from an oblique, metacomic angle. Their films are

sw: Didn't that scare you going into it?

pm: A little bit. A little bit. But what the French taught me is that an homage is a wonderful thing. They can salute Jean Renoir or whomever, but in our society, saluting somebody meant you were inadequate. But Hollywood can make sequels and it's okay? *Spiderman 3*? *Shrek 3*? It's silly.

sw: Willie and Phil meet at the Bleecker Street Theater after a screening of *Jules and Jim*. The shot that follows them out is one of the most amazing shots you've ever made.

pm: It's one shot. They talk in the lobby and then come out onto the street. As they emerge, the camera lifts up and we see the whole thing from above. Here's how we did it: The camera was handed to another operator on the crane. Sven [Nykvist] lit it in no time. He was the fastest guy I ever worked with. It must have taken him two hours to light the whole thing—the lobby and the exterior. It's a fabulous shot. [*Thinks*] You know, it wasn't a very successful movie. Maybe it was a bit perverse of me to make it. I knew how difficult it would be for a movie that's that sophisticated to be successful for the masses—the mass doesn't know about Truffaut—and there are subtleties in the movie—I'm not saying they're brilliant—where you're expecting a lot if you think they're all going to get it.

sw: I think you ran into trouble with your leads. Was Michael Ontkean your original choice for Willie?

pm: I had originally cast Richard Gere and then I had a nightmare that he was wrong for the part and I changed my mind. I had to call him up in Malibu and said, "Look Richard, I had a dream that I made a mistake. Forgive me, but I go by my dreams."

sw: You also had—I read—Woody and Pacino at one point.

pm: Woody would have been interesting, but I couldn't get him. Pacino I never had.

sw: Meryl Streep?

pm: Meryl was going to do it, but she didn't want to do it with Ray Sharkey [Phil], so I said to hell with her. My attitude was, "Who the hell is she?" She wasn't that famous then, but boy, she was brilliant. She was at the

---

primarily character studies that stress the importance of those off-moments when revelation takes the form of the smallest smile, or an unexpected caress, or the lighting of a pipe. Because of this emphasis, both men know how crucial an actor's contribution to a movie can be; more than that, they love actors, and love to act themselves. Finally, both occupy that select circle of filmmakers who deserve to be called great."

19. *Willie & Phil (1980) Ray Sharkey, Margot Kidder, Michael Ontkean, and Paul.*

reading I had with Juliet Taylor and Ray. Willie was read by Mandy Patinkin. I didn't feel Mandy was doing it the way I wanted him to. And at one point, I also met Bob De Niro. I thought he could play Willie.

SW: Willie? The Jew, not the Italian?

PM: I met with him at Caffe Reggio, which is in *Next Stop, Greenwich Village*. It was a rainy night. He said, "I don't want to play the Italian guy, I want to play the Jewish guy." I said, "You're perfect for Phil." He said, "If I don't do Phil, who will you get?" I said, "I'll get Ray Sharkey." He said, "I can do this part in my sleep." I don't remember what he said exactly, but he wanted to play Willie, but I didn't see him in the part. If I got Woody, it would have been a thrilling and sensational curiosity, but he didn't want to act in other people's movies. He doesn't do it very often. But I later got him for *Scenes From a Mall*.

SW: So, after *An Unmarried Woman*—I want to go back to the beginning—which was a critical and commercial success, did you find yourself in the position you were in after *Bob & Carol*? The *Alex in Wonderland* predicament?

PM: Yeah, yeah, but I wasn't blocked the way I was after *Bob & Carol*. And this time I had no partner. Larry wasn't there. It was all on me. Now I was suddenly in a place where I wasn't sure what to do. And then I don't know what happened—I saw a rerun of *Jules and Jim* or something—I started thinking about how much the times were getting to be where we could have two guys fall in love with the same girl and I started writing it, and I gave it to Fox and they said great.

SW: Just like that?

PM: Yes. That was Laddie. [*Thinks*] You know, Sammy, *Willie & Phil* is not a masterpiece. It's an interesting movie, I'm proud that I made it, and I stand by it. It's no more like *Jules and Jim* than *Alex* is like Fellini. [*Beat*] In the middle of writing I suddenly realized that I could be bicoastal with it, the way that my life has been bicoastal. I even had the thrill of being able to type into the script: "He goes to India." So I went to the studio and said, "I want to go to India." They said, "How much would it cost?" I said, "About a hundred and fifty." That wasn't much, so I went.

SW: They didn't resist?

PM: No. I insisted. I said, "I've got to see him on the Ganges. It's got to be real. I've got to believe Willy is really on the search."

SW: Did you ever have one those searches? Did you ever drop out?

PM: I've never dropped out. I've fantasized about it, but I never have. You know, in writing you get to realize your fantasies . . . but I like nice toilets. If you want to go to the Ganges, you have to have a lot of guts. I don't have that. When we got there the crew, which was Indian, said I had to go into the waters. It was supposed to purify me. I told them that I'd do it and then I changed my mind. I just couldn't. It was polluted with chemicals and you'd see dead bodies floating past.

SW: But there's a part of you that wanted to.

PM: Oh, yeah. And I've always been attracted to what I would call "crazies." Always. I still am. I'm talking about people who go outside the norms. You know, there's this book called *The Fifty-Minute Hour* by Robert Lindner, a psychotherapist. It's a great book. He wrote about society in terms of a series of ripples in the water. You know, when you take a pebble and throw it in? The pebble creates a series of ripples, so that you end up having . . .

Paul reaches for paper and pen. He draws as he talks.

PM: In the middle is the power of society. [*He points to the smallest circle*] The other ripples represent people who want to be in the power. The outermost ripples [*the biggest circle*] . . . the one on the outside, is where the crazies are, the antis. See them out here? But as the decades go by, the crazies get into the power and a new group replaces them. You understand? The crazies become the visionaries. I suspect Bill Clinton was pretty far-out at one point. Einstein, too.

sw: What about a guy like Elmo, from *Blume*?

PM: For sure, but he'd never quite get into the middle because he had already achieved a kind of beatitude. "Nothin' to it." We all have a lot of baggage that we can't let go of. As we get older, we get more baggage until we can't carry all of it. We have to let some of it go. That's what it's like to attain wisdom.

sw: If there's any wisdom in *Willie & Phil*, it comes through the voice-over at the end of the movie. It says something like, "Willie and Phil got married, had kids, and went on to live a very normal life."

PM: A lot of the people you'll meet from that generation are now square. They're not young anymore. You can't be that way forever. There were guys like Ken Kesey and Ginsberg who were doing that until their last breath. And then there are the guys who are the fakes. Charlatans. There are some good crazies and there are some just crazy crazies. What can I say? These people have always attracted me. I want to spend time with them. I believe that the far-out people in this universe—whatever those words mean—have a little madness in them. These are the people who go the next steps.

sw: Willie's not one of these people.

PM: No, no! Willie goes to the Ganges, but then he realizes that that's never going to work for him. We took Michael Ontkean to Varanasi on the Ganges and in the middle of it all, I think it began to affect him. He started to get weirder and weirder. Maybe that's why I cast him— because I knew on some level . . .

Paul throws his arms in the air—merry exasperation.

Hey, *Willie & Phil* got me to India. Know what I mean? In *Alex in Wonderland*, I typed in Fellini and I get him. I write it and I get it—it's amazing. Now I don't know what to type in. Should I write, "Assisted living"? [*Laughs*] You know, I will be seventy-seven years old tomorrow. Part of me feels like forty-seven. Not twenty-seven. I never feel like twenty-seven anymore. But definitely in my forties. I have bursts of great energy and still have a passion to see everything and do everything, but I'm still realistic enough to know that I can't. Physically, there are limitations. I can't climb up to Nepal. Not now. That's the catch-22 of getting older. You can't do much, but if you don't do anything, you'll get down. You know? [*Laughs*] Why am I asking you that? Of course you don't know. You're eleven years old. Forget it. Ask me another question about my career as an award-winning filmmaker in Hollywood.

Laughter.

SW: I want to talk more about Nykvist. How did you meet him?

PM: I met Sven . . . [*Thinks*] How did I meet him? [*Thinks*] Oh, here's how it happened! I had just done two movies with Arthur Ornitz and I wanted him to do *Willie & Phil*. I loved Arthur, you know. He could be a difficult man, but he was very gifted. The Cinematographers Union, which was awful, said he could work in New York because he was a New York cameraman, but he couldn't work in L.A. And *Willie & Phil* had locations in both places. I said, "How dare you? I have two weeks in L.A. and six weeks in New York. Do you expect me to change cameramen in the middle of the movie?" They said, "You've got to have somebody that has both cards." So I went with Alan Ladd, Jr. to a meeting at the Union. We tried to beat them, but we couldn't do it. We offered to pay a California cinematographer to stand by for the three weeks, but they wouldn't let us. So they give me a list of cameramen who have cards in both places. I read the list and I don't know one from the other. Suddenly, I see the name "Sven Nykvist." I said, "How the hell did he get two cards?" They told me that he had a manager who got it for him because he did commercials on both coasts. So I had a meeting with him.

SW: Were you nervous?

PM: Yeah, a little bit. I mean, he's one of the great men of the movies. Maybe the greatest cameraman in the world, and he had worked with Bergman, the greatest filmmaker in the world. So the meeting took place in Mia Farrow's apartment in New York, where he was staying. Mia was at her mother's place—her mother was the actress Maureen O'Sullivan. Sven had met Mia when he was doing *Hurricane*. Back then he was in a deep depression. His son had committed suicide. Mia helped him through it.

SW: They were together?

PM: Sort of. This was way before Woody. So I gave Sven the script and he loved it. He said he wanted to do it. He was a wonderful guy, you know. He stayed with me in California for the two or three weeks we shot. I would play practical jokes on him to a degree you can't imagine. Did I tell you about this?

SW: No.

PM: I got fake sushi—I knew he liked sushi—so I got fake rubber sushi on Hollywood Boulevard and I'd buy real sushi and put in two fakes and serve it to him with the sauce and everything. Sure enough, he's chewing the good ones and loves it. [*Swedish accent*] "Paul, Paul, this is the best sushi I have ever tasted!" I said, "Try one of those tuna rolls." So he goes for one of the fakes. [*Swedish again*] "Paul, Paul, I don't like this one." I fooled him with that. Then I fooled him with fake fried eggs. I put them in with hash browns and the whole thing.

SW: Had you ever done that before?

PM: No, no, never. But there was something about him. I'd ask him, "Does Bergman know who I am?" "Ya, ya, Paul. Ingmar has seen *Next Stop, Greenwich Village* and he loves it." I said, "Let's call him. I want to meet him." "Oh Paul, I can't call Ingmar, I can't do it." I'd say, "But doesn't he have a sense of humor?" "Oh, ya, ya, ya, ya, Paul. Sometimes Ingmar has a funny nightmare." [*Laughs*] Well, that put me away. Sven was a great guy. He met one of our friends and starting dating her. He loved women. He used to ask me what to do with his money: "Should I buy this apartment in New York, Paul?" I said, "Sven, you can't go wrong. Buy it. It's right next to the Museum of Natural History, it's eighty-five thousand dollars, and it will be worth half a million dollars in four years!" I don't think he did it. Then I went to his house in Stockholm, right on the water. Gorgeous! I had great times with him. He lived a hard life, you know.

SW: Did you ever connect with Bergman?

PM: No, never saw him. The two I never connected with were Bergman and Kurosawa. I was publicizing *Harry and Tonto* in Tokyo and I said to the Japanese Fox representative that I wanted to meet Akira Kurosawa. He said I couldn't meet Kurosawa because his last film, *Dodesukaden*, got bad reviews and he cut his wrists. He tried to commit suicide. It must have been a feeble attempt, but he did it. *Dodesukaden*! Have you seen it?

SW: No.

PM: It's a masterpiece! Absolutely amazing. But bad reviews. Maybe just one review, but who knows? Maybe it was the *New York Times* of Tokyo, but Kurosawa took it very seriously. You know, I don't think Fellini was that way. I don't know if Federico was actually that bothered by it. But one bad review—not by a schmuck, but from a notable critic—can put you in the toilet. Anyway, I never met Bergman. I never met Godard, either, but I am going to try to nominate him for an honorary Oscar this year. He's a fantastic figure. I don't love every movie he made, but I like a lot of them. He should be a lesson to all of us who claim to be serious on any level that if you want to keep doing it and you've already earned some recognition and some money, there are a lot of things out there you can do to keep it going. [*Beat*] You know, if you've made two great movies in your life, maybe that's a lot. Like Coppola made two *Godfathers*, *The Conversation*, and *Apocalypse*—maybe he doesn't have to do anything else. Friedkin made *The French Connection* . . . Do you want a sandwich?

SW: I'd love one.

PM: [*To Lauren*] Darling . . .

She comes in from the reception area.

PM: I would like a ham and cheese—

LAUREN: From Subway?

PM: Yeah.

LAUREN: No meatball?

PM: That's too much for me. [*To me*] You want ham and cheese?

SW: Sounds great.

PM: [*To Lauren*] Okay, get one big one and we can cut it in half. Put everything on it.

LAUREN: Okay. Water's fine?

PM: Yeah.

SW: Great, thanks.

PM: Thank you, darling.

She leaves.

SW: You mentioned Nykvist's invisible zooms . . .

PM: Particularly when he operated, which was only in California.

SW: You can't do that in New York?

PM: You're not supposed to. Every now and then he would just do it. In New York, they were very strict about those things. Here's how it would go: Say we're shooting a scene between two people in a bedroom in L.A. Sven is the operator. The two people are seated in a way to give us a master with both of them in the shot. Sven would say to me, "If I see something I like in the shot, do you mind if I go for it?" I said, "No, as long I as I won't see the zoom." So he'd find moments here and there that he'd love and he'd zoom in ever so slightly, and as he'd zoom, he'd make a gentle move with the camera and he's ending up with another place in the same shot. He'd do that for Bergman, too. You know, Bergman is the king of the human face. His portraits are like none other. So Sven did some of that in *Willie & Phil*. He adds a lot, believe me.

SW: Any diffusion?

PM: He put a little diffusion in the movie. I was against it, but he begged me, and I gave it to him. He wanted to try it because he was using a new lens and he shot a test and told me that I shouldn't worry because I wouldn't be able to tell the difference. I said to him, "If you can't tell the difference, why bother?"

SW: Right.

PM: He said, "Well, I can tell the difference." I finally surrendered.

SW: Why don't you like diffusion?

PM: Well, because it represented what you saw in all those movies that had a certain look *except* when you cut to the woman. She'd be soft. You were aware of the fact that there was a camera. I don't want the audience to be aware of the fact that's there's *anything*. It's difficult enough for me as a filmmaker to watch a movie and not see the crew and the shots and the track and the crane. I want to be involved and forget everything. I don't even want to know that it's a movie.

SW: All throughout *Willie & Phil*, we see the practicals have a slight glow.

PM: I don't know. I never thought about it, but if it was there it was intentional on his part. I never said, "I want a slight glow." I like a harder look, but you're dealing with the great Sven Nykvist. I think Sven, without using words like "romantic," saw it as a love story between two men, a man for a woman, another man for the same woman, and the love of the trio. [*Beat*] You know, I know of two couples who switched their mates. Academics. One guy fell in love with the other guy's wife and they did it. I suspect the midlife crisis has a lot to do with that. You start to wonder, "Is this it forever?" That didn't happen to me, but I see it happen all the time. I mean, after I started writing for Danny Kaye I thought, "Am I going to be a comedy writer for the rest of my life?" That's when I started seeing Don Muhich, my old therapist, who I later put in the movies. He was very helpful. He's the one that blanched when he met my mother. He said, "You're a miracle. I've never seen a more classic case of the Oedipal complex. You should have been a homosexual." After that, I stopped seeing him regularly, but I'd call him now and then for a phone session. Like getting a B12 shot. Somehow it helped. He was like the priest or rabbi. There's very little actual advice, just talking about it gets it out of your system. But I haven't been to a therapist in years. [*Beat*] I'll tell you something else about Sven. He was so confident. Even Connie [Conrad] Hall, who was great—he did one night of shooting for me on *Faithful*—said to me when it was over, "I'm keeping my fingers crossed."

SW: Well, he goes dark.

PM: *Very* dark.

SW: At the time of *Willie & Phil*, you said the following: "I don't believe there is a perfect shot or scene. I've never felt driven to carry on and on looking for a certain effect or look. You just get as close as you can in the time that you have."

PM: Well, I would say this about me: My tendency was always to try to complete the day's work. That doesn't make me a great director. That's the opposite of, say, David Lean, who I don't think would have settled if he didn't get something fancy he had in his head. He was known to wait a long time for what he wanted. Look, if I really couldn't get it, I'd come back for it, but generally speaking, I'd find a way to get a shot and then that would be it. But most of the time I accepted what I shot. I was not insane about a little mistake. Sometimes the cameraman would say, "I could do better," so you do it again if you have time. What you want is the perfect performance. You can't cut corners there.

SW: You have a scene in the movie when they all get together and drop acid. What would you do if an actor were in situation where he could not draw on his own experience for the scene?

PM: Well, I had done it, so I was very well versed—I haven't had acid in a month, you know—so I think I talked about it with them, but I can tell you that both Michael and Ray had done it. I don't know about Margot, so I'm not sure.

SW: What if she hadn't? How would you have directed her if you hadn't had that experience?

PM: You just talk about it and you let them do things and you just keep redirecting it if it's going off in the wrong direction. For me, acid produced extremes: a lot of laughter one moment and then crying the next. There was also a certain amount of awe at the beauty of things. "Look at that tree. It's been right in front of me this whole time and I've never really *seen* it." Also fear: I remember I thought my arm left my body and I was afraid it would never come back.

SW: That's in *Willie & Phil*, except it's her hands that fly away.

PM: I had that. I also had one where I had the face of a wolf. Once I told Don Muhich that I had done it. He suggested we do it together, that we find a place out by the woods in the country or by the seashore where we would have absolutely privacy. He believed it was beneficial to the psyche. He used acid to help Vietnam vets. I only did it five or six times.

SW: Was *Willie & Phil* the first of your movies to have significant use of the Steadicam?

PM: Yes. It was developed by Garrett Brown, and Garrett was the operator on *Willie & Phil*. He's about six foot four and he handled it like it was nothing. He was fabulous. That was the first time I used it. It was new then and it made it easier knowing that you didn't have to lay track or do it handheld. To do a long handheld shot would be hard on the operator and you wouldn't be able to hide all the little jerks and movements. Unless you're interested in a shot about energy, where maybe someone's being chased, you'd want that wobbly feeling of handheld. Otherwise, for straight walk-talk, you don't want the camera moving. It keeps you from knowing it's a movie.

SW: There's a beautiful, long Steadicam shot that begins when Willie and Phil are playing chess in Washington Square Park and then ends with Jeanette's flip of the coin.

PM: The art of operating is a special art, but they very rarely get the credit they deserve from the critics. You know, the operator is a poet. They tend to look like teamsters, but they have hands of butter. They remind me of cowboys.

SW: This may be nothing—

PM: That's a good title.

SW: —but in Willie's apartment we see the "Don't Worry Be Happy" poster that's in Josh Mostel's character's room in *Harry and Tonto*. Does that have special significance for you?

PM: I used to carry around a small card that said that. And that was my religion. The guy's face made me laugh. I saw some film about him once that was very amusing. He took a vow of silence. I don't know how he did it. It's Willy's preparation for his trip to India.

SW: There's no cut to the poster. It's just part of the *mise-en-scène*.

PM: You just have to make the milieu as specific as possible. I would often say to the actors, "Go to the library and get five books you think this person reads and bring them in. What are this character's interests? Put that in there."

SW: There's a great deal of buildup to *Willie & Phil*'s inevitable threesome, but we don't see it. We get the scene before and the scene after. Were you afraid that it was just too hot?

PM: I don't like sex scenes unless there's a real reason for it. The reason being it's going to take you forward somewhere. In the case of *Willie & Phil*, I suspect that talking about it the next morning was enough. In other words, if you're showing a sex scene, you had better do something that is going to change the story or something that scares the wits out of the audience.

sw: There are a lot of after-sex dialogues in *Willie & Phil*. A lot of sex goes on, but they talk about it more than we see them do it. What do you—

pm: I thought the movie would have been received better. By that time, they were into focus groups. They were scared of it, I think. [*Thinks*] Let me give you a bit of advice, as a writer: Never try to figure out the critics. [*Beat*] *Willie & Phil* needed good reviews. It didn't get them. A good review early on might have convinced the studio they had a shot with it. How else do you think they know? That's why they have test screenings, you know, with the cards. If they get a certain percentage, they get behind the movie. Who's making that decision? The audiences. So Fox dropped the movie. I should've fought more for it, but I didn't.

sw: How do *you* feel about it?

pm: I like *Willie & Phil*. I don't know if I love it. Emotionally, I'm closer to *Next Stop, Greenwich Village* and *Harry and Tonto*. I love *Enemies*; it makes me weep every time I see it. I like *Winchell*. To be honest, it's impossible to have the same zest for every movie you made.

Willie & Phil is Mazursky in transition. Struggling to broaden his comic perspective, and perhaps even push himself beyond the great streak of his seventies films, the movie breaks from his long-standing engagement with satire and naturalism. There is a touch of theatricality about *Willie & Phil*. Paul calls it romance. But with what? Willie, Phil, and Jeanette are always talking about love, but are they actually in it? What the picture needs is an encounter session at Esalen, from *Bob & Carol*. "People talk about love," the group leader says, "but do we really know what it means?" Maybe that's why *Willie & Phil* feels soft, because Mazursky feels closer to these characters than they are with each other.

With stronger performances, it's easy to see what *Willie & Phil* might have been: a nostalgic hymn to love and friendship and youthful folly. Unfortunately, Ontkean, Sharkey, and Kidder aren't always up to it. Human spontaneity—what we see from George Segal and Jill Clayburgh, that arresting sense that anything's possible because it's happening now, for the first time—has fled the scene. Instead the performances seem to have come to the screen ready-made, as if they were all decided off camera around a conference room table.

So what happened? Is this an error? A director out of touch with his work? Paul was after something different here, something more wistful in spirit, and maybe even a touch—though it doesn't sound like him—mannered. Consider an uncharacteristically specific line of direction Paul put into the script. Generally, Paul's screenplays are free of editorial; he's writing them for himself, he doesn't need to direct in the margins—but in this one he did. The phrase "rapid-fire dialogue," which appears before the scene when Willie and Phil discover they're both after Jeanette, suggests his mind was veering from the "realistic" performance style both he and the critics had become accustomed to. This heightened quality speaks to a larger trend in his films, something we can trace back to *Bob & Carol*— though it doesn't get rounded out until now. I'm referring to Mazursky's sometimes dialectical, sometimes synthetic approach to the worlds of Reality and Romance, of Naturalism and Sweeter-Than-Naturalism. As far back as *Bob & Carol*, Paul has gently (and sometimes not so gently) drifted into the latter. By *Willie & Phil*, his transmission of human weirdness is nearly obscured by the glow of hearts. At Mazursky's best, the boundary between weirdness and glow is so easily crossed, we don't know we've stepped from one into the other until we've gotten there. But it doesn't always work out that way.

Donn on Mazursky

Editor, *Blume in Love*, *Willie & Phil*, *Tempest*

On the bottom floor of the Warner Building at AFI, Donn Cambern sits in a dark office, speaking softly to one of his students, an editing fellow fretting about his thesis. As I walk in, they're examining the still frame frozen on the TV before them. With his finger, the professor draws invisible circles across the image, and the student, nodding, begins to loosen—it's going be fine. Cambern's voice is soft and soothing, the kind you want to hear when after six cups of coffee you realize that you didn't shoot enough coverage and your rough cut is four and a half hours long. It's a doctor's voice, and what I'm watching is emergency surgery.

SW: There's something pejorative in the phrase "actor's director," an implicit criticism that says the director who is good with people is weaker in cinema.

DONN CAMBERN: That's not true in Paul's case. In each one of his films— certainly in the ones I've edited—he tells stories that are mounted in such a way that, cinematically, everything about them is supported. I've done films with magnificent cinematography, but it's very difficult to get the story. Paul's different. He tailors his story to his cinema view.

SW: What is his cinema view?

DC: He always wants to capture the essence of a person. Somehow the frame he uses surrounds the people in such a way that your eye is always with them. And he allows the eye to rest comfortably, so that it can flow with the emotional rhythm. That's what engrosses an audience. When you step out of it, audiences get bored and confused. Paul's stories and his direction indicate to me that he always understands the rhythm of the scene. That's extremely helpful to me as an editor. When we would look at Paul's dailies, we would never have to talk about the intent of a scene. It was always clear right away. He's always so clear about the point of view of the scene, it leaves very little to discuss. Paul would say, "I really like this" and I would say, "This is working right here," and we would talk just back and forth and then I'd have at it.

SW: When the dailies came in, did you find there was a lot of variation from take to take?

20. *Paul and Donn on the set of* Blume in Love, *Los Angeles 1972.*

DC: That's the best. And with Paul, it's absolutely, absolutely true. There are variations in the actor's vocal rhythms, there are variations when they make a turn to look at somebody . . . you look for those variations. The worst kind of actor is the one who never does it differently. That gives me one hell of a palette. [*Thinks*] Let me tell you a story about *Blume in Love*, which was my first film for Paul. We were at Warner

Brothers. I had prepared a first cut of the film for Paul. He hadn't seen any of it, which was his wont.

SW: You're not cutting scenes together before the first cut?

DC: No. I just present him with the first cut. Some directors can't stand it, but the most usual thing is that within two or three weeks at the very most, you're looking at the first cut of a movie. The whole idea of a first cut is to see what you've got, to see what the problems are, and then solve the problems. That's what the editorial process is—solving problems. So anyway we were at Warners to screen the first cut and Paul wanted to sit by himself. I sat by the control panels so I could control the sound because we were playing it single-track and the levels kept jumping around. Well, during the screening, I'm hearing these strange sounds from Paul. He's whimpering. I think, "What's going on? It isn't that bad! This is a good first cut!" So we got through the whole thing and I walked down there and I said, "Paul, is everything alright?" And he says, "Yeah, I was just happy to see it up on the screen." He was crying. That's so Paul. He's very emotional.

SW: Did you spend much time on the *Blume* set?

DC: Whenever I could. I wanted to watch Paul work. The reason why is because it gives me insight into what to look for in performance. I learn a lot about performance from Paul. Just watching him. Whatever I learned would come into play when I was looking at dailies and when I was editing. I gained insights. Also, I would talk with the actors when they were relaxing. I was listening to their voices, to the way that they expressed themselves, and then I would see that kind of a natural expression in a particular line and I would say, "Ah, okay, I got it. We're gonna go for this take." Here's what happens: In the space from the first cut to the second, you're beginning to look through the scene through different eyes. Now you aren't seeing the scene as itself, you're seeing it within the entire film. You begin to identify little things you may not have been tuned in to. That's where Paul and I would begin to make the corrections. Each time you go back, you go back with another set of eyes.

SW: Can you remember an example when you were on a set talking to an actor and learned something that directly informed a decision in post?

DC: Yeah. I can. I got to know Susan Anspach on *Blume*. Sometimes I would talk with her, just talking—we would talk about psychoanalysis—I was in it, she was in it, and I remember that her husband at that time really wanted to get into it, and I suggested my therapist and then he started going to him! That was the kind of ease you felt on the set. And I remember that the way she expressed the difficulties in her own relationship with her husband . . . she could get this wonderful look . . . her eyes would convey a lot, they were very expressive. Sometimes her eyes actually played the opposite of what she was feeling. When I looked at the scene of the rape, I remember thinking that I had seen that look when she was talking about her husband. I had seen that look. That's why, whenever I could, I would get on the set to look around.

sw: Was the rape scene difficult to cut in any way?

dc: No. You knew exactly how to go on it. The only choices were when to cut from Susan to George, and whether I was going to cut on the line or let the person keep speaking. Cutting in the middle of the line, which I did, created more tension. It compresses the time and increases the emotional rhythm.

sw: Paul describes your editing style as musical and lyrical.

dc: Yeah. Well, my mother was a professional harpist and my father was the West Coast manager for Carl Fischer music publishing, which was one of the two largest publishing firms in the United States. When I went to college, I thought I wanted to be a film composer. I studied composition and conducting. That's when I met my wife, who was also studying music. One of my earliest jobs at Disney was as a music editor.

sw: There is an analogy between music and editing.

dc: My feeling of emotional rhythm in editing is very much attached to the emotionality of music. I'm very in tune with that.

sw: How do you create that rhythm?

dc: With the use of imagery, with movement within the images, with the frequency of the cut—all of that boils down to rhythm.

sw: One of the rhythmic patterns of *Blume* is tied to hard cuts. There are a great many in the picture.

dc: [*Professorial*] Define hard cuts.

sw: A hard cut is where, I would say, opposing images and opposing sounds are right up against each other.

dc: Mmm-hmm. Mmm-hmm. Very much. Very much. Looking at *Blume* from that point of view, the hard cuts develop a certain emotional rhythm, and then you might come to a cut and take a whole beat [*takes a long beat*] before the actor speaks. That pause breaks the rhythm of the hard cut. Right there, that gives the audience a bit of surprise, and they have an emotional reaction to it. If that same beat were preceded by pauses, this significant pause is lost. It has too many pauses before it!

sw: You're sparing with it. You save it for when you really need it.

DC: There's a scene—this is really fun, I remember when I ran it with Paul— when Nina first meets Elmo, when he comes into the office. They sit down, like we are, across from each other. She's not being particularly friendly toward him and he's just being himself. Now that is a relatively long scene, probably three or four pages, and it's covered in a very, very, very, conventional way. Direct. A master, a tighter two-shot, overs, singles, singles. That's it. So how do you get a scene shot that conventionally to breathe? I would start with the master, go in for the tighter shots, and then probably tighter, and then open the scene back up again to the wide shot, and then again I would work my way in again. That's another kind of rhythm. A visual rhythm. When Paul saw it he asked me, "Why did you do it?" I said, "It's because there's a moment when you wanted the scene to breathe."

SW: The cuts to close-ups build tension, and the cuts to masters release it.

DC: That's right. Yeah. So you open up, breathe, and then build tension again.

SW: What were some of the problems that you faced cutting *Blume*?

DC: When the three of them [Blume, Nina, Elmo] sit down and sing "Chester the Goat." Because all that was recorded live, from setup to setup, the singing is a little bit different. The words are alike, but the rhythm of the song is a little bit different. The way Nina strums is always a little bit different. There are a lot of continuity problems. So you just have to find your way through it. When I saw those shots in dailies, I knew it was going to be a problem, but I didn't doubt ever that I wouldn't get it together. It just took some time.

SW: Were there any disagreements with Paul? Any fights?

DC: No. Bob [Robert] Wise taught me a very valuable lesson. He taught me that it's much easier to try something. Rather than get into an argument, why don't we just try it? Then we'll know if it works or if it doesn't. [*Thinks*] Sometimes with Paul I would cut too often. Paul would simply say, "Look, we've got to slow up here," and I would say, "I've got it. Of course." Nothin' to it.

SW: That makes sense. Paul loves the masters.

DC: And I learned that from him. Paul's priority in the editing room is always performance. Always. And that's the best priority of all. In order to get the best performance, sometimes you have to cheat. Sometimes when you're looking at dailies you'll see a wonderful moment and you'll say to yourself, "I want to be at that moment." You don't always know how you're going to get to that moment, but you know that's where you have to be. In *Blume*, in the scene in the yoga class, when it ends, the screen goes dark. Completely. And then there's a beat and then you're into the beginning of the fight. When I saw that beat in dailies, I knew that's how I was going to make that transition. With that beat. And when we saw the dailies of the scene when Blume goes sport fucking, when he reacts to that couple, he gives a look—that look—when I saw it in dailies, I knew we had to be there. And the scene with Shelley Winters, after she says "Men!" and spits, George Segal's look was wonderful. I knew we had to be there. When they shot that scene, Paul fell down laughing off camera. I remember it from the dailies. And that spit Shelley did was completely spontaneous. She only did it in one of the takes. "Men!" [*Spits*] That was gold.

SW: So that was real saliva, not stunt spit?

DC: That was Shelley's real spit! They didn't know it was coming.

SW: Did you get to know Sven Nykvist on *Willie & Phil*?

DC: I got to know Sven very well. He was a lovely man. And he had a real sense of editing, too. We talked a lot about that. His son, you know, was an editor. He would say something like, "I'll make sure and get what I know you need." And of course I would look through the lens with him at times and he would describe to me what I was seeing, but with his eyes. He made sure that I knew how soft lights were supposed to be, or had my attention directed to an actor passing through the light or stepping into it. You know? He taught me how to look for things like that and therefore, on a take-to-take basis, to recognize which was the best— for him, I mean. That could be extremely important, but Paul and I would always go for performance.

SW: But what would you do when you had performances, like the two leads in *Willie & Phil*, that were problematic?

DC: Michael Ontkean was the more problematic of the two. He didn't use his palette, you know? I'll tell you something, and I really honestly believe this: In dailies, you weren't acutely aware of it. It was only when you saw the whole thing cut that you began to realize. It's the accumulation. We spent the most of the time in the editing room searching for performance for Michael.

SW: What can you do at that point?

DC: You can only go back to your dailies. Behaviorally, Paul adds to the subtext of a character. With Michael, unfortunately, there wasn't a lot of that. Ray Sharkey had more of it. In fact, Paul had to bring him down.

Like in the opening shot of that movie—a beautiful shot—Ray Sharkey was doing a lot of expressive Italian motions with his hands. In the middle of the take, Paul called out, "Ray, stop acting! Stop acting!" And Ray was caught. So he stopped. See, Paul knew exactly what to do. He knew that giving that note in front of everybody would really put it in his mind, would really make him aware of what he was doing. Paul understands that. [*Beat*] One of my favorite shots in *Willie & Phil* is that shot of Michael Ontkean in India, that wide shot with the long horns looking over the Ganges. Not only is it beautiful, but it's emotional and informational, too. That's tough to do in a master shot as big as that. Intellectually, we understand the piece of the story that's being put across and we relate to it emotionally. In other pictures that I've done, you have so many shots that are expositionally functional, but lack the emotional intimacy of the characters.

SW: An emotional master shot.

DC: Like that shot in *Blume* when he's looking through the window at Nina and Elmo. That's when you begin to ache for Blume.

SW: How did you become Second Unit Director on *Tempest*?

DC: We were in Greece and there was stuff that needed to be shot that Paul simply didn't have time for. There was a Second Unit cameraman who was trying to do it, but he just wasn't getting it. So Paul asked me and I said, "God, yes. I'd love to do it." So there were things to do with the dog, Nino; there were things to shoot in the storm—

SW: Did you make the shot with the umbrella?

DC: Yep.

SW: That's a beautiful shot!

DC: Isn't that a wonderful shot? I talked to Paul about that and he said, "Go ahead. Go ahead and do it." I got the special effects man to come out with his team so I could get the wind to blow it off. We wanted it to land upside down so it would just keep floating off like a ship sailing out. I told Alexi, the cameraman, just to follow it, just to let it go out of frame. We did about two or three takes. It was very easy.

SW: Well, it looks quite difficult. Were there any strings on it?

DC: No, but there was a release. The wind just carried it. And the opening shot of the film, I got. The sun coming up over the black sky. When Paul was finished with that beautiful boat in the film, the one that Gena Rowlands and Vittorio Gassman are on, he gave it to me and said, "Take it out and shoot whatever you want to. Get some stuff that you think might help us." So we get out there at like five o'clock in the morning and shoot the sunrise—and the sky was black. Like nothing else I've ever seen. And we just sailed around. Paul was very generous that way.

sw: What originally drew you to Paul's material?

dc: You feel like you know his characters so well that when they change— even the slightest change—you're interested, you're hooked. [*Beat*] You know, when Paul shoots, the eyes are never lost. You may be in a profile shot, but the eyes, which are so important to a performance, are always the center of the frame. When you cut to somebody on the screen, the audience always looks to their eyes first. The only thing that will change that would be if after the cut, the actor makes a movement. In that case, the audience's eye will track the movement. That's built into our dna. It's our survival technique, because when we meet a stranger, a quick movement is dangerous. But if that isn't there, you go to the eyes first. Paul may not be thinking that when he shoots, but it's obvious take after take when you're watching dailies that that's what he's interested in. The eyes do it. Knowing that, one has a wonderful tool when editing. Say you have a conversation between two people and you cut from one to the other and then back again to see that the first speaker has turned his eyes away. Some directors wouldn't care to insert a shot telling you why. Not Paul. He would want you to see the motivation for why they looked. If you study movies, you'll see that that happens a lot. But not with Paul's movies. If you can see an actor make a decision about something before he does it, you've added to the subtext of the character. Those details are the things that add depth.

sw: Can you think of an example when that has been applied in a Mazursky movie?

dc: Yes. The way people look at each other. In *Willie & Phil*, when Jeanette goes to meet Willie's parents, which is a favorite kind of Mazursky scene, the way that the mother looks at her son and then looks back, you know, those things, they're little gifts Paul gives the audience.

sw: He's deepening the behavioral complexity.

dc: You're absolutely right. He's always adding something more. Musi- cally, you would say that his harmonic structures are very, very complex, very thick. The Impressionist composers are that way. They would often build a chord all the way up to a thirteenth. You'd have the seventh, add the ninth, add the eleventh, and then add the thirteenth. Then you'd have a very thick kind of a chord. In a way, that's how I see adding behavior. Yes, Paul plays with complex harmonic structures.

Toward the end of the interview, Donn's wife, Pat, walks into the office, crosses to her husband, and gives him the kind of lingering kiss I could compare only to the one Grace Kelly gives Jimmy Stewart in *Rear Window*. When I get up to go, Pat stops me. "I love that scene in *Willie & Phil* when they drive the Volkswagen up the ramp," she says. "That's *Blume*," Donn says. "Oh yes, but . . . don't both movies have Volkswagens?" "*Blume in Love* caught that so beautifully," Donn says. "It was such a strong moment, a moment that I happened to be in the midst of myself. I had hair down to my shoulders, and Pat . . . well, she had hair down to her shoulders too." At the door, Donn says, "People always ask me what my favorite of my movies is and *Blume in Love* always pops up first. Always. And it's such a romantic movie. I'm very romantic."

Tempest (1982)

Phillip Dimitrius: We're all nervous.

I walk past reception into Paul's office to find Lauren on the floor, rummaging through a stack of large envelopes. Paul's sitting beside her. He's uneasy.

PM: Where is it? We can't do it without it. [*Pointing*] Is that it?
LAUREN: That's *The Monkees* pilot.
PM: I've got to find this thing.
SW: What are you looking for?
PM: It's a bag with the thing in it. It's a little kit.
SW: What thing?
PM: I've got to call the doctor so he can take a reading on my pacemaker. I put this thing around my neck and hold it up to the phone.
SW: Could you have brought it home?
PM: I leave it here. Oh, shit. Is it in there, honey?
LAUREN: No.
PM: This is horrendous. And stupid. We're going to find it. Don't worry.
SW: What about in there?
PM: Check. I think that's paper, but let's check.

I check.

SW: There's nothing in here.
PM: I always sit right here and do it!
LAUREN: The last time you did it you did it over there.
PM: Where?
LAUREN: In there. [*She points to the front room*] On that phone.
PM: There's no phone in there.

Lauren's dog Gucci comes in and starts jumping and yelping.

PM: [*Laughing*] What's going on here?
SW: Is that it?

A big yellow envelope behind a stack of scripts sitting on the floor.

PM: That's it. That's it. Okay.

The office settles down. Lauren returns to her desk at reception. Gucci follows.

PM: Okay . . . What are we up to?

SW: *Tempest.*

PM: Fabulous.

SW: The story that became *Tempest* was on your mind a long time before you got it made.

PM: A long time. I don't know exactly how long but I know I had a meeting with Mick Jagger a couple of years before I shot the movie. We met down at the old Plaza Hotel and behind him I saw this chick with hot pants and a big hat walk in and I said, "Man, look at that babe." He said [*Mick's accent*], "That's not a babe, that's me wife, Bianca."

SW: But you were thinking about it before even then. I read a treatment you wrote from 1972. That's ten years before the movie was released.

PM: At first, the idea was to do a kind of Marx Brothers version of the play. But I didn't know how to do it. I wanted the irreverence of the Marx Brothers where it's never really real. It wasn't a sound idea; it was just a way to get me started.

SW: So what was it in Shakespeare's play that appealed to you?

PM: I guess it was the idea that Prospero was somebody who would do something very far-out. That's when I started thinking about midlife crises, which is something I consider myself something of an expert on. I say that as a joke. Here is a man of forty-five or fifty with a beautiful wife and an adorable daughter and successful career, but something's wrong. He's unhappy in his life. Everybody living can identify with that problem. In the end, after the storm, they reconcile. Maybe it's a little like *Blume in Love.*

SW: What do you mean?

PM: Well, in the end he rapes her and she forgives him. People were always criticizing me for that. "Why did he rape her?" "Why did she take him back?"

SW: They've got a point!

PM: Life is strange. That's how it goes. It's very easy to take someone back who forgot the milk or some banal thing. But when it's profound, and it really hurts, and *then* you forgive . . . that's big stuff. So Phillip's forgiven at the end of the movie. When he gets off the helicopter, what does he do?

SW: He winks into the camera.

PM: Yes.

SW: Why?

PM: It's all a dream. It's all a play. At the end of Shakespeare's play, the guy at the end says, "This is all a dream, it's all a play, and I hope we haven't bored you" et cetera. So my thing is, I use a helicopter with those fantastic shots of New York. It's Phillip or Prospero's farewell.

SW: That explains the curtain call.

PM: After I see a movie, I'm always wondering who played what. They have that fast credit crawl and I can't tell. This way each person steps down and you see twenty players. And it's fun! It's nice to know. But John [Cassavetes] wouldn't bow!

SW: Why?

PM: Who knows? He said, [*mumbling*] "I don't want to bow. What do you want from me?" I just wanted him to take a really elegant bow and he wouldn't do it. You want my guess? I think he was saying that I was the one who should be taking the bow.

SW: With all you borrowed from Shakespeare, there's a lot that's been invented, stuff that has nothing to do with the original play.

PM: Shakespeare has clowns. I've got Alonzo's doctor and his comedian. The girls sing "Why Do Fools Fall in Love?" *Fools*. That's Shakespearean. They're all fools. Alonzo is the king who sends his brother off in a boat. You know, I wanted *Tempest* to be funnier than Shakespeare's play. The only humor in Shakespeare is Trinculo. I almost ended with Prospero's last speech when he says, "Now my play is done" and says good-bye to the audience. In my case, I have him go back to New York with the wife. They're reunited. He's forgiven. They both forgive. At that point I suddenly realized that the play is about forgiveness, a profoundly difficult thing to do, forgiveness. To forgive. Can you forgive?

SW: Let's go back to the *Tempest* treatment of 1972, when the movie was still called *The Tempest*. It begins with a troupe of actors on a boat. The storm comes, they get shipwrecked, and their play begins.

PM: But I didn't meet Leon [Capetanos, co-writer of *Tempest*] and start writing until 1979 or so.

SW: That's seven years of putting it off. Why did you keep delaying it? You had it in mind since *Blume*—both movies about forgiveness.

PM: I thought about this story after every movie I did. But I don't know why I kept putting it off. You know, while they're directing a movie, most directors are already being fed material by their agents for the next movie. They're reading new scripts while they're still working. I never did that. What I did was I'd finish the movie and then start dreaming about what I was going to do next. If I got lucky, I had an idea already and I'd take a month or two off and start writing the idea. I guess it took me time to feel qualified to do *Tempest*.

SW: So maybe there was a little bit of anxiety about taking on such a—

PM: Yeah, yeah. *Tempest* does not follow the pattern of a commercial and successful Hollywood picture. The normal elements aren't there. I have goats dancing to Liza Minnelli.

SW: Did that make you nervous shooting the picture?

PM: I was exhilarated. When I finished it, the first people I showed it to were John [Cassavetes] and Gena [Rowlands]. John said, "That's the picture you wanted to make, buddy, and you made it. Congratulations." He wasn't one of those phonies.[17]

SW: The budget was thirteen million dollars.

PM: Yes, and they left me alone. The studio paid me one visit on the location. They were thrilled.

SW: No interference?

PM: None.

SW: *Willie & Phil*, your last picture, cost six million dollars. How did this enormous increase in budget affect your filmmaking?

PM: *Willie & Phil* was double the previous movies not because I did anything rash, but because the union prices went up. Everything had gone up. So the Hollywood of you could make a really good movie for two and a half million bucks became you can make a really good movie for about six. So *Tempest* was perceived as a big picture. Thirteen million dollars was a lot. They paid Raul [Julia] $500,000 and John $750,000 and Gena $500,000 and Vittorio [Gassman] $350,000 or something. Those were big salaries. I must have gotten a buck and a half. Above the line alone was something like five or six million. But what I'm saying is that Frank Price must have had faith in me and the picture. The budgets confirm it.

SW: In an early draft of the script, Phillip is a writer. In the movie, he's an architect. That reminds me of something Cassavetes said about his character, Phillip. "Why isn't he a director?" he said. "Why doesn't Paul say what he really means?"

17. Cassavetes on Mazursky: "Mazursky is crazy, of this I have no doubt. But he loves. He loves the grips, the electricians, and the actors, with the same ferocity with which he protects the ideas that spring out of his head a mile a minute. It's never boring because he won't let it be. He tells jokes during rehearsals, makes fun of himself, does impersonations, disguising and covering the pain of the real love that is the basic structure of *Tempest*."

PM: Yeah, he knows, he knows. John was wonderfully smart, but not very articulate. He could sometimes take you from the material at hand to electrical storms and Yankee games and cheeseburgers and you don't know what the fuck he's talking about. But when he had to speak clearly, he did. Look, if I made Phillip a director it would have been *8½*! I couldn't go that far! I had already done it in *Alex in Wonderland*!

SW: You met Leon Capetanos after Jeff Berg sent you—

PM: *White on White*, Leon's script, and I liked it. We were thinking about doing it. [*Beat*] You should know, there are long gestation periods before making a movie when you're doing a dance about doing it. It's the same dance, in a way, that certain actors who have been wrongly criticized do. I'm thinking of Warren Beatty and Dustin Hoffman. All that dance is they want to see if they can really do the movie. They're trying it on in their heads. Sometimes it takes months to realize that you don't want to do it. Do I really understand this? Do I really see this? Do I really want to go on this journey for the next six months or year? Whereas there's no dance when you're offered the next *Spiderman* movie. "Seventeen million? Okay, I'll do it." You just put on the *Spiderman* yarmulke and that's it.

SW: *Spidermensch*.

PM: He goes *glatt* kosher. So I met with Leon because I liked his script. We're talking and I tell him that I'm fooling around with the ideas in *Tempest*. This was like 1979. I didn't need another writer but I liked him. He had a wonderful imagination. He saw himself as a bit of a poet. I think he still does. That was refreshing because he didn't worry about box office and all that crap. But, yeah, Leon is a poetic guy. Together we came up with a new treatment, and I pitched it to Laddie at Fox and he gave us some money to write it.

SW: But *Tempest* ended up at Columbia.

PM: When the script was finished, Laddie had now come up against the fact that even though he had discovered *Star Wars*—which Universal rejected—this plum, and brought it to Fox, they offered him only a $75,000 raise. He was deeply offended and quit. He went off to form his own company, The Ladd Company. Whatever financing they had—I don't know the details—he said *Tempest* would be an awfully tough one for them to start out with it. It would be a tough first movie. And he wasn't wrong. So I brought it to Frank Price at Columbia and Frank says yes immediately. Just like that. He even set the budget. The guy with him was an executive named John Veech. John picked up the script and weighed it in his hands. He actually picked it up like this [*Paul demon-*

strates with a script on the table] and said, "Yeah, I think this is about twelve-point-five." [*Laughs*] And that's what it cost until the minute I realized we were short $500,000 for special effects. They said to me, "Paul, the board has already approved twelve-point-five. Don't shake the boat." I said, "Do I have to pay a penalty if it goes to thirteen?" They said no. So we went up to thirteen.

sw: What was your collaboration with Leon like?

pm: He would write, I would polish. Sometimes I would write a scene, but I don't remember how much. Now and then we would disagree, but that didn't cause us any kind of writing pain. You know, my attitude toward a writer who really disagrees is, go direct it yourself. Leon knows that.

sw: How did it compare to writing with Josh Greenfeld and Larry Tucker?

pm: Larry was the funny guy and I was more the story guy. I'd map it out and then we'd get into it. I was funny too, but I know story. With Josh, our relationship was wonderful. I wrote the story after we had talked a lot, he started hammering out a first draft, I liked it, I continued it, and then we sort of mixed and matched and put it together. Leon works best at the typewriter after very intense meetings and discussion. He would write it, I would read it. Some I would accept as it was, some I would change, and some I would totally rewrite. That's the way we worked together. It was healthy. When he finished the first draft, I knew it was going to work. I just had to trim it down. I had to make Aretha more interesting. And then when I'm on the set I would make some changes. We've written so many scripts together besides the four that have been made.[18] There are about four or five others.

sw: You once said, "Leon is always looking for an island." It made me wonder if you see Phillip and Leon as surrogates.

pm: There's a little bit in there, yes. They're dreamers. But I'm Phillip, too.

sw: How?

pm: We both want to make magic.

sw: That's the name of your book.

pm: *Show Me the Magic*. I probably should have called the movie *Show Me the Magic*. I think the Shakespeare title scared people.

sw: Why was it a harder movie to write? I mean, harder than the others?

pm: We kept changing our minds. We threw out draft after draft. At first, we had a group of traveling players that went from island to island to do

18. *Tempest, Moscow on the Hudson, Down and Out in Beverly Hills*, and *Moon over Parador*.

Shakespeare's play at resorts. On one trip, the boat gets stuck in a storm and that's the movie. That was one of the original concepts. Then I had the totally musical version with Mick Jagger as Ariel. Finally we decided to make him an architect, because architects, I thought, are like magicians. Who could imagine what Frank Gehry has done, for example? He puts up this building and he says, "It's really a ship." So I got into architects and I interviewed a guy named Solari who was trying to build a city in the desert somewhere out in Arizona. He was pretty far-out. I went to visit him and I told him about *Tempest* and asked, "Do you believe a guy would believe he could make a storm?" He said, "I do it every day." You've got to have guts to throw out drafts. It's a great feeling when you finish and say, "Look, there it is! Now all we have to do is get the money!" But throwing it out, that's tough.

sw: At one point you had Paul Newman in mind for the lead.

pm: Right. I took it to him and he said to me, "I don't get it, kid." He called me Pablo.

sw: I know you don't have anyone in mind when you write, but do you see a face?

pm: I see myself.

sw: Is it startling then to see somebody else playing it?

pm: If they do it truthfully, it's always a wonderful revelation and it feels great. If they're not doing it in a way that's working, I think, "I should be playing this."

sw: After Newman, you went to Brando.

pm: I sent him the script and then I went to meet with him. He said he read it, but when I got there I realized that he hadn't. After we talked for thirty minutes I said, "What about *Tempest*?" He said [*dead-on Brando*], "What? *Tempest*? What is that?" I said, "It's the movie I wrote. That's why I'm here." He said, "Is it historical, comedical, tragedical, romantical?" I said, "All of the above. And we can do it on an island! *In Tahiti*!" He said, "I'd love to read it!" [*Laughs*] I think he was playing a game with me. When I got there, for the first thirty minutes he asked me about Russian composers. [*Brando*] "Do you like Tchaikovsky?" "Yes." "Do you like Mussorgsky?" "Yes." "Mazursky—is that Russian or Polish?" "Both." "Are you hungry? Would you like something to drink?" "Sure, I'll have a beer." He says into the phone, "Myrna, get Mr. Mazursky a beer." She says back to him, "We don't have beer," and he asks me, "Would you like a glass of water instead?" On and on and on like that.

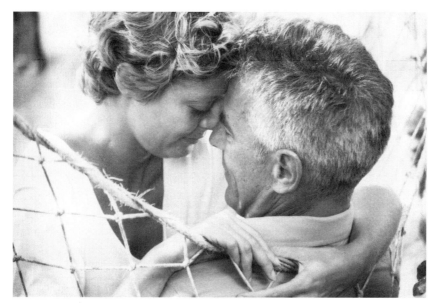

21. Tempest *(1982) Susan Sarandon and John Cassavetes.*

SW: How long was the meeting?

PM: About an hour. I think he was manipulative and rude.

SW: So what brought you to John?

PM: I knew him from New York. He was the guy that told me they were casting for *Blackboard Jungle*, remember? More than that, I had seen him in *Husbands*. I loved his look and I said to myself, "Jesus. He's not a big, big star, but I know Frank [Price] likes him." So we went after him and we got him. From there, it all fell into place.

SW: And did Gena come with John?

PM: No, I had to get her. He said, "If you want Gena, you have to go after her yourself." I also met with Giancarlo Giannini in his apartment in Rome. I wanted him to play Kalibanos, but he didn't want to play it. He said he had played a part like it in *Swept Away*. And then I thought of Raul Julia, who I had seen in *The Threepenny Opera* on Broadway. That was it.

SW: Raul Julia has turned out more than one terrific performance, most of which are uncelebrated, and this is one of them. He was a remarkable performer.

PM: He had it all. I really mean it. Raul could sing, dance, act, and play all kinds of parts. When I was casting *Enemies*, he said, "Why can't I play the Jew?" I said, "You can't do it, Raul." He said, "You're prejudiced!" [*Laughs*] I said, "I can't see you as a Jew." But I bet he could've done it. God bless him. [*Beat*] Yeah. Raul.

sw: There was also a point when you were thinking of Elia Kazan for Phillip's father.

pm: He was writing a novel [*The Anatolian*] and wouldn't do it. He just didn't want to stop writing.

sw: From what I understand, you rarely ever had difficulty with actors on the set, but Susan Sarandon, apparently, was a little tricky in *Tempest*. She thought her character was too much of a sexpot.

pm: Yes. It was at the beginning of the feminist stuff. I tried to explain to her over and over again that being an aggressive female doesn't make you a sexpot. Was Simone de Beauvoir a sexpot? But Susan is a wonderful actress and they have a right to disagree or to have a problem. I tried, with John's help, to get her to see it. I changed some of the words to make it work better for her. But I never saw her as a sexpot. I saw her as a free spirit, like Shakespeare's Ariel. She and I had a few arguments, but nothing terrible.

sw: I want to read you some things Cassavetes said about you. He said, "I really don't think I acted that part alone. If I got a haircut, Paul got a haircut. If I tried to lose weight, Paul tried to lose weight. If I went swimming, he went swimming." What is he talking about?

pm: Well, I wanted to play the part!

sw: He also said, "The picture became so much a part of us in our relaxation hours that we never got away from it. As the characters got angry with each other, the actors got angry with each other."

pm: It's true. They were into it. John might have been saying that when his character is having some trouble with his wife, he might have been having a few cross words with Gena behind the scenes.

sw: "I love Vittorio Gassman," John wrote. "I think we could probably be friends, but he was my adversary in this film, and every time I came to talk to him nothing would happen. Paul would always invite Gena and Vittorio and me to dinner. We would always have one of the worst evenings."

Paul chuckles. He picks up his cap and ruffles out his hair.

pm: It's all true. I loved him. [*Beat*] Vittorio was probably doing that purposely with John. He was a great guy. You know, we used to have these shows on Saturday nights. We would entertain ourselves. I would be the emcee, Jackie Gayle would do his routine, and Vittorio would do poetry and handstands. John would do all kinds of weird stuff. Molly Ringwald would sing—she was a great singer. Susan sang too. They were hilarious shows. I would do imitations of everybody. I would do Cassavetes: "I hate these fucking rocks, I hate 'em! I hate every fucking rock there is here! Why did you pick this fucking location?" Vittorio: "I'm not threatening you. You'll know when I threaten you." Gena: "*Hey*. Don't you ever talk to me that way again. Ever."

sw: What were John and Gena like off camera?

pm: Loving. Beautiful. Like Lunt and Fontanne in your imagination.

sw: So you had a sense that it was a good marriage.

pm: Wonderful. Wonderful. Did I tell you about the killing-of-the-goat scene?

sw: No.

pm: Gena said to me, "Paul, we have a real problem. When we shoot the scene, John said he's going to kill the goat." I said, "You're not going to kill the goat. It's fake! John holds the knife to the goat's throat, I cut to you watching, we hear the slashing sound, and I cut back and we see blood all over. It's a *fake* dead goat." "No," she said, "he's really going to kill it." I said, "He's not going to kill it. I don't kill animals on movies." She said, "I'm just telling you what he said." So I go to John and I say to him, "Stop this. Tell her you're kidding." He says, "I'm not kidding. I'm going to kill that measly fucking runt goat and I'm going to kill it real good." I said, "John, I know you're kidding. You're just doing this to rile her, to get her angry." But he wouldn't stop. Finally, on the day before we were to shoot the scene I took them to an Italian restaurant and said, "It's time to stop the game because I'm getting exhausted. I can't sleep at night because of what you're doing to *me*." John says, "I'm sorry, Paul. I'm killing the goat." Gena says, "Please excuse me, I have to go to the restroom." She's gone for fifteen minutes when John gets up and goes to the ladies room and knocks on the door. "I'm going to kill the goat!" he shouts. "You hear me, Gena? I'm going to fucking murder it!" But no answer. He quickly peeks inside and sees she's not there. He calls the hotel. She's in the room. He says, "Why did you walk out on me? [*Listening*] Uh-huh . . . Uh-huh . . . Well, I want you to know I will be *killing that goat*." He hangs up. The next morning I get there early and try to figure out what I'm going to do. That's when I see them walking toward the set, arms around each other, deeply in love.

SW: The whole thing was a put-on?

PM: Either the whole thing was a put-on or he finally told her. I'll never know. [*Paul looks at his watch*] It's time. They're late.

He takes off his shirt. I get up to go.

PM: No, no, no. Sit down. I want you to stay here. This is going to be funny.

He hangs the blue receiver around his neck. Oh, I see: It's pacemaker time.

PM: [*To Lauren*] Call Armando. [*To me*] This saves me the trip of going in. What happens is, I put this thing here [*he moves the receiver to his heart*] and then I put the phone on it and then after thirty seconds they can read it. It's like my pacemaker is talking on the telephone.

We wait.

SW: Now what's happening?

PM: Lauren's dialing. We're waiting for them to pick up.

Waiting.

PM: I have this scene in *Tempest*.

SW: This scene?

PM: When he's on the treadmill and gets the phone call. [*To Lauren*] What's happening?

LAUREN: [*From the other room*] I got the answering machine.

PM: Call back.

LAUREN: They said they'd put me through, but I got voice mail.

PM: Try them again. Armando's supposed to call me.

Waiting.

PM: Shit.

Waiting.

LAUREN: Okay, line one.

Paul picks up the phone.

PM: Amando? Oh, Eli, how are you? [*Listening*] Yes, today's my day for the phone test and I'm trying to get in touch with Armando. [*Long pause*] Museum of Tolerance? Really? When? [*Beat*] Really? [*Beat*] Tuesday? Tuesday in the afternoon . . . Okay. Okay, thanks Eli.

He hangs up.

PM: [*Laughing hard*] I wish you could've heard that.

SW: What happened?

PM: [*Still laughing*] His wife is doing a one-woman show about the Holocaust at the Museum of Tolerance. He wants me to go. He said, "I was trying to get a hold of *you*." [*Laughing*] Is this great, or what? [*To Lauren*] Try them again, sweetheart.

LAUREN: Line one.

Paul picks up the phone.

PM: Yes, dear . . . Yes . . . This is the day for my test. I'm sitting here in the office with my shirt off. [*Beat*] If they can't do it, just let me know . . . Should I hang up now? [*Beat*] Okay.

He hangs up, laughing.

[*To Lauren*] Honey, can I have a cup of coffee? [*To me*] Okay, let's go on.

SW: In the scene when John and—

Phone rings.

LAUREN: Okay! Now!

Paul picks up the phone.

PM: Here we go!

He holds the mouthpiece to the blue box hanging around his chest and closes his eyes, breathing slowly. Buddha Mazursky. The little box is beeping like mad.

PM: [*To Lauren*] I've got to do the magnet now. Tell me when it's twenty seconds.

LAUREN: I will.

Paul holds a magnet against his shoulder. Waiting.

LAUREN: Okay, twenty seconds!

PM: Thank you, dear.

Paul hangs up.

PM: Okay, now for the penile examination. [*Beat*] I'm kidding.

Lauren laughs from the other room while Paul puts his shirt on.

PM: I'm sorry you had to see my breasts.

SW: That's okay. It's my pleasure.

PM: [*Raising an eyebrow*] Really?

SW: *Tempest* was your first collaboration with cameraman Don McAlpine.

PM: Yes, but it was originally going to be photographed by Sven Nykvist. Sven called me and said, [*Swedish accent*] "Ya, Paul, I have a problem. Ingmar has called me to do a movie called *Fanny and Alexander*. I have to do it." I said, "I understand, don't worry about it." So I called Peppino [Giuseppe] Rotunno, Fellini's cameraman, who said, [*Italian*] "Paul, I would love to do this picture but Federico has called me to do this picture, *And the Ship Sails On*." So I was screwed. That week I was at the movies and I saw Bruce Beresford's movie, *Breaker Morant*. It was clean, crisp, I loved it. I got ahold of Bruce through Tony Bill. Bruce gave me Don's number and I called him, though I didn't understand a word he said—thick Australian accent. I sent him a script, and he said he wanted to do it. We did four pictures in a row. He was a wonderful guy. *Down and Out in Beverly Hills* is as well photographed as anything, but he got no Academy nomination. His photography had satire *in* it—it has gloss and sheen.

SW: Was Fellini around when you shot *Tempest* in Rome?

PM: I'll tell you the story. We built the interiors of the island cottage on Stage 22 in Cinecittà. It was the biggest stage—Fellini's stage. One day I'm shooting, I happen to be up on a crane, and Fellini walks in. I shout out to him, "No visitors, this is a closed set! I don't know who you are, but get off my set!" Fellini says, "Please, Paolino, let this poor man stay here to see what you are doing to his stage!" The crew was hysterical. Everyone applauded the Maestro. And Raul was there. He had been on Broadway in the musical *Nine*, which is based on *8½*, so he had been asking me everyday, "Paul, is there any way I could meet Fellini? Any way?" I said, "Well, Raul, let me think about it." I wanted to give him the business. So I set up a trick. I asked Fellini to come to the hotel to meet Raul, but I told him that I'd have Jackie Gayle, the comedian, there too. We set it up. I told Fellini that when he comes in he says hello to Raul, but to be cold to him. When he sees Jackie Gayle, I told him to fall all over him, to tell him that he was the funniest man he had ever seen in his life. Federico got it. So a few days later, the afternoon it was planned,

Raul was getting his hair done, he was actually primping, and then Fellini comes in. The door opens—it was the Maestro—he's got the cape, the hat, the whole thing. Raul goes over to him, fumbling, "Maestro . . . it is a pleasure . . . an honor . . ." and Fellini cuts right by him to get to Jackie, screaming, "Jackie Gayle! You are the funniest man alive! So talented!" It was hysterical. I couldn't stand it.

SW: Was there ever any talk about you and Fellini collaborating again?

PM: I tried to get Fellini to do a three-part movie with me. Sometime around the time I was doing *Tempest*, I had this idea to do a movie of my Rome—Mazursky's Rome. I wanted to do the Rome of a guy who comes from America to live there. I wanted to show the fight I had with my wife on the Spanish Steps when she hits me with her purse and all the shit goes flying out of it and the guys are singing those beautiful Italian love songs. An American trying to be an Italian and really failing. I wanted Fellini to do *his* New York and maybe Kurosawa to do *his* Paris. Fellini said, [*Italian accent*] "What would be my New York?" He loved New York, but he didn't think he could make a movie about Americans because he didn't know how they wiped their ass. I said, "Well, you'd have to build 42nd Street at Cinecittà with all the porno shops and bums and everything, but it would be Fellini's 42nd Street." I told him that Marcello would play a toilet seat salesman from Rome who was in New York for a convention. One night he wanders out on the street. That's all I knew.

SW: What did he think?

PM: He liked it. I told him that I could raise ten million bucks—I made up some number—three million for each little episode. For a short while it went along. We'd call each other and talk about it. "I'm thinking, I'm thinking," he'd say. And then it just disappeared.

Quiet.

Yeah. You know, I don't want to kid myself—and I don't think I am—but I would say that we had a very close relationship.

Quiet.

SW: Cassavetes.

PM: Go ahead.

SW: Was he difficult to work with?

PM: Not at all. Not at all. All that stuff you read about John being difficult, I tell you it's not true. I directed John Cassavetes. I spent seventeen weeks of shooting with him and I had maybe a day and a half that was strange. He was irritable. And he was probably getting sick. You can see it in the movie.[19] He was a wonderful, funny, great pal. He *wasn't* difficult.

SW: What about the goat story? He gave you a hard time.

PM: He was doing it for the part. He wanted to get Gena in a state.

SW: Ray Carney, the Cassavetes scholar, wrote, "Cassavetes' description of Mazursky's directorial methods is the closest he ever came to describing his own way of working with actors."

PM: That's probably true. And I was never directed by John. Okay, go on. What does he say?

SW: This is something else Cassavetes wrote: "Interpretation of character and motive is not something you can just design like an architect can design a building. There are feelings that go back and fourth and a sense of creativity and comfort. I think comfort is very important. I was enormously comfortable with Paul. He allows you to make your work your own. You never know with Paul whether he wants you to be upset or make a jackass of yourself or what. You have to constantly think and adjust your feelings. You become alive, not just as an actor, but as a person who is dealing with a situation." And then he said this, which I find particularly interesting: "With Paul, the work is important, but it's also not important." What does that mean?

PM: Well, I don't want to speak for him, so I can only hazard a guess. It's important that we're really enjoying the process, as difficult as it may appear to be sometimes. It isn't just the work, it's the experience of creating. It's not like at the end of the day you say, "I did a good job of acting today." It's more instinctive. And I'm permitting the actors to be instinctive in their way, not in my way, even though I am trying to lead them. Since I am the co-writer of the script, that's a right I sort of have. It gets tricky when you're doing someone else's script.

SW: And how does that apply in Sarandon's case, when she was having difficulty with where you were leading her?

PM: Sometimes I think when you're acting in something you have a hard time seeing the bigger picture. You just see you. But that's okay. Sometimes it's better. When I'm acting, I often don't read the whole script. I don't want to know what happens. I just want to know what my character knows. Of course, an actor who's playing the lead has to read the whole

19. Cassavetes's belly is distended from cirrhosis of the liver. He died from it on February 3, 1989.

thing. You know, Carl Zucker, who did some scouting for me in New York, also did some for Woody. I think the first one he did for him was one of the Bergman ones, you know, *Interiors*. Woody told him that he wanted a place in the Hamptons. Carl said, "As soon as I get the script, I'll have a better idea . . ." Woody says, "You don't have to have the script, just find me a place on the beach." He didn't want him to read it. What I'm saying is, you just need to know your part. In my case, not only do I show them the script, I talk about it with them. I collaborate in that sense.

sw: You gave Pato Guzman co-producer credit on *Tempest*. How did that come about?

pm: I wanted him to have more time on the movie. If you tell the studio you want to pay your production designer more money, they don't want to do it. If I made him the co-producer, there's an extra twenty-five grand in there for him, so I can ask him to be around four or five weeks more, because what I like to do is talk out loud when I'm thinking about a movie and who else am I going to talk to? Pato. You can't get the camera guy because they get ten thousand dollars a week, it's too much, and they don't have the same head even. They're brilliant, but they don't always understand the script. Pato did.

sw: You say you talked out loud to Pato, but how did it work? What kinds of things would you talk about?

pm: How to shoot it. And as an actor, I was able to act out scenes. I was actually able to play the whole movie for him.

sw: So the entire process of *Tempest* was intensely collaborative for you, from script on.

pm: Yes. But it all began with Paul Mazursky in Stanley Kubrick's movie, *Fear and Desire*. I sing in it, "Full fathom five thy father lies, / Of his bones are coral made: / Those are pearls that were his eyes . . ." you know the rest. That's from Shakespeare's play *The Tempest*. I was only twenty-three, but somehow it stuck. Years later, after dozens of drafts, Leon and I both agreed that *Tempest* would start it in New York and we wouldn't make it about actors, but about an architect. I didn't want it to be about show business. The character of Phil might have been a variation of me, who, having been tempted to do *The Flasher*,[20] found himself deeply unhappy. Alonzo was the studio . . . [*Beat*] Did I tell you the story about training the goats for the goat dance?

20. For one sleepless night, Paul agreed to direct Burt Reynolds in *The Flasher*, a movie about a cop who secretly flashes. He ended up making *Blume in Love* instead.

sw: No. Where did that idea come from?

pm: I don't have a fucking clue. Just one of my weird, crazy ideas. I'd just seen *All That Jazz* and in my mind I saw goats flying in the air. I wanted Sinatra singing "New York, New York," but it was too expensive so we got Liza instead. [*Beat*] The trainer was an Italian guy who spoke almost no English. I liked to fake him out and pretend I spoke Italian, but I don't. I said, "Can you teach goats to dance?" He said, "Yes, yes, of course. It's easy." And I came back six weeks later to the location and he's got a carrot on a stick and one goat. He holds the carrot up, the goat stands up; he brings the carrot down, the goat goes down. I said, "Is that it?" He says, "*Si, si* . . ." I said, "Well, how can you do this with twenty goats?" "What?" he said, "I thought you meant make the *goat* dance." "No, *goats, goats*, plural, it's like a chorus! *Capisce?*" Anyway, finally the Italian grip—who was one of the greatest grips you could ever have—had the idea to tie wires around the ankles of all the goats and give them shocks at the same time by attaching the wires to these nails and then playing "New York, New York" on the nails by hitting them with a hammer. Each time I hit a nail, the goat leaps. I said, "Will the goats die?" He said, "Oh, no. It's just a little shock." And that's what we did. So they played the record and I would play the goats like they were an instrument. And then I tossed them—

sw: What do you mean you tossed them?

pm: We literally had two grips throw the goats in the air so that they would fly over the camera. [*Laughs*] Anyway, that's part of the entertainment aspect of *Tempest*. And it makes the movie twenty minutes longer. If you wanted that movie to move and be a fast-paced, 2007 cinematic spectacle—*Jews of the Caribbean*—if you wanted it to be that, you'd take those out. You could get *Tempest* down to an hour and forty-five and make it move like a bullet. You could also take out the *Blume in Love* trick of being in the present and cutting to the past. Just stay on the island. But that's a different movie.

sw: I want to talk about one of the most ambitious shots you've ever made. You probably know what I'm talking about: It's the tango shot at the end of the movie.

pm: Well, we built the exterior of the seaside villa on location in the Mani, but the shooting of everything that takes place at night was shot on a rock-for-rock replica that Pato built in Cinecittà. So, with the control of being in a studio, I could do all kinds of things with the crane—up, down, in, out, pushing it—and that's what I did.

sw: When did that shot come to you?

pm: Early on I wanted it to be a continuous shot. I want to show the way the tango was continuous. There's something about the tango—and these are the risks you take—that I thought was Shakespearean. It's saying in its own stylized way that they're all one. They all need to be forgiven. Better have that in one shot than in a bunch of little ones. That's what the whole movie is about: forgiveness. Phillip overreacted and he realizes now that it's all over and he still loves her. He's sorry.

sw: And there isn't even a reconciliation scene. It's just a moment.

pm: You don't need it. You know already how much he cared for her and how passionate they were about each other. You saw John and Gena joking in bed in the earlier scenes—and only they could have pulled that off—when he's playing with her hair and kissing her. By the way, that's marital behavior. I didn't direct that. I just let it happen. They did it without me ever saying anything.

sw: It's interesting that Phillip doesn't see a shrink. Considering he's in a Mazursky movie, he's a perfect candidate.

pm: I didn't see him as a guy who would be going to a shrink. He's much more daring than Blume or the people in *An Unmarried Woman*. He's a guy who sees big buildings. He's a dreamer.

Paul takes a sip of coffee and adds a small packet of sugar.

There's no question in my mind that therapy is a combination of three things: science, art, and mystery. Okay? When you're in the water and somebody throws you a life jacket, you grab it. It works. That's therapy. It helps you to get through it. Eventually, hopefully, you can get back to the boat on your own. I think that's the aim of it. Here's what therapy is and here's what life is—it's a very simple metaphor—you're in a boat and you're going downstream, rowing along nicely, and you feel a little water coming into the bottom of the boat. So you cover one leak with one foot and the other leak with another foot and you've got to get rid of one oar to hold the third leak. By now, there's so much water in the boat, you're barely holding on. And then, by a miracle you reach the shore. You're soaking wet, you're dripping, but you fix the boat and spend the day on the shore, and then you take the boat with you back into the water and you start downstream again. But you can be sure of one thing: It's going to leak again. If you think it won't, you're kidding yourself. No therapist is going to make it leak-proof.

sw: So what does he do?

PM: Nothing. You just keep going. You learn. You learn to be stronger. If you learn anything, you learn that nothing lasts forever, the good or the bad. And if you're not so shocked by it, you can learn how to live with it. [*Whispering*] Do you know the song "Is That All There Is?" by Leiber and Stoller?

SW: Sure.

PM: Peggy Lee. It's fantastic. It's *fantastic*. It's the story of life.

SW: One more question?

PM: Okay.

SW: Okay. How do you feel about *Tempest*?

PM: I'm very proud of it. [*Beat*] It's long, though.

Every director has his long-in-the-works-and-courageously-overambitious intended masterpiece. Coppola's *One From the Heart*, Scorsese's *Gangs of New York*, and Spielberg's *A.I.*, for instance, are impressive in reach, but sadly short in grasp. At best, we congratulate the filmmaker for his wholesome chutzpah and vision; at worst, we're chucked out mid-dream, promises unfulfilled, and wishing the movie were more like the trailer. Odds are these sorts of pictures split the difference and leave the audience with a sense of awe and bafflement rolled confusingly into one.

Tempest is a lot of things. It's odd, charming, exhausting, sincere, striking, and generally all at once. You wonder at it. "How," you think, "could this have happened?" How could John Cassavetes, the most frighteningly spontaneous of screen actors, seem, as he seems here, so uncharacteristically tame? A little more story might have helped. (Penelope Gilliatt: "We never get a clear impression of what accounts for his fame or of the dissatisfaction that he runs away from or why he's ready to go back when he is.") To address the problem, we might go back to *Blume in Love*, a movie which, in structure and content, looks like it could be *Tempest*'s older brother. Where the former was focused by a razor-sharp attention to personal detail, the latter is brought down by scope. Mazursky is after the big picture here, and it's a strong picture, but the moments, the sweet and sour Mazurskyisms, get lost along the way. It's hard to find the love story between Phillip and Antonia.

What endures is the work of Raul Julia. If ever there was an actor—actually, performer is a better word for it—suited to the hedonistic pangs of Mazursky's fantasies, it would most certainly be him. He's Mazursky's id, his Falstaff. Julia does everything in the extreme, and always with plausibility. His smile breaks open the entire screen with hot-blooded human delirium and he dances around the frame like a wildcat. He represents the late, Felliniesque side of Mazursky (Jill Clayburgh represents the early, neorealist side). If only the *Tempest*'s tempest belonged to Julia and not Dimitrius, the movie would be the full-bodied, crazy, semi-musical love-fit it only sometimes is.

This is still Mazursky in transition, but what a transition! We miss Paul Mazursky, master of contemporary American idiom, and Paul Mazursky, satirist. What we get instead is another crack at theatricality (see *Alex in Wonderland* and *Willie & Phil*), the part of Mazursky that wants life bigger and to drink in more of it. Right now that impulse is overwhelming his observational insight, but in time (see *Down and Out in Beverly Hills* and *Enemies, A Love Story*) he'll be able to bring them together. He'll be grand *and* specific.

Stay tuned.

Moscow on the Hudson (1984)

Cop: This is New York City. A man can do whatever he wants.

Just about every morning, Mazursky and his cronies get together at the Farmers Market for coffee and donuts. They've been doing it for something like twenty years. By now, the little breakfast group has become a destination for movie people of all kinds. Not just the writers and directors of the glorious American seventies (De Palma used to show), but now new blood, folks like the director Mike Figgis and Jeff Garlin (of *Curb Your Enthusiasm*) have been known to make an appearance and trade stories with the regulars, which include Charlie Bragg, a painter in a fisherman's jacket; David Freeman, the screenwriter, novelist, and playwright; Greg Pritikin, a youngish director; and comic Ronnie Schell. As I approach the table, which is as intimidating as the Friars dais, Mazursky tells me that there are only three relevant topics of conversation: box office, health (generally bad), and pussy. "Either it's some piece of shit that made $350 million in twenty-four hours, or it's blood pressure, or the hot forty-year-old girls in their little yoga pants." When Charlie arrives (dancing), Paul turns back to him and mutters, "I thought you were dead." "Nope," Charlie says, "just sleeping." The painter sits down next Schell. Noticing the pair, Paul leans into me and whispers, loud enough for everyone to hear, "Charlie and Ronnie here just joined West Hollywood Gays Against the War—" The rest of it is lost in Ronnie's story; he's on his feet now, reenacting his run-in with Tony Bennett backstage at the Sands. Charlie: "Ronnie, do we have to hear this fuckin' story again?" Greg: "Let him have it. He's got nothing else." And when they get going they really get going—it's jazz—the shtick explodes from all directions. ("We call them *shpritzes*," Paul tells me back in the office. "You get on one idea and you just go. You *shpritz*.") An hour later, most of the coffee has been spilled. "Where do I get this shit validated?" "You believe this Jew?" / "I'd pay fifteen thousand dollars for her to sit on my face." / "Would you please take Larry King's dick out of your mouth for just one moment?" On the way back to the car, Paul says, "That's my medicine," and then a moment later, "The rest of the day is downhill from there." And it was.

PM: I'm trying to find a new secretary.

SW: Oh, Lauren's leaving? Why?

PM: She got a job at an ad agency. It's okay, it's not for a couple of weeks. I'll find someone. Look, I read the *Tempest* chapter and I think it's good and interesting. I don't agree with all of it . . .

SW: What did you disagree with?

PM: No, I like what you're doing. You don't expect me to agree with everything you do, do you?

SW: No, no.

PM: You have opinions. I don't want to censor you on any level. Just keep doing what you're doing. [*Beat*] By the way, I'm reading a masterpiece right now: *The Yiddish Policemen's Union*, by Michael Chabon. It's fantastic. It's a great comic machine. The guy imagines that Sitka, a city in Alaska, is given to the Jews instead of Israel. Wow! Chabon has got some courage. He's a genius. Wait until you read it. [*Beat*] I wonder if Scott Rudin owns it.

SW: I think he owns *Kavalier & Clay*.

PM: He does. [*Beat*] Want to see me do something funny?

SW: Yeah.

PM: Open the door and see what I do.

Paul points to the door leading into the reception area. I open it.

PM: Dear, would you do me a favor?

LAUREN: Yeah.

PM: Call David at ICM in New York and ask him how I can get in touch with Scott Rudin.

LAUREN: Scott Rudin?

Paul shoots me a look.

LAUREN: R-O . . .

PM: R-U-D-I-N.

LAUREN: Okay.

PM: Thank you, darling. [*To me*] He'll know how I can get in touch with Chabon. I want to send him a copy of *Yippee*. You know, I gave the book to Betsy and she read forty pages and says, "I don't want to read any more." So I said, "I would rather you move out. Right now. Leave the building." She says, "I don't have to like what you like. All that Jewish stuff." [*To Lauren*] You got it?

LAUREN: Yup.

PM: Try him. Let's go.

Paul takes a long sip of coffee.

PM: I love this book. The main guy's a detective, he's suicidal, and his ex-wife is his boss. His descriptions of life in Sitka are so meticulously imagined and so brilliantly written you will think you are there.

LAUREN: Okay, Paul, go ahead.

Mazursky picks up the phone.

PM: Hello? Yeah. Ernie, you know what I'm calling Scott about? This is a bizarre call. Does he buy Michael Chabon's books? [*Waiting*] I'm trying to send a documentary I made called *Yippee* about Hassidic Jews to Michael Chabon. I've just read his new book—did you read it? [*Waits*] Well, it's unbelievably brilliant. It's beyond brilliant. I made this documentary about Hassidic Jews in the Ukraine and I want to get it to him. I thought maybe Scott knew how to get in touch with him because Scott knows everybody. [*Waits*] Yeah. [*Waits*] Yeah.

Paul reaches for a pencil and starts taking down information.

PM: Okay. Okay. [*Writing*] Thank you. Well, I'm going to put this e-mail through to Rudin and send him a copy just for fun. I know he isn't busy. I'm kidding, Ernie. [*Laughs*] Okay, bye-bye.

Paul hangs up and leans back in his chair.

PM: [*To the door*] Lauren?

LAUREN: Yeah?

PM: Let's do an e-mail to Scott Rudin.

LAUREN: Okay. Ready.

PM: Okay. [*Paul rubs his hands together*] "Dear Scott . . .

Long pause.

PM: Okay. "Dear Scott . . . I'm trying to find an address or phone number for Michael Chabon so I can send him a copy of quote *Yippee* unquote, my documentary about Hassidic Jews who go to the Ukraine once a year. Period. I'm sending you a copy as well. Period. But having just read quote *The Yiddish Policemen* dot, dot, dot, unquote by Chabon—

LAUREN: That's "Yiddish Policemen dot, dot, dot—"

PM: *Yiddish Policemen's Union*. Just say *The Yiddish Policemen's Union*. By Chabon. C-H-A-B-O-N. [*Beat*] I thought he'd enjoy it.

LAUREN: Put that in?

PM: Yes. To Scott. "I thought you'd enjoy it." And then, "Hope you're well, comma, Paul Mazursky." Okay?

LAUREN: Okay.

PM: Thank you very much. [*To me*] I think he'll like the movie. Okay, let's do *Moscow on the Hudson*. Let's start with the idea—I'm getting good at this, aren't I, Sammy boy?—I was lecturing at NYU on *Willie & Phil*, this was right before I made *Tempest*, and this Russian guy stood up in the audience and said, "I'm Vladimir. I studied camera in Moscow. I want job." I said, "This is not the place to ask for a job, sir. I'm doing a lecture for students here. Are you a student here?" "No. I want job." People started to laugh. I said, "I don't have any jobs for you." Finally, he wouldn't shut up, so I said he could call for an appointment at the office. Eventually I met with him and I told him that we didn't have the money to take him on *Tempest*. He was so insistent and there was something about him. I thought it might be amusing to have this Russian fellow there—if the union didn't know about it, who gives a shit? Anyway, so I told him that we'd pay his airfare and he would have to figure out the rest. So we brought him to Greece to work on *Tempest*. He carried things around the set. And he slept on the roof. One day he told me the story of a Russian orchestra that played in Pittsburgh and somebody tried to defect. That's where I got the idea.

SW: You say *Moscow* began with this guy, and yet *Willie & Phil* ends with Jeanette actually making a movie called *Moscow on the Hudson*. The idea must have been around before then.

PM: When I was shooting *Willie* I would meet all these cab drivers, guys from all over, and I began to think about their lives and how they got to New York.

SW: And you pitched *Moscow* to Frank Price?

PM: Right. He bought the pitch, but when he read the script, he said, "Seventy-five percent of the American audience cannot read. How are they going to read the subtitles?" That version of the script began in Russia and he was afraid audiences were going to think they had walked into a foreign film. So after Price told me his concerns I spent a day or two rethinking it and then I thought, "Why not begin on a bus in the United States and then cut to a flashback?" And then we came up with the device of having the clown [Elya Baskin] learn English so we know he's going to defect. We know America is coming.

SW: You had an unusual approach to research when you were planning the movie. You wrote the script and *then* you went to Russia.

PM: Yes.

SW: It was you and Pato [Guzman] and Leon [Capetanos]?

PM: Yes, but they wouldn't let Pato in because he was Chilean. We met a
Russian film representative at Cannes who told us that we had to go to
Vienna to get Pato a visa. So we all go—Leon and Pato and I. Pato fills out
all his forms and gets his photo taken. A few days later, Pato went back
to pick up his form and they told him that his visa was denied. He didn't
know why. And when they gave him back all his papers, he found that
the picture they had of him wasn't the shot they took a few days before,
but a shot of him from when he was twenty-two years old. How the fuck
did they get it? So Pato was scared shitless. Now, I'm in Russia. I spend
the first two days there alone and I take a driving tour with a regular tour
bus with tourists and I see some of the sights of Moscow. Except for the
Red Square, it's not a very beautiful place. The food was terrible. The
hotel was not very good. I went to the Aragvi Restaurant, where I was told
I could meet some sophisticated Muscovites. I met a guy named Vladimir something, who told me he was a real estate lawyer and seemed
liked a pretty nice guy. He took me to some restaurant and told me not
to speak English. "Better they don't know you are an American," he said.
We went to his apartment. There was cat piss in the halls; it wasn't very
nice. Afterward, he brought me back to the hotel and asked me what I
wanted to do tomorrow. I said, "I don't want to impose on you. My
friend Leon is coming tomorrow and—" "No, no," he said, "I'm happy to
do it." I didn't know why he was so eager. I said, "I'd love to go to the
zoo." So the next day, Leon shows up and this guy took us to the zoo.
We're watching as the attendant puts meat into the tiger cage, and when
he walks out, a well-dressed gentleman with a fur-collar and a cane and
a briefcase approaches the cage, looks around, and quickly slips his
cane between the bars and pulls out the piece of meat and puts it into
his briefcase. Then I knew I was in the right place. That's how bad things
were. On the last day in Moscow, I'm sitting in the car with Vladimir—
he's driving, I'm next to him, and Leon's in the back—and we pull up to
the hotel, and Vladimir, who has tears in his eyes, asks me to take a
package across the border and give it to his brother in Queens. It was
wrapped, but looked clearly like an icon or something. I said, "I can't do
it. I love you, Vladimir, but if I get caught smuggling . . . I don't know
what would happen." And as I pulled my hand away, my elbow hit the
glove compartment, which fell open, and a Beretta fell onto the floor. I
picked it up. It was a gun, a real gun. The guy takes the gun from me and

goes, "That's my child's toy," and throws it back in the glove compartment. Now I'm saying to myself, either he's a gangster or a KGB. I never found out, but in discussing it with my friends, they said KGB for sure. His job was probably to find out what I was doing there. I knew our script was right.

SW: Are you and Leon reworking the script at this point? Are you going back to the hotel every night and writing?

PM: Not exactly. We were taking notes a little bit, but not much because we knew we might be searched at the border. As it is, Leon was reading the book *Space* by James Michener. When we left through the Finland Station, the guards found the book and didn't know what it was. "*Space?* What the fuck is this?" They opened it up, turned it around, looked at it. It's just a book about going to space! They were nuts.

SW: Why didn't this trip happen *before* the writing?

PM: What I'm saying was, we didn't need Russia to get us started. When the script was written and the studio bought it, they paid for our trip. During the course of the trip, several things happened to us that made their way into the script. We met a guy in St. Petersburg, in Leningrad. We said something to him in English and he said, "Oh, I speak English." He said, "What do you do?" We said, "We make movies." He said, [*Russian accent*] "Do you know Doostin Hoofman? I love Doostin Hoofman." I said I know him and he went crazy. So he asked us, "Would you like to see my apartment? [*Whispering*] I have blue jeans." I said, "Yeah." So we went to his little apartment, he's got a wife and a little baby in one room. Under the bed he pulled out a rolling display that had a pair of blue jeans.

SW: He was hiding them?

PM: Yes, to sell. We said we didn't need any blue jeans, but told him that if he'd like to meet us the next day we would give him American magazines and soaps and little luxury items. We went the next day, but he never showed up. I think he got scared. Life was tough. They sold wine on the street in Coke machines.

SW: The movie isn't shot on location, right?

PM: They wouldn't let us shoot in Russia, I didn't like what I saw in Finland, then we heard about Bavaria Studios in Munich that had build a special street in the back lot with a European-style trolley on it. They called it *Bergmanstrasse* because they built it for Ingmar Bergman, who had used it for *The Serpent's Egg*. So Pato went to Bavaria and found this back lot. And then we did a fantastic thing—I think I'm probably the first director to do this—you've heard of day for night? Well, I shot night for day. Moscow is always dark. It's so dark in the daytime that it looks like night. So we had to shoot this scene where it's snowing and it's supposed to be daytime. Well, I shot the daytime scenes at night. I shot some of it in the studio and found a few odd places in Munich—tunnels, archways, underpasses—and I did some of it there, on locations. But the funny thing was, after a few Russians saw the movie, [*Russian accent*] "I lived there! That's my street! How'd you know? Paul! That's Gorky Street!" I said, "No it's not, that's the fucking back lot." Russians!

SW: *Moscow on the Hudson* is extremely patriotic. It's in love with America.

PM: Sometimes you don't know what you're doing until you do it. It struck me that *Moscow* was really about the fact that this is a great, great country. It's openly done in the movie. In this country we take in people from everywhere and they bring the place a *juice* that if you are lucky enough to absorb and make use of its pleasures, you can have a much richer life than if you stayed in the same neighborhood for your entire existence. In New York, you're within minutes of the Black experience, of the Russian experiences, of the Yiddish experience, of the Italian, German, Swedish . . . It's all over the city in restaurants, in music, and shops. The only thing they don't have is a good Eskimo neighborhood.

SW: At what point did you decide that the movie would have this vision of America?

PM: In Leon's first draft, the girl [Lucia, played by Maria Conchita Alonso] was American. It seemed too dry to me so I changed her into an Italian. In rewriting it, I saw that I could make a few other changes of ethnicity, and before long, they were all immigrants.

SW: Was Bloomingdales in it from the beginning?

PM: Yeah. I could have done it in any other department store, but I knew as a comedy guy that "Bloomingdales" is a great name. Funnier than "Lord & Taylor." "Macy's" is okay, but not as good. So I had to go before the head guy who ran Bloomingdales. He read the script and had one or two little objections to what we had written, so I took them out. I said, "They're gone. Trust me. I want your store. If the movie is as funny and wonderful as I think it's going to be, everyone's going to want your business." So they gave me the exterior of Bloomingdales in the daytime and certain interiors at night. The shots of the escalators you see in the movie are from the actual Bloomingdales, but the other parts of the defection scene we built in a studio in New York.

SW: So that had to be very carefully storyboarded.

PM: Pato. Pato. He made it easy. Now, watching the movie, you can't tell the difference. And I'm very good at understanding how to execute it. It's smooth as silk.

The phone rings. Lauren gets it.

LAUREN: I got Ernie from Scott Ru—!

Paul picks it up.

PM: Ernie? Go ahead . . . Uh-huh . . .

Paul reaches for a Variety and scribbles across the masthead.

PM: Thank you, Ernie. [*He hangs up*] I got it.
SW: What?
PM: Chabon's information. Everything. Should we call?
SW: Yes!
PM: You know Rudin read *Moon Over Parador* in 1985, a second after we handed it in to Universal. I have no idea how he got it. "What do you mean you read it? No one's read it." "I read it," Rudin says. "How'd you read it?" He says, "I know the guy at the copy center. How do you think I get all my scripts?" I said, "You're a fucking thief!" He says, "I'm in this business, what do you expect me to be?" Then there was this movie—I think it was a Belgian movie—about some kid who survives a firebombing. He wanted me to switch it to here. He had the rights to it and wanted me to do it in America. I said, "How can I switch it to here? There's been no firebombing in America!" He said, "You can do it! You're great!" I never did it. [*Laughs*] Should I call Chabon on his cell phone?

He dials. Waits.

PM: [*To me*] It's the message. [*Into phone*] Mr. Chabon, my name is Paul Mazursky. I just finished reading your incredibly brilliant novel, *The Yiddish Policemen's Union*, and I just wanted to chat with you for a few minutes and tell you about a documentary I made called *Yippee* about the Hassidic Jews in the Ukraine. Call me if you get a chance. Bye.
SW: Try him at home.

He dials again and waits. Waiting.

PM: [*Into phone*] Oh, this may be the second message I've left. My name is Paul Mazursky, I'm an American filmmaker and I just finished reading

Mr. Chabon's novel, which I think is one of the great experiences of my life, and I made a documentary about the Hassidic Jews that I think he may find amusing. I just want to send you a copy. Please call when you can. Bye-bye. *Abi gezunt.* [*Hangs up*] Onward.

SW: Before you had Robin Williams, you thought of Dustin Hoffman.

PM: Yeah. Dustin was interested and then I got a call from [Michael] Ovitz [then head of Creative Artists Agency] that he was passing. By then I had also met with Dudley Moore, who said, "Wish I could do it, but I don't think I could . . ."

SW: What was it in Dudley Moore that you responded to?

PM: He was such a wonderfully funny guy and sympathetic. He could have played it, but he couldn't do a Russian accent. He just wasn't up to that kind of stuff. And then I met once with Bill Murray—a very offbeat idea— it didn't work. Then came Dustin and *then* Robin. He and I were talking about it and we reached a point when he said, "Can we meet one more time before I give you an answer? Can you come to New York?" I told him that I would, but that he would have to guarantee that after that meeting he would have a definite answer. He said okay. I said okay. That was on a Thursday. Five hours later, Ovitz called and said Dustin had reconsidered—he wanted to do it. I said, "Well, I'm flying to New York tomorrow and if Robin says no, I'll call you right away." That was it. When I saw Robin in New York, he said yes right away. We didn't even have a meeting.

SW: So what was all that about?

PM: I don't know. I guess he wanted to see how much I wanted him.

SW: Was it difficult to get him away from going for the laughs? From shtick?

PM: There was a tendency in the early rehearsals for him to be a little shticky, but nothing much. It was quite easy to help get him on the path to the performance he gave. He deserves enormous credit for that character. Watching it now, I see that he understood it better than I thought he did at the time. He's right in there.

SW: What did you communicate to get him to come down?

Paul picks up a box of Altoids.

PM: When you pick this up and you get a candy out and you're having trouble getting it out, you don't have to have it fly up in the air—[*Paul throws it*]—and make a big thing out of it. Just get it out.

He opens the box and removes a mint.

That's all.

He eats it.

He would do a little more. He got it. Simple. Art Carney. I like to use Art as a measuring stick.

SW: But it's not just that you got him to do less; you got him to go in.

PM: Robin is smart. He understood the pain. One of the good things that happened was, without me knowing quite why I did it, the teacher who I got to teach him Russian—a guy named David Gumberg—was very familiar with life in Russia. So when Robin worked with him for three months to learn the language, he must have learned a lot of good stuff along the way about how tough life was there. He is a very intelligent man, and as you know, he's a very humane man. He did Comic Relief. [*Beat*] You know, he could be the guy in the Chabon book. He could be Landsman. He's a little too old, though, but not by much. [*Thinks*] No, Robert Downey, Jr. is the guy. He's filled with irony. They're both addicts. Anyway . . . Robin turned me down for *Moscow on the Rocks*.

SW: That's the sequel?

PM: Yeah. I approached him with it about five years later.

SW: You wrote it with Leon?

PM: And got well paid—$750,000. We wrote it for the studio. Vladimir, his character, is now driving a BMW. He has a vanity plate: VLAD 2. He now owns a whole company. He's the boss of all those people selling that shit on the sidewalk. All that stuff he used to sell. He lives in a loft in SoHo. He's getting a little pussy. He's a little mean. He's lost his Russian soul. He doesn't know what he is anymore. He's no longer an immigrant, he's a bitter American. I think he goes down to a Russian club at some point—I don't quite remember everything—and he gets a phone call in the middle of the night. It's his mother. She tells him that his sister is getting married in Moscow. She tells him he has to be there. "Mama, they'll kill me," he tells her, "I defected!" She says, "No, that's all over. They don't care. They're not going to bother you anymore." So he's scared, but he goes over. He's met at the airport by the clown, Elya Baskin's character, and he's driving a stretch limo, but the limo breaks down; nothing's perfect yet. He stays with his family in the tiny apartment. There isn't much room and so he has to sleep with the father and the grandfather and there's a lot of farting. That's where we put in the farts. You know, they're asleep in the middle of the night and then out of nowhere you hear these quiet little farts. Little ones. Next thing you know, they're at the wedding. It's held out of town in the Russian countryside. One of the guests there is a very attractive Russian woman and the arrow goes right through his heart. And she likes him. She's a doctor, a friend of the groom. They begin an affair. He begins to experience Russia again. He's getting excited about the new Russia, but then he tells her that he has to go back to America to his work. Should he stay or go?

SW: What did Robin say when you gave it to him?

PM: He said, basically, that he was afraid he would be kidnapped in Russia. I wanted to shoot New York for New York and Moscow for Moscow, which you could now do, and he said he was afraid to take his family there. I didn't believe it, so I said, "I'll tell you what I'll do." I said, "All I'll need in Moscow is two weeks"—I made that up, but I knew I could do it—"for exteriors. And I'll build the interior of Russia in London, where you will be safe. You'll just have to do two weeks in Russia." He didn't do it. To this day I can't tell you if he was just saying that he didn't like the script, if he was reacting to his new wife, his managers, or maybe he didn't like *Moscow on the Hudson*. I offered to go through the whole script with him, which is quite an offer. I told him that I'd read all the parts out loud with him. [*Beat*] I felt he should have been loyal and gone on this journey. Together we could have made a beautiful movie. A beautiful movie about the pain of going home again.

SW: Williams said, "Working with Paul was interesting. We used to yell at each other. It's only when we get in tiny rooms where it gets real hot that he gets crazy."

PM: Every now and then I guess I thought he was doing shtick and I would shout, "No, no, no!" I don't remember exactly, but if he says it, it's probably true. There were times when he might have been difficult to hold down because he's such a genius. He could do a riff now about anything—about your shirt—that could put you on the floor. We had a good time, though. We genuinely liked each other. We did. I mean, I went to his wedding afterward.

SW: So there's no struggle here?

PM: No, no, no, no, no. None. I would never say we had the equivalent of a fight except for once. It was in the scene when he brings the record to his

22. Moscow on the Hudson *(1984) Family à la Mazursky.*

family. He was doing stuff, big stuff, but I never had trouble with him in the States. He was straight on with the black family and Maria Conchita. He was realistic. He really was. I don't remember getting crazy. My style in general, I would say, is that I don't hide my feelings with actors. Years later, on *Faithful*, I said to Ryan O'Neal, "Ryan, can you bring it down a little?" He said, "What did you say?" I thought he hadn't heard me—we were outdoors—so I said it again, louder, "Could you bring it down a little?" He said, "I quit. I'm off this movie." "Why?" I said. He said, "Why did you say that in front of everybody?" I said, "Say what?" "Bring it down," he said. I said, "I'd say it to Cher, I'd say it to anyone." He said, "I quit." I said, "Do you mean it?" He said, "Yeah." I said, "If you quit— and I know you're strong physically because you have a boxing ring in Brentwood—if you quit, I'm going to take this fist and break your fucking nose and break your teeth in." And then he started to cry! "Really?" he said. He was crying. So he stayed. With Robin, I may have done the same kind of thing. "Robin, please don't do the shtick." So I tend not to hide my feelings. I don't kiss ass, but I'm very complimentary when I think they've done well. When I'm moved, I cry; when it's funny, I laugh. It's okay if Robin says I'm crazy. I don't think he meant anything terrible. Who knows what crazy means to him?

sw: There seem to be two acting styles in the movie. There's a tendency toward broad comedy, some of it slapstick, and then a great deal of it is restrained and naturalistic. I bring this up because in an old interview, you said that you wanted the movie to have the quality that a real defection situation would have—one bordering between slapstick and terror.

pm: Slapstick? No. No, I wanted there to be humor in it, so I came up with the notion of him getting behind the counter and putting his head up her skirt. If you want to call that slapstick you can, but it came out of a reality. It all comes out of a reality. He's trying to get away and not be seen. I wouldn't call that slapstick.

sw: What would you call it?

pm: I don't know that I have to label it. In other words, you could have him tiptoeing, you could have him running, but I thought it would be funnier—and more realistic—to see him on his hands and knees. Don't forget, he's defecting for his life. I don't consider that slapstick. It's a heightened reality.

sw: Yes. That's the quality. What's wonderful, I think, is that it coexists with these moments of everyday reality.

pm: It's real, yes, but it's also very heightened.

sw: More and more in this period, I think your films are moving in that direction.

pm: I don't know, I've told you this before: I don't like to analyze my work. All I do is do what I think is going to work and try to put in a little bit of humor, but I don't look for humor. For instance, in the last scene, when he's out playing his saxophone, I don't want to make it funny. I want to say he's doing okay now. I could have thought of a few jokes to throw in there, but I don't. [*Thinks*] You know, it's an unusual movie. They don't generally make comedies in this country with such political resonance. At least not since Capra. In Europe you get it more. We get stuff that's aimed more at the kids. I got this one under the wire.

sw: Were the studios becoming more difficult?

pm: Look, I didn't have any trouble in the eighties. Frank Price made *Tempest* and *Moscow on the Hudson*, two of my most difficult movies. *Tempest*, as you know, wasn't an easy sell, and the first twenty minutes of

Moscow are in Russian. But Frank said yes. It was a daring move on his part. No, the eighties were, like the seventies, a golden period for me. My trouble began in the nineties.

sw: *Moscow* is very sad, even for a Mazursky comedy. You're not shy about really getting in there.

pm: I'm explicit about it. But I wanted it to be funny, too. You can't take a straight line to pathos. You've got to have funny in the middle of it all. One of the most popular scenes in all of my movies is in *An Unmarried Woman* when Martin tells Erica he's having an affair with another woman. He tells her on the street, out in public, and starts to cry. There's no more serious moment in any movie I've ever done, and yet it had humor. That's the human comedy. That's what Chekhov and Woody do. And Fellini.

sw: I know you like to use paintings to inspire your cinematographers. What did you show Don McAlpine before you shot *Moscow*?

pm: Chagall. It's weird and odd and strange. Somebody's flying over the roofs, the colors are big and bright . . . I don't know if it's in every shot, but it's in there.

sw: Would it be safe to say that *Moscow on the Hudson* is less autobiographical?

pm: Yes. The movie is not in any way based on my experience. Even though the stuff in *Bob & Carol* never happened to me, I did go to Esalen with Betsy. But here, in this movie, I had no real experience. It's fiction. If there was any autobiography, it's from my memories of my grandparents getting out of this country. [*Beat*] You know, even though we complain about all the bullshit that goes on in the United States, we're actually in paradise. I understand the joy that immigrants feel when they get their citizenship. I understand them. Right now, Betsy and I are trying to deal with helping these Latin American people from Honduras try to get work. They're about fifty, they both have green cards, but they can't pay the rent. It's a nightmare, but they *are* free. So we'll see . . .

sw: It's difficult to be cynical about this country when you think about it in those terms. You begin to understand your connection to Capra, who you mentioned earlier.

pm: The unabashed patriotism of it, of the ending—the scene in the diner. And a little sentimental too, like Capra. I have that rack-focus from the guy's sparkler to the Empire State building. It's the only rack-focus in the movie. I hate rack-focuses, but I did it deliberately because I didn't want to cut. But yeah, there's a lot of unabashedly political stuff that we have coming out of the mouth of the Cuban lawyer, you know. And we play the song "Freedom" in the end. Yeah, it's Capra-esque. An Italian immigrant, wasn't he?

Mazursky's gotten a lot of flack for drawing from the greats. *Alex, Willie & Phil*, and even *Down and Out in Beverly Hills*—movies rooted in Fellini, Truffaut, and Renoir respectively—all suffered, in one way or another, at the hands of critics unable to come to terms with their revisionist assertions. But flip it over and you'll see Mazursky honors his idols—when he steps away from them. Pauline Kael thought *Next Stop, Greenwich Village* greater than *Amarcord*; Richard Corliss sensed a bit of Truffaut in *Willie & Phil's* love of love, and David Thomson considered *Enemies, A Love Story* worthy of Renoir.

I should add another name to the list. The director I have in mind isn't a European, and Mazursky's work never references his, so calling him one of Paul's "idols," I think, would be a stretch, but the overlap is too strong not to mention. George Cukor. Like Mazursky, he was a brilliant performance shaper. One need only think of Cukor's Katharine Hepburn, of Cukor's Cary Grant, and of his Judys (Holliday and Garland). Under his watch, actors discovered latent personae. We should think of Paul Mazursky in these terms.

There are the women: Natalie Wood, Dyan Cannon, Marsha Mason, Shelley Winters, Jill Clayburgh, Lena Olin, Angelica Huston, all of whom turned out their most complex performances in Mazursky's company. (And has there been a better cinematic spokesperson for America's modern woman?) And then there's the career-topping work of Elliott Gould, George Segal, Art Carney, and others. But there may be no better example than what *Moscow on the Hudson* did to Robin Williams. It's been over twenty years since the film was released, but it's still his strongest performance. Williams's evocation of the innocuous is so complete, at times we forget we're watching a titanic personality. Never once does he plead for our empathy, or defer to the cute, or take a shortcut through charm; rather, Williams seems uncharacteristically camera-blind, and as a result allows us to see more of what's inside than what's out. When Paul says he did very little to produce this result, what he means is that the work he wants from his actors has more to do with being than imagining. To get that, he fosters an environment where actors can feel safe enough to trust themselves. As Cukor once said to Jack Lemmon, "Don't act."

Behind its occasional lapse in focus, *Moscow on the Hudson* has a great big wide-open heart, happy to take in just about anything. But dramatically speaking, Mazursky's wholeheartedness weighs heavily on *Moscow*. As he says, he's sentimental. Fair enough. But I like my Mazursky with a twist.

Laddie on Mazursky

Studio Executive, *Harry and Tonto*, *Next Stop, Greenwich Village*,
An Unmarried Woman, *Willie & Phil*

Laddie and I meet in the office he shares with Jay Kantor, on the very floor of the very building where Laddie worked his very first job—for Freddie Fields. "I was in the mailroom," he explains. "Sometime later I left Freddie because he wouldn't give me a raise to I think four hundred dollars a week. A couple of months later, he tried to hire me back for twelve hundred dollars—and I didn't go. But we always remained friends. Me, Freddie, Jay, Paul, Mel, Michael Gruskoff . . . that's The Table."

sw: Paul says you green-lit his movies quickly, easily.

ALAN LADD, JR.: Yeah. Paul had given me *Harry and Tonto* and I read it and I liked it, and I called Paul and said, "Yeah I'll do it." Mainly because I have just always been a great admirer of talent and I thought that Paul had a tremendous amount of talent. And I trusted Paul and I liked the script, and I believed it was going to work. And I knew he would do it on time. I mean, I was never surprised or afraid of what is he going to do next.

sw: But a movie about a man and his cat?

AL: Well, I was charmed. And I was satisfied with the cast and the price it was costing wasn't outrageous, and Paul did have a reputation of being on time and on budget and stuff like that.

sw: So when a Mazursky movie comes back and it does nicely but it isn't a blockbuster, what do you think?

AL: Well, I think I know Paul did the best he could and if it didn't work, so be it. I went along with it. I'm not resentful because it didn't make money, because all pictures don't make money. But I mean Paul was never outrageously over budget or anything like that. And he always shot the script the way I'd read it. We made it together and we were both in it together. It was both of our faults. Maybe he shouldn't have written the script in the first place. Maybe I shouldn't have said yes in the first place. But I did and he did, so you know? Who's to blame? [*Beat*] I mean, in that time we all had good relationships with one another. It's a whole different business now. Now it's "How can I screw the next guy?" Now each guy hates the other guy and everybody wants everybody to fail. At that point in time, when I was making movies with Paul, I think everybody wanted everybody to succeed. And certainly I wanted [Columbia's] Frank Price to succeed and [Warner Bros.'s] John Calley to succeed. And we were all good friends. We didn't hang out. I can't say that we had dinner together once a week—we didn't. But we'd see each other and be glad to see each other. It was a wonderful business at that point in time. It was like a community and it was like, when I grew up in the business we were all . . . [*trails off*] That's not the case anymore today. Now it's "So and so I hear got *x* amount of dollars, why aren't I getting *x* amount of dollars?"

sw: While we're on the subject of a better Hollywood, I want to ask you about Paul's former agent, Sam Cohn. He was a legendary figure in the industry, practically ran New York show business, and from what I've heard there hasn't been anyone like him since. What did he do that was so good?

AL: All Sam Cohn cared about was talent, which Paul had. Therefore, Paul could get him on the phone. And Sam liked me because I would hire his talent. If I was hiring one of these action hotshots today, I couldn't get Sam Cohn on the phone—he wouldn't return my phone call. I mean, Sam loved talent so much he would be pushing talented clients who he didn't even represent anymore. I am not kidding. "You got to get Mazursky," he'd say. "Or you got to get Mike Nichols." And I'd say, "Well Mike Nichols left you three years ago, don't you remember?" "Yeah, but he's talented." That's all Sam cared about: talent.

sw: Do we have agents like that anymore?

AL: No.

sw: No one?

AL: No. Agents now are saying, "How much does the guy make?" Was it a good film? Bad film? Doesn't matter.

sw: In Sam Cohn lore, which is vast, one hears stories about how he would actually eat paper. Was that a nervous thing?

AL: Well, no. One time I made a deal with him—I think it was for Fosse, actually—and he called me and he said, "You remember that deal we made?" I said, "Of course." He said, "What was it?" I said, "Don't you have it there?" He said, "I ate it." So I said, "Do you remember what the deal was?" He said, "I ate it, I'm sorry." And at that point in time

I was much younger and had a much better mind than I do these days and I was able to rattle off to him what the deal was. And he said, "Thank you, bye."

sw: Fabulous.

AL: But it was at that time when things were honest. I probably could have said, "Well, Sam, we made the deal for a hundred thousand dollars." And he would have said, "Oh I believe you." But you didn't cheat people. You didn't cheat your friends, you know?

Down and Out in Beverly Hills (1986)

Barbara Whiteman: I want you to know, Jerry, that I am trying to overcome my middle-class prejudices. As my teacher, Yogi Ran Bir, says . . . we are part of the same oneness . . . the same electric, universal tide . . . we flow into and out of everything . . .

Monday, June 4th, 2007. Lindsay Lohan is back in rehab, and according to *The Hollywood Reporter* on Paul's desk, *Knocked Up* took in $29.3 million over the weekend. It's only 10:30 a.m., but Paul tells me he's had three calls about it already.

PM: Okay, listen to this.

He presses the voicemail button on his speakerphone.

MICHAEL CHABON: Hello, this is Michael Chabon, I am returning calls from Mr. Mazursky, and I am sorry I haven't had a chance to call back earlier, I'm in the middle of a book tour—I'm actually on my way to London in about an hour and I will be there through next Friday—so I don't know how or when I will get a chance to speak with him before then, but, in any case, my cell phone number is [*leaves number*], um, I am also on e-mail at [*leaves e-mail*] and I would love to speak to him and I am a *huge* admirer of his work, so I was very excited to get a call from him and again I'm sorry it took so long to return his call.

SW: Was that all one sentence?

PM: That's flattering.

SW: He's nervous. You can hear it. Believe me: I had to make that call to you.

Lauren pops in. Gucci follows.

LAUREN: Paul, can you talk to Alan Ladd?

PM: Yeah. [*Picks up the phone*] Hello?

After that, Paul doesn't say anything for a long time. Laddie does the talking.

PM: Okay, wait a second. I'm getting exhausted from retrospectives. It's a lot on your shoulders. You get the feeling everyone thinks you're dying. [*Listening*] A Bar Mitzvah? I don't know why they do it. It's a waste of money. Just say to the kid, "Today you are a man." That's what they did to me. I remember mine; I read the thing, we had tuna fish on Ritz crackers, and I got a fountain pen. Then I stopped being Jewish. [*Beat*] Wait, listen to this, you know what my wife did? You know I'm always fighting my weight, and I had a nice suit that I wore to the Oscars, a nice dark suit, and it was the only suit I had that fit. It was one of those Zegnas, you know? I guess it must have cost a couple of Gs for sure. She must have seen it sitting on a chair and thought that I meant to give it away, so she gave it to the gardeners. [*Laughs*] So I've got to go buy one tomorrow. It's not a joke! So I see the gardeners walking about with it . . . [*Laughs harder*] I can't ask for it back! It's a typical Beverly Hills story. You know, once we got a care package from Sarah Dylan—Bob Dylan's ex-wife—and she gave us a half-dozen jackets of Bob Dylan's, and we didn't know what to do with them so we gave them all to the free clinic. So there are kids walking around town not knowing they're wearing Dylan's jackets. [*Laughs*] Alright. I'll talk to you later.

Paul hangs up.

That's the guy who said okay to *Star Wars*.

SW: And *Harry and Tonto*.

PM: Pretty good, pretty good. Okay, I'm ready for you. Let's go.

SW: Okay. You said this in a press interview around the time *Down and Out* was released: "Leon and I wanted to make a comedy that we laughed at, not the kind of movie where the kids are laughing and we're not. We didn't laugh at *Ghostbusters* and we didn't laugh at *Spies Like Us*. That doesn't mean they're no good, but we wanted to make a movie we laughed at."

PM: That's true. The way this movie came about was very simple. When I was in my twenties, around 1952, 3, 4, 5, I used to go to the Museum of Modern Art and see all the great old movies. They had everything. One day I saw a film by the great humanist, also an actor, Jean Renoir. It was funny, sad, and clever—all those qualities I most admire personally. It was like Fellini, but less magical. The movie was called *Boudu Saved From Drowning*. In it, Michel Simon, the great French actor, played a *clochard*, a homeless man. Another way of saying it was a vagabond, someone who didn't work, someone who had no *intention* of working. He had a little dog. He was fed up with life, but there was a charm about him. At the period of time in which this movie was made, being a *clochard* was an accepted part of French life. It wasn't like the poor homeless people who live down in Skid Row here—the guys who make you want to cry. No, he was more . . . romantic. [*French accent*] "Ah, *oui*, *oui*, *oui*, *oui*. We have Pierre, he is doing very well in the merchandizing business, Albert is doing so-and-so, but Claude, well, Claude, you know, he is a *clochard* . . ." Well, I see the movie and I love it. Very simply, the movie has a scene with Boudu, who tries to kill himself by jumping into the Seine. He's tired of life. It has no more meaning to him. By coincidence, a man who sees him jump is a bourgeois shopkeeper looking through a telescope. We don't know much about him except he has a wife, and a maid, and a little shop by the river. "*Mon dieu!*" and he runs out to the river and jumps into the water and they pull out the bum. They carry him into the shop, he's soaking wet, and, to make a long story short, he ends up staying in the shop and he really upsets their lives. In the end, he can't take the constraints of bourgeois life. They all go on a picnic and he decides he has to get away from it all. The way he decides to do it is, he fakes his suicide by jumping in the river. In the last shot, we see him on his back floating down the river, looking up in the trees and the birds and flowers and he's never been happier in all his life. I couldn't end my movie that way. Anyway, now it's 1984 and I'm living in Beverly Hills and behind the houses that I live on north of Santa Monica Boulevard—at the time I was living at 707 North Alpine Drive—I'm in the alley to throw some garbage away. The alleys in Beverly Hills are really nicer than the homes that most people live in and, you know, the crap that people throw out in these big bins contains everything from furniture to clothing to food. Certainly a homeless guy could live on it and clothe himself and do quite well. Every now and then I might find something there myself. [*Laughs*] So, I see this homeless guy pushing a shopping cart full of tin cans and some other crap of his and a little dog following him. And suddenly I got one of those little cartoon bubbles floating over my head where the light blinks on over you. I think *Boudu*. Boudu tries to kill himself in a swimming pool.

SW: *Jerry Saved From Drowning*.

PM: That was the original title, yes.

SW: And when you got the idea to adapt it to Beverly Hills, you hadn't seen the movie in thirty years?

PM: I hadn't seen it in thirty years. So I ordered a print of it at Columbia and I called Leon Capetanos and I told him my idea that we're going to do it in Beverly Hills. He said, "That sounds like a good idea." When we see the movie, it's better than we even remembered it. It's kind of a

23. Down and Out in Beverly Hills *(1986) The End.*

masterpiece, which made me a little nervous, but I knew that what we were doing was going to be so different, because in our movie, we quickly came to the conclusion that our vagabond has done everything. Or you think he has. We start working through the idea and inside of a day or two days, we've got it. We go pitch it to Guy McElwaine, who has taken over Columbia. We make a deal in about half an hour and we're overjoyed. We were going to get a lot of money. Two weeks later, there was no deal memo.[21]

sw: It was a verbal agreement.

pm: Yeah, but that's an agreement. It's legal and binding. There's no two ways about it. Jeff Berg says, "I can't get ahold of Guy. He's in Hawaii." Finally he gets ahold of him, and Guy says that he just can't remember the story the way we pitched it and asked to get out of the deal. So Berg calls me and tells me this and I say, "I want the money. To hell with him."

21. A deal memo is a record of the negotiated terms but not yet a binding contract. Because contracts can take forever to draw up, some begin working with a deal memo. But it's not ironclad.

SW: You were going to sue him?

PM: Yeah. We made a deal and I wanted the money. Jeff says, "Let's not bother. This thing is so strong, I think you can make a deal in five minutes." So we go to Frank Price at Columbia and halfway through the pitch Frank says, "Okay, it's a deal." So we wrote it for Frank—it's a great script, if I may say so myself—and Frank loved it, but he had trouble with the ending. He wanted me to somehow change the ending so the bum went off with the girl. I refused to do it. I told Frank that it's better if Jerry stays with the Whitemans. He's had his fill of eating trash. In 1932, Renoir would have had the bum go off with the dog. But that wasn't the world anymore, and this wasn't France. Things were bad in America, very bad, and we couldn't just let the guy walk away. So that was that. I wasn't going to do it with Frank. At the same time, I had already given the script to Jack Nicholson, who wanted to do it, and who wanted to do it with me playing Dave Whiteman, but that scared me a little. I said, "Jack, it's going to be hard enough for me to direct you . . ." Jack said, "No, no, no, it won't be hard for you to direct me. I want you to play Dave Whiteman and that's that." I was thrilled. I said, "Okay, when do we start?" He said, "That's the only hang-up. I'm committed to Bobby Evans to do *The Two Jakes*. I owe it to him." I said, "That's no problem. Shoot that and then we'll do this." He said, "That's the other problem. We don't have a script yet." I said, "Jack, that means we're talking about at least a year here. Let me think about it." That's when Jeff Berg and Sam Cohn said to me, "We really think you should go with this new company called Touchstone. It's Disney's new company and it's going to be run by Michael Eisner—he's leaving Paramount—and Jeffrey Katzenberg. They want to do it. We let them read it." So I go take a meeting with them and they were terrific and we did it. That was it.

SW: You and Frank couldn't compromise on an ending?

PM: Nope. I wouldn't change it. I offered to make the movie on the condition that I would shoot another ending if mine didn't work in previews, but he wouldn't do it. By the way, I love Frank. This just wasn't the script for him. Anyway, after Nicholson, I went to Warren [Beatty]. I said to him, "Just imagine yourself as a dirty, filthy bum living in the garbage, and about twenty pages later you've cleaned up in an Armani suit. You can't miss!" He was wavering . . . So I got Nick Nolte, who was great.

SW: He's very real. Threateningly real.

PM: Yes, but he understood the humor. He played it with total honesty. In order to get Nick, I had to go down to his house in Malibu and spend an afternoon reading all the parts. He played the bum and I played everyone, including the dog. He was very shaky at first—his hands were shaking—but in time he got used to it. So he said yes. And then, he and I would take walks down to Venice Beach where the other bums hang out. He spent most of a night downtown at the Mission, but he only lasted until about two in the morning. I had a friend of mine, Michael Green, go with him just in case . . . just in case.

sw: Did Nolte go in character?

pm: They both did: two bums. They were going to try to sleep outside in a box, but they got a little scared. [*Chuckles*] It was tough.

sw: When did Dreyfuss come in?

pm: I saw Richard in a play and I knew he was back on his feet.[22] I had always liked him—I originally wanted him for *Next Stop, Greenwich Village*—and when I offered him the part, I hadn't yet cast Nick. I said, "Do you want to play the bum or Dave?" He said, "I'll play the dog if you want." [*Smiles*] Richard Dreyfuss is very smart. He can handle those bourgeois parts, but he can also play a fallen man. Then I thought of Bette Midler. When I told Michael Eisner that idea, he got up from his chair in the office and touched the ceiling with both hands. That's how happy he was with it. He said, "I'll see you in April," which was when we were going to finish the shoot. That's what happened. He never bothered me again. They were wonderful, very—

The phone rings. Paul picks it up.

Tecolote. [*Mouthing*] Alan Ladd. [*Into the phone*] What? Oh, *you* saw *Knocked Up* . . . Jesus Christ. [*Listening*] Alright, Laddie. Alright . . . [*Beat*] Ciao, darling.

Paul hangs up.

He tells me he saw *Knocked Up*. What do I care?

sw: I'm telling you, everyone's into it.

I open the Variety *on Paul's desk.*

Listen to this: "*Knocked Up* is uproarious. Line for line, minute to minute, writer-director Judd Apatow's latest effort is more explosively funny, more frequently, than nearly any other major studio release in recent memory."

22. Dreyfuss had a widely publicized drug problem in the early eighties.

PM: Wow.

SW: I think you should see this movie.

PM: Did you see it?

SW: Yes.

PM: You liked it?

SW: No, but it's hilarious.

PM: So why should I go?

SW: I think this type of comedy is going to keep hitting big. It's new.

PM: What's new?

SW: Well, the vulgarity of it is so extreme, and yet it's charming at the same time. It's contemporary and ballsy and it's also shit.

PM: Jill loved it. She said it was funny as hell. Meg hated it, though. *Hated* it. Do you think it's pushing it farther than *Bob & Carol*?

SW: No. See, *Bob & Carol* was about people. Nothing pushes farther than that. This movie's about jokes. It's two hours of funny television. Watching it I was thinking, "Why am I watching this on a fifty-foot screen?" It's a sitcom with a good, dirty mouth.

Paul sighs.

PM: Jesus, what a town.

Another sigh.

The DGA [Directors Guild of America] wants me to do a funny article. So I thought I'd do something like the following: "The most frequent question I got was did I think I could get these pictures made today. When I started to think about it, I realized I'd have to alter the pitch somehow. Starting with *Bob & Carol*, this is how I would pitch it today. First of all, it wouldn't be Bob and Carol and Ted and Alice, it would be Bob and Ted and Jack and Tom. Two homosexual couples who go to Vegas and get loaded on acid and booze and switch couples. Then we come to *Harry and Tonto*. Today, I'm pretty sure this new version would excite them: Harry is a drug dealer. He has to get fifteen pounds of cocaine across the country so he shoves it up the cat's ass and takes the cat to L.A. But the cat gets diarrhea along the way and the coke spills out all over the highway. It ends with a shoot-out with a Columbian mob. *Blume in Love*: A man comes home and finds his wife in bed with another woman. *An Unmarried Woman* becomes *An Unmarried Transvestite*. The woman becomes a man but can't get laid, so he becomes a transvestite and goes out into the red light district where there are a lot of care groups and ends up free and on his or her own or whatever the fuck you want to call it and he's independent. Wait, where were we?

SW: So Eisner and Katzenberg have the script . . .

PM: Eisner and Katzenberg have the script . . . This was their first movie together. They were two, youngish gung-ho fellows. I think Michael had made his reputation on movies of the week. Katzenberg was a clever and ambitious guy. Very hardworking. I don't think he had much movie experience.

SW: And the idea behind Touchstone . . .

PM: Adult movies. Disney wanted to make movies for adults. But Katzenberg then became the king of the animated movie. *Shrek* and all that. He's very smart about it because he doesn't have to deal with actors and he doesn't have to deal too much with writers and directors. He has to work with them, but in essence, you are the *real* producer. And he's done wonderfully at it. I found both of them to be very good.

SW: Why?

PM: They knew the script was good and they trusted me. They never bothered me.

SW: No pressure to keep the movie family-friendly?

PM: Touchstone was Disney's attempt to compete with the other stuff. When I was making *Down and Out*, they never told me to cut anything or change anything. It was an R movie.

SW: Disney's first.

PM: You've got to understand something. Then didn't give me a hard time. I rarely got shit. That should be the title of my next book. I really mean it. It's a good title.

SW: Can I use it for this book?

PM: Sure. *He Rarely Got Shit: Paul Mazursky Talks About His Movies*. The first shit I encountered was when *Harry and Tonto* got an R rating for the word "cunt." They told me that if I changed it to "bitch," I would have gotten a PG rating. I should've done it. It was my mistake; my ego and my pride got me. I told you all that. Then there was *Moon Over Parador*, where they wanted me to do a few things to the picture after it was locked. That was a little annoying. Universal. Once, when I made *The Pickle*, when the studio had no confidence in the picture, they did not screen it for the critics. That was a knife in the back. I was very angry at everyone. You don't do that with a Paul Mazursky movie. You just don't. You're better off getting bad reviews. Their rationale was, "This way we might have a better opening." When I was doing *Faithful*, Cher didn't want to do publicity unless she could recut the movie. And then I found out that she was recutting it behind my back, which is illegal. And the studio was helping her. I'll tell you about all this when I get there. So that's three out of eighteen movies. That's not bad.

SW: Let me read you something Leon said: "One day I was over at Paul's house and he was floating on an air mattress in his pool. His family was there and it was a wonderful ambiance. He said to me, 'I'm so sick of this town.' I said to myself, there's the movie. That's what we're looking for. Here's a guy who is living life like a king, who is still unhappy, who is in this disaster mode, this guilt mode. I said to him, 'This film is really about your discontent.'"

PM: Well, yeah. There's no two ways about it. Dave and Barbara are versions of me and Betsy, but so extreme, I can't consider it autobiographical at all. Dave was guilty about all his money and all that, but Barbara's not. Betsy's more like Dave in that way.

SW: *Down and Out in Beverly Hills* is a different kind of Mazursky comedy. We're not looking at the world as we recognize it, but the world cranked up a few notches. It's flamboyant. Until now, your satire has been more subdued, more naturalistic.

PM: With *Down and Out*, most of the movie we shot on the set. Pato and I could not find the Beverly Hills house we wanted, so finally we decided that the best way to make the movie would be to use the real exterior of a real house in Beverly Hills where we could shoot the cars going down the street and then shoot the rest on a stage. We ended up with a house at 802 North Bedford Drive that was owned by an agent. But everything else was built. The interior was a set. We took the staircase from one house, a bedroom from another, and other elements from half a dozen houses. And we built the backyard on the back lot at Disney. We built the swimming pool. We rebuilt the exterior of the house at Universal so we should shoot the night scenes. It's all pieces. Don McAlpine, the cameraman, did a fantastic job of making it look wonderfully superficial. It's like expensive candy.[23]

SW: McAlpine had what is called the Nettmann Cam, which is essentially a mini-crane, controlled with a remote. That means it didn't have to be big enough to accommodate an operator.

PM: That's standard now.

---

23. Pauline Kael called *Down and Out* "one of the most sheerly beautiful comedies ever shot."

sw: But it was new then. And it's all over the movie.

pm: It let us do things that you couldn't do with a normal crane.

sw: You can get really low and really high with it. You mentioned the word "heightened," and I think this technique—all the swift camera movement—enhances that feeling. The camera moves *a lot* for a Mazursky movie.

pm: We move when you're supposed to move. One of the things I like least in movies in when two people are sitting and talking and the camera is going 360 degrees around them. It's on all the television shows now. It's very "impressive," but why is it moving? All I'm aware of when I watch those scenes is the camera. I'm not aware of a single word. You've got to have a reason for it.

sw: Well, in *Down and Out*, you have a lot of highly physical behavior. That seems like a good reason. The camera movement heightens that energy.

pm: When I say "heightened," I'm really talking about the characters. Dave is a little larger than life. There's satire there.

sw: But compare it to *Bob & Carol*, for instance. Both are satires, but *Down and Out* is almost a parody. It's bigger.

pm: They have one thing in common: In both cases, the situation is a heightened situation.

sw: What I'm saying is that I see moments of pure farce here. That's a long way from *Bob & Carol & Ted & Alice*.

pm: I have farcical elements in it, yes. When Barbara has her orgasm and the fountains go off . . .

sw: The sprinkler in Dave's face . . .

pm: The hot coals . . .

sw: All that stuff. This is slapstick. And that's a new direction for you.

pm: But there is a similarity in this movie, which you haven't noticed, to *I Love You, Alice B. Toklas!* In that movie, he can't stand his bourgeois life so he gives up his marriage and runs away with a girl who has a butterfly tattooed on her leg. Can you blame him?

sw: Not remotely.

pm: And then he gets into the hippie life in a very exaggerated way. He grows his hair down, he's taking walks with the guru on the beach, and he's totally into it. As it goes on, it starts to invade his life in a way that makes him uncomfortable. It's a little too much. The bums are sleeping in his bathtub—

sw: You mean the hippies?

pm: Right. And it reaches a point when he stops enjoying it. Dreyfuss, in

Down and Out, is thrilled that he ate dog food and slept on the beach and all that stuff, but as the movie goes on, you see he's starting to get a little pissed with the bum. He starts to transform.

SW: Right. The way you use the dog is very interesting, and it takes me back to my point about this being a different kind of comedy for you. Matisse, the dog in *Down and Out*, is portrayed in a way that is completely opposed to how you show us Tonto. The dog is actually acting. The cat is just being a cat. Do you see what I mean?

PM: Bourgeois life has made that dog neurotic. Living in Beverly Hills has pretty much destroyed this collie.

SW: There was an early test screening in which the dog got the highest ratings in the movie!

PM: Bette knew it. She knew the dog would steal the movie. [*Beat*] He auditioned for me. He sat on the couch in my office the way you're sitting now. I mean he really *sat* on the couch. I'm standing there with the trainer, Clint, and Clint says, "Well, say hello to Mike"—the dog's name was Mike—and I go, "Hello, Mike" and the dog barks. He was talking to me.

SW: So Mike knew he was an actor.

PM: Oh, yeah. And he had the ego of an actor. Clint would actually discuss him in Method terms. He would say, "Tell me what you want the dog to do in every scene so I can prepare for it." One instance I gave was in the scene when Jerry is talking about how he got out of the draft that the dog comes up to him and puts his chin on Nick's knee. Clint said, "No, the dog would never do that." I said, "What do you mean, the dog would never do that?" He said, "The dog would know that Jerry was lying. He'd never do that." I said, "The dog would know he's lying?" And Clint would say, "I think so. He's a very smart dog." Anyway, I loved the dog. He would do very long takes. And we had another dog who swam. Mike didn't swim.

SW: His paw prints are at Grauman's Chinese. I think he was the first dog to get cemented.

PM: Oh my God. I didn't know that . . . [*Laughter*] I didn't know that . . . [*Laughs harder*] When I went to France to publicize the movie, I get on Air France with my wife, my two daughters, a publicist, Clint the trainer, and sitting in the first-class chair next to me with his seatbelt on: Mike the Dog. The first thing I say is, "This dog is going to fly eleven hours without taking a piss?" I say to Clint, "How are they letting him do it?" Clint says, "He will not urinate. As soon as we get off, he'll have to go really bad. If it was an emergency, he'd signal me." I said, "What is he going to do, piss out the window?" [*Laughs*] Wait a second! The entire plane makes its way to the front of the plane, not to look at the five-time Academy Award nominee, Paul Mazursky, but to look as this fucking dog sitting there like this [*Paul daintily folds his arms*] with a fucking magazine. We arrive in France and like *that*, the dog takes a leak. All the press are there and they run right by me with their cameras, all wanting to get a shot of Mike the Dog. Now, when we got to Deauville for the film festival, *Down and Out* was already a big hit in America. My daughter Jill, who's very tough, came upstairs to see our room and said, "My God! How come you got such a crappy room, Daddy?" I said, "I don't know. It looks alright." She said, "It's a dump. There must be some mistake." So I called up the concierge and said, "Are you sure this is my room?" He says, [*French accent*] "Monsieur, there has been a terrible mistake! I am so, so sorry. You are in the wrong room. You should be upstairs." So we go upstairs and open the door and Mike the Dog lying there in this huge king-size bed in this huge suite and Clint looked up and saw me and said, "I thought it was a mistake. Let's go, Mike."[24]

sw: Did the French like the movie?

pm: Yes. It was huge there. They adored our take on *Boudu*. There were no complaints that we took a masterpiece and ruined it.

sw: You must have been nervous.

pm: I was. I realize that when I made *Alex in Wonderland*, I invited the critics to savage me. People have thought of me as a kind of European director in Hollywood, but I'm not. I'm an American director making American human comedies. If that's European to some people, then that's their choice, but all my subjects are very American subjects.

sw: You called Nolte, Dreyfuss, and Bette Midler "the Betty Ford Kids." We're talking about three actors who were at lulls in their careers and had had histories with drugs or alcohol.

pm: Yes. I would say, "I cast the movie at the Betty Ford Clinic." My favorite line. I wasn't nervous about it, no. I have never really been nervous about almost any actor. I don't know why.

sw: Did you rehearse *Down and Out* longer than normal?

pm: No. I rehearsed about the same amount of time. It was really important that Bette got some good rehearsal in because I wanted her to feel

24. Also from the preview screening of 10/30/85: "The highest-rated performance in the movie was received by Matisse, played by Mike the Dog, as she (or he) received a very high 70% 'excellent' rating over all. (NRG has not yet established a norm for a canine in a supporting role, but a human would be average at 25% 'excellent.')"

secure with these two highly trained actors. Don't forget, she had already done *The Rose*, but she was nervous about doing this, because in *The Rose* she was playing something she knew very well. I would say to her, "Come on, Bette, you know this Beverly Hills woman." She's not one of those people. We played it moment to moment, and it helped. Also, Richard and Nick were very helpful. They really looked after her. Also, I made sure she never did outrageous things. Remember she's the Divine Miss M. She was fucking brilliant. [*Beat*] And Nick was brilliant, too. It was an unerring performance. You know he wore those clothes to the set?

sw: I did know that, actually. He took his role off camera. But did he bathe?

pm: No. Bette said to me, "He stinks! I'm not going to go to any more rehearsals unless he changes." I said to her, "Look, Bette, I can't make him change clothes." She says, "We can get him to take a shower! I know how this Method stuff works!"

sw: Do you respect that decision—when an actor goes to such extremes?

pm: I was the one who told him to do it!

sw: You said, "Don't shower for three months"?

pm: *Try* not to. And I thought it helped.

sw: There's one other major cast member we haven't discussed: Little Richard.

pm: I was a little nervous about Little Richard knowing his lines. He was one of the most unique people I've ever worked with. I'll tell you the story. He couldn't learn his lines, so I put up big cue cards. It was the first big scene he had outside the house, when the helicopter's overhead and he's shouting at the cops. I had cue cards all over the fucking place. I was yelling "cut" all the time. I said, "Richard, you've got to go through the whole take." He said, "Well, who's that kid who keeps waving a camera in my face?" I said, "That's the kid. He's part of the scene!" He said, "But I'm so distracted!" so I said, "Look, we're reaching a point when it's going to get light soon." It was five in the morning. I said, "Richard, if you can't do this, I'm going to get Sidney Poitier." [*Laughs*] He says, "Paul, Mr. Mazursky, I'm sorry, God bless you . . ." I said, "Okay, well, if you don't know the lines, make something up. Just try to go in the direction of my lines and then I can cover it if I need to." Finally I got one.

sw: And he was scared of the dog.

pm: Scared to death. He thought it was going to bite him. I assured him that the dog wouldn't bite him and then I had the trainer get the dog to go over there and bite him. He ran like a fucking thief. Anyway, we now reach the point when the sun is coming up. He would get only two words out at a time. We can't reach anymore. "Cut," I say, "We'll finish this tomorrow, Friday night. I'm thrilled with everybody's work. It's fabulous." Richard came up to me and said, "Paul, I can't work tomorrow night. I just can't." I said, "Why?" He said, "It's Shabbas." [*Laughs*] So I say, "Are you telling me you're Jewish?" He says, "I'm a Jewish man. God bless you, I'm a Jewish man!" I said, "Are you kidding me?" He said, "I don't kid about my Jewishness. Tomorrow I have to go to Sacramento and do a service at the synagogue up there. God bless!" I said, "Richard, I need you to work tomorrow. If you don't, I have no coverage. It will cost you $120,000 to pay for the night." He said, "Good God Almighty! Let me think about it." So he went into his white stretch limo and sat in it with two of his "cousins"—who knows what *that* was—then they call me over, his manager's with him too, and Richard says, "Paul, I spoke to the Good Lord about all this and the Good Lord says I can work until two o'clock in the morning." I said, "Thank God!" The next night we worked until about four in the morning.

SW: It's a first-rate bit of casting.

PM: I'm very good at that. I had to loop him months later, and between the time when we finished the movie and the looping, he had been in a big car accident. They found him in a red roadster and he had a lot of pins put into his leg. When he arrived at the studio to loop, they had to carry him in. I said, "I saw that picture of you in the red roadster, but didn't you say to me that when you got off the plane, you got into a *limo*?" He said, "Yeah, I did." I said, "Well, how did you get from the limo to the red roadster?" He said, "I don't know. That's the one thing I can't figure out." [*Laughs*] Who knows? And then I used him in *The Pickle* and it was the same thing with the cue cards. But it's worth it. [*Little Richard voice*] "Whhhhhhhooooooooo-weeeeeeee!"

SW: For a white guy, you cast a lot of black people in your movies.

PM: The guy at the alarm base that answers the calls is an African-American guy. I always like to cast African-Americans in movies if I can when they're not playing what I call "slave parts." Hollywood is filled with slave parts. It's just horrible, horrible, horrible. So I always wanted to beat that. I made Blume's mistress an African-American woman. She was a gorgeous girl. Boy did I envy George when he got into bed with her. There was also the judge in *Moscow on the Hudson*. I couldn't make her an immigrant, but I could make her someone who experienced the pain that some of the immigrants experienced.

sw: When we spoke about *Bob & Carol*, we talked about the master shots, which pretty much continued through your next half-dozen movies. Now, with *Down and Out*, it looks like you've moved away from that in favor of something a little cuttier.

pm: *Bob & Carol* was a satire, and satire permits longish scenes with a lot of reality. You don't want to cut that. *Down and Out* is more a comedy—a social comedy or whatever—and requires more energy and so it requires cutting.

sw: And movement—from both camera and actors.

pm: I've noticed that camera movement is a *thing* now with cameramen. Somewhere along the line, maybe ten or twenty years ago, it became a thing to start moving on establishing shots. They don't just cut and there it is—like David Lean did. Now they cut to the exterior and there's a little glide with it. Why, I don't know. Of course, I began to do it too.

sw: That's in *Down and Out*. There are establishing shots with a little crane down—the movie opens that way—and also, some shots outside the Whiteman's house that drift a little. It's much different than your establishing techniques for your earlier movies, like *Next Stop*, for instance.

pm: That one's just stills. When he's going into New York, I do like little photographs. It's more classical. It's my opinion—and I've said this before—that all those big, sexy camera moves are often a substitute for depth. tv does it all the time. They're doing it because they're saying nothing. But there should be a reason for the movement. A reason. If there isn't, don't do it. [*Beat*] Michael Mann moves the camera all the time. It's always moving. But you know, I'm not as aware of that as you are. I'm sure you're right, I just never really think about that.

sw: You added something new to your comic repertoire in *Down and Out*. You have *gags*.

pm: What did I do after *Down and Out*?

sw: *Moon Over Parador*.

pm: That's got a lot of gags.

sw: Yes. So, I'm seeing a kind of arc here—I know you hate that word—

pm: But what did I do after *Moon Over Parador*?

sw: *Enemies*.

pm: Right. From farce to the Holocaust.

sw: Yes, but in your films the two are closer than you think! Pauline Kael called *Enemies* a "post-Holocaust farce." Your satire is becoming physical as well as verbal.

PM: Maybe. Could be. I never thought of that. But don't forget, you're talking to a guy who started out as a nightclub comic, so I was used to wanting laughs. That's different than being a graduate from film school, like you. That's one thing I share with Mel Brooks. He and I both want you to laugh. Now, I won't go to certain lengths that Mel goes to—he's got scenes with ten guys farting around the campfire. I'm a little bit more like Billy Wilder. He gives you the broadest farce in *Some Like it Hot* and then gives you a thing like *The Apartment*.

SW: Can we go back to the script? *Down and Out in Beverly Hills* is the least free feeling of your films to date.

PM: What do you mean?

SW: The way the script is designed. It's structured in a rigorous, classical, three-act way. It's more traditional Hollywood.

PM: Sure.

SW: Again, I'm going to make a comparison. A script like *An Unmarried Woman* isn't as concerned with moving the story forward—

PM: But everything takes it forward if it has information in it that's psychological, that's emotional, that's behavioral. If it adds to the picture of who these people are, then it makes it richer. For example, she throws up in *An Unmarried Woman* and the marriage is over. Then you cut to her with the women. I don't know if it moves the story forward, but it moves *her* forward, it moves the character forward. We just see them talking, but it does something. It sets her up for the moment when she says "fuck you" to the guy who flirted with her in the earlier scene. The Erica you've seen up to now would never do that. When the marriage was good, that was okay. Then we see her with the daughter, we see her with the therapist—I don't remember the order . . .

SW: Yes! The order, the plot, is less important than the change in character.

PM: You're getting pictures of her as a different person. What would you do without that stuff? Cut to her on her first date with Cliff Gorman? That changes her.

SW: Yes, yes, yes. *An Unmarried Woman* allows the time for that. *Down and Out* does not. It's moves at a fierce clip.

PM: *Down and Out* builds to a pyramid.

SW: It has a narrative muscularity. My question is, did you feel, in writing the screenplay, under a certain amount of pressure to write in this traditional format?

PM: No, no. In *Down and Out*, Leon and I had the luxury of knowing where we were heading, which was for the moment when, slowly but surely, the bum has an effect on everyone in the family, including the dog. All of those things added up to the moment when Dave is going to find out that Jerry has slept with his daughter. That's the one thing he can't do. Now you have this big slapstick scene when you have everyone at the party jumping into the pool. I have all these people, who I've set up very carefully—set up the way Billy Wilder would have set them up—jump into the pool. Even the dog, who has set off the alarm again and again—

SW: You have running gags.

PM: *Down and Out* requires a certain kind of building, yes. But *An Unmarried Woman* requires a *different* kind of building. That's a psychological building. If you went right to that scene after the breakup, you have a different movie. I don't do that. We take a long time to get there. She plays piano with the kid, she goes out on a date. Whereas in *Down and Out in Beverly Hills* I want laughs to get me there. It's a broader comedy. You could call it a farce.

SW: And that changes the way you constructed the script.

PM: Yeah, but I don't know that we were consciously thinking that. When you hit joke, you know you hit joke, okay? What I did do with *Down and Out in Beverly Hills* is that I rehearsed every scene with the cameramen and the crew before we started shooting. Unheard of.

SW: Why?

PM: I wanted them to know how funny this picture was and how great it could be and I wanted the actors to get a sense of it, too, by all these people watching them, laughing their brains out. I wanted them to be very confident that this was going to be something.

SW: You have a scene in the script with Jerry taking a few of his homeless friends to the Sunset Boulevard restaurant. You shot it, but it didn't make it to the final film.

PM: It was too long. We were getting away from the movement of the picture. In other words, we had already spent a whole night with them in Venice, and we had already seen the bum come over to them and steal a roll from their table, which is a great piece of activity.

SW: What you lost, though, is an interchange in which Jerry's friends say to him, "Look at you! You're living the greatest life!" and Jerry says, "I don't know . . . it's tough living in Beverly Hills . . . the pressures . . . the guilt . . ."

PM: That I got from *Boudu*. I don't know if Boudu ever said it, but Boudu didn't like the constraints.

SW: I was reading an interview with Dreyfuss and he was joking about how you wouldn't let the actors in to see dailies.

PM: Well, that became a big thing. I offered Richard *Enemies* and it came down to, "I'll do it if I can see dailies with you." I said, "I don't do that, Richard, you know that." He said, "*Why* don't you do it? Why can't *I*, the star of the picture . . ." He didn't use those words exactly, but what he meant was, the cameraman was there, the costumer was there, this one and that one was there . . . I said, "For that very reason. I want to be able to talk to these people openly about what I like and what I don't like. If the actors are there, I am going to be inhibited and it will be a waste of my time. When I say, 'Use take two' and you're there with me and you say, 'Jesus Christ, I fuckin' like take three,' I'm going to have a nightmare." I said, "You're welcome to see the dailies every single day in a separate screening room." He didn't want to do it, so I said good-bye. I got Ron Silver.

SW: Has that been a rule of yours since the beginning?

PM: Yes. I've let them in for a day. On *Bob & Carol*, I let them in for a day. Elliott didn't want to see it, I don't think, but Culp saw it and Dyan and Natalie, and after one day they were satisfied. They never came again.

SW: So most actors didn't fight you on that?

PM: No. Cher had someone see it for her. Bette had her partner, Bonnie Bruckheimer. They could come and report back to them, but not the actors. Once in a while I'd show them cut footage. I'd put something together and show it to them.

SW: I know you wrote a sequel to *Down and Out in Beverly Hills*. Whatever happened with it?

PM: In it, Dave's business goes bust. The Chinese thing goes bust and all of the Whiteman's money goes into trailer parks in Miami and then a hurricane comes and wipes it all out. His business manager—the part I play—steals whatever is left and he runs off with it to Bali. They are broke. They have a garage sale and Little Richard, out of kindness, buys a lot of the stuff. They get a cheap apartment in West L.A. The son is living in San Francisco and sends them his latest video of his marriage— to a guy. The daughter is married to an Iranian and wears those masks. There's a scene with her and Bette Midler at the Ivy when they have to eat like this. [*Paul mimes lifting up a cloth in front of his face*] It's fucking hilarious. Dave can't find a job. He goes on unemployment until finally he gets a job at the hamburger place. He's the manager. It's killing him. Bette has a job on Montana Avenue at a dress shop. One day Dave comes home and he sees a hooker on Sunset Boulevard. He stops for a light and it's his ex-maid, the one he's been fucking. He says, "I guess the revolution didn't work." She says, "Mr. Whiteman, how are you?" He says, "Things are bad. Things are very bad. We lost everything." She says, "Let me give you a blowjob for old time's sake." She gets in the car and goes down on him. The cops catch it all on video, and when Bette's home preparing the Thanksgiving turkey, she sees her husband being arrested on TV. He gets out of jail on bail and Bette forces him to live in the Rolls-Royce like a bum.

SW: Where's Nolte's character?

PM: He's a golf pro now. He got hot with the gal who showed them the apartment. Remember, he fucks everybody. He's doing good, and he's sorry for Dave. You know, his part is not as good. In the end, there's a terrible flood in L.A. and Dave is missing. Everyone's worried about him. "Where's daddy?" They find him eventually, he comes back, and they try to straighten themselves out—I don't remember exactly—then Little Richard sees them and gives them the money to start a car wash.

SW: So they're not living with Nolte?

PM: I couldn't do it. It wouldn't work. I didn't believe it because they're broke.

SW: The last question I'll ask you is about the Talking Heads song. You use "Once in a Lifetime" in the front and back of the movie.

PM: Bette Midler. She told me to listen to it. She said, "You might like it." And I heard it and said, "That's it. There's nothing to talk about." So I tried it and it was fantastic. I decided that I wasn't going to buy it, that I wasn't going to do anything until I showed it to David Byrne. I showed the movie to him with the song in it and he loved it. He's great, by the way. He's a *menschy* genius.

Down and Out in Beverly Hills, like Preston Sturges's daffiest pictures, is a bottomless grab bag of riffs, quips, juicy gags, and assorted adorable incorrigibles. When the movie begins, Mazursky shoots them into the air like a rocket—they go everywhere, in every direction—and as it wraps up, you can see them twirl down like snowflakes settling back to earth. His workmanlike attention to structure is, for better or for worse, a model of setup and payoff, but Mazursky and Capetanos get Hollywood storytelling to work for them here. *Down and Out* is so full of gifts and so hell-bent on entertainment that we never have time to worry about its conspicuous architecture. Moment to moment, the picture's 103 minutes are too fun to let that happen, and so, with the bounce-back of a veteran comic ("You don't like THAT one? How about THIS?"), Mazursky broncos up Rodeo Drive for a little L.A. target practice. Along the way, he delivers some of the biggest catchwords of the 1980s. AIDS, gay, guru, aerobics, low-cal root beer, and anorexia are woven in so artfully, we're almost unaware of them—it's Beverly Hills administered intravenously. In fact, Mazursky is so attentive to the fads and fashions of the day, *Down and Out* sometimes looks a little like a period piece, a contemporary film set decades earlier. Somehow, it simultaneously defines as it derides, which is why we can regard it, as we regard *Bob & Carol & Ted & Alice*, as one of the essential comedies of its era, *My Man Godfrey* for the neon decade.

Down and Out in Beverly Hills was a sixty-million-dollar monster hit. With the studios at his feet, Mazursky went ahead with another satire of Reagan-era decadence. This time, though, the part of the president would be played by a good actor.

Moon Over Parador (1988)

Madonna Mendez: You gave a nice speech today. Very emotional.
That's why Roberto needs you. We Paradorians are so romantic.
It makes us fools.

Paul is in high spirits this morning. His mood is always up, but today it's electric. His kidney test looked great, he's skipping a meeting at the Academy (to take his grandson Tommy to see the Mets), and *Yippee* is in its fourth week in Brazil. "Len Klady saw me at the Farmers Market this morning," he says, "and said *Yippee*'s doing good." That last bit he says carefully. After years of trying to get distribution, his documentary is finally playing in Rio and São Paulo. "Yeah," he says, grateful and yet unsurprised, "They love me in South America." (It's true: Mazursky has a Latin love for revolution and romance.) "But I'm not gonna worry about it," he says, throwing his hands in the air. Mazursky makes his own rapture, and it's the most compelling case for happiness I've ever seen. Forward, forward, always forward. Maybe humor doesn't come from neurosis after all. But bliss? From a Jewish comic?

PM: Did you see *The Da Vinci Code*? It was on TV the other night. *The Da Vinci Code* should have been if you know the code, you get your money back. Tom Hanks needed a haircut. What was with that? The girl—I didn't understand half of what she said. The albino—I just didn't get what the fuck was going on. And it made eighty-five billion dollars. What the fuck do I know? I'll tell you what *does* work—*Titanic*. It has corny and unbelievable moments, but it works. It's only when they fall in the water, which you've been told fifty times is forty-four below zero and you'll die of hypothermia in six seconds, that it falls apart. They're floating around like dolphins! What kind of movie is that? But the stuff on the boat is fantastic. Okay, let's talk about me. [*Calling to Lauren*] No more calls unless it's my doctor or my agent.

SW: *Moon Over Parador.*

PM: Who made that? Oliver Stone?

SW: I think it was Dreyer.

PM: Oliver Stone could use a little fun. He should do an *Evan Almighty*. Did you see *Alexander*? It was so bad it was beyond belief.

SW: How does a director let that happen? How does a movie get *that* bad?

PM: Look, making a good movie is very, very hard. And when you get obsessed with a movie and you're really as strong as Stone is, I don't know if you'd call it a faux pas, it's just that that's the trip they went on. It's very easy to sit and criticize—I make fun of it too—but he's still out there trying. Stone has made some wonderful movies. And in order to make the wonderful ones, you've got to make . . . you know what I mean? Fellini wasn't perfect. But he was courageous. The best are. Bob Altman was very courageous. Also, he liked to stand in the back when he screened his movies. That way you'd have to talk to him on the way out. When he screened that movie *Quintet*, the one that Paul Newman did in the ice—which I didn't like—I didn't know what to say. We were in a small screening room and after the movie I'm walking up the aisle and I see Bob and I don't know what the fuck I'm going to tell him. I ended up saying some banal thing like, [*with conviction*] "That's the picture you wanted to make and you made it." Coppola stood in the doorway after *One From the Heart*. Everybody had to pass by him. "Fabulous, Francis!" "Great!" "What a movie!" "You did it again!" No one liked it.

SW: Before you started on *Parador*, you and Leon were talking about doing a movie about a spa.

PM: That's *Nirvana*. It just didn't get made.

SW: Was it an Esalen-type place?

PM: No, not really. You go to lose some weight and do some exercise and change your diet and do some yoga. You get a recharge of your battery and learn a little about your being. You go to get revitalized, to start over.

SW: The idea of nirvana is very important in your work. People are always going to new places in search of happiness. Parador, I think, is one of those places.

PM: *Moon Over Parador* is a masterpiece. I'm kidding. Ask me a question.

SW: What is it about Dreyfuss that makes his portrayals of actors so resonant? He won the Oscar for *The Goodbye Girl*, you were going to cast him as Lenny in *Next Stop*, and he plays an actor in *Moon over Parador*.

PM: Well, he's got that smart, spunky energy. He gets the humor of actors.

SW: The insecurity.

PM: That's his hallmark. His characters look tough, but they're a mess on the inside. [*Singing*] "Parador, oh Parador . . ." I think it's a wonderful movie. Not wonderful meaning *perfect*, but I really like it. The question you always ask of a movie you like a lot that does okay—not great, but *just okay*—is, What is it that I could have done or might have done to take it on to the next step? But you can't always answer that, so you just have to go on to the next movie. At the time, I was a little disappointed. I thought, "Why doesn't anyone appreciate this?"

sw: How did it happen? Where did *Parador* begin?

pm: The idea's from an old movie.[25] Here's how it happened. I got a phone call from a guy [Gary Shusett; he gets Associate Producer credit on *Moon Over Parador*] who says he's got videos of old movies that were total failures, but had brilliant ideas. He was a strange guy. I said, "Tell me a couple of them." So he started. "There's one with so-and-so and so-and-so . . ." I said, "That one's not for me." I said, "How'd you get these, by the way?" He said, "What's the difference, I have the videos." He didn't have the rights. Then he told me one with a South American country, a terrible dictator, and there's an acting troupe appearing, and one of the actors is a terrific mimic. The dictator dies in an earthquake or something, and they can't let the people know that he's dead because the country will fall apart, so they force the actor to play the dictator. I heard that story and I wanted to do it.

sw: Why didn't you make it for Touchstone?

pm: Universal had the rights. I showed the movie to Leon. I thought it would be a chance for us to do something about the unbearable South American politics, the Pinochet world and all of that stuff. So we saw the movie, I pitched to Universal, they bought it right away, and we wrote the script. We changed all kinds of things—it's not like the movie we saw. In any case, we started and ended the movie in New York. That was vital.

sw: Why?

pm: He's a New York actor who shows up at the Public Theater to audition for Shakespeare. He's got that kind of actor's ego.

sw: This was expensive for a Mazursky movie.

pm: They gave me about eighteen and a half million bucks.

sw: The most expensive movie you had made up to that point.

pm: By far. By far. They were very generous in letting me look for locations. They paid for it. I took Pato and Leon and the three of us went to Mexico City, a couple of other places in Mexico, and I couldn't breathe. The air was so bad that I couldn't do it. I spoke to [John] Schlesinger, who had done *The Falcon and the Snowman* there, and he said, "It is hard to breathe, but it's cheaper." It didn't matter, though, because I didn't find the plaza I was looking for.

25. *The Magnificent Fraud*, 1939.

sw: What about building it?

pm: It was possible to build it at Universal, but it would be tricky. After Mexico, we went to Guatemala. In Guatemala City, I asked the senior attaché at the embassy if it would be safe to make the movie there. He said, "Well, it's like Central Park." He was a New Yorker. I said, "You mean it's dangerous?" He said, "Yeah. I wouldn't take a chance," or something to that effect. While we were there, we saw the people demonstrating against the government. Anyway, I didn't like their plaza. Then we went to El Salvador, which scared Pato because El Salvador was at civil war. Duarte was the president. We stayed at an empty hotel. The only people there were airline crews. I got the manager of the hotel to take us in a car to the village where his grandfather lived. He warned us that we might get pulled over by the army. Pato was sweating now. [As Pato] "Paulie, can't we stay at the hotel and have a swim? We know we don't want to shoot here. . . ." But I was fearless. After that we went to Jamaica, which was gorgeous, but it wasn't right. Our driver there was a guy the studio got for us and he took us to Kingston, which was so dangerous we couldn't even get out of the car. He showed us the countryside and some other beautiful places, but again there was no plaza. It was good for the beaches, but nothing else. We asked the guy if he could get us a good smoke. He said, "They have cigarettes—" and we said, "No, we want a *really good* smoke." [*Laughs*] "Ah," he said, "I'll come back later." So he comes back later with what looked like a pound of grass. We gave him like twenty-five bucks. He said, "It's very strong. Very." So I roll a joint and Pato is laying down towels at the bottom of the door so the smoke won't be smelled and Leon is just watching it all, very amused. Pato and I took about two puffs . . . soon he was paralyzed but with a slight grin. I was pretty far gone, too. Finally, we got up and Leon had to steer us back to the car. The guy said he wanted to take us to a river for a great ride. So Leon's on a raft and Pato and I are on another and we're out of our minds. We don't know what we're seeing. Then, at the end of the trip, the driver says to us, "At the airport, they have drug dogs. You better not take that with you." We said, "Well, what should we do with it?" He said, "I don't know." So we give it back to him. A block away from the airport the driver pulls over to the side of the road and goes over to a tree where there's a rock and he puts the grass under the rock. We get to the airport and we thank him profusely for giving us the warning and the advice, and he leaves and now we're looking around for the dogs. But there are no dogs. He went off with the weed! That's his scam. So we go to Trinidad, and there we had the good luck to meet the Mighty Sparrow, who is the hero of Trinidadian culture. He has his own theater in his house and improvises lyrics as he sings. He's great. He's so far-out I can't describe it. The first thing he does is offer you some weed, so now we're stoned in Trinidad. [*Laughs*] But there was nothing there, either. So we come back to L.A. and I'm a little depressed. I hadn't found the plaza. I begin to think seriously about shooting on the back lot. Then somebody, I can't remember who, tells me to go to Brazil. So I go to the Brazilian Embassy and tell them what I'm looking for and the guy says, "Well, there's a town called Ouro Preto." It was designated a World Heritage Site by UNESCO because of its unbelievable Baroque architecture. It was in a mining town in the mountains called Minas Gerais. So we contacted some movie people in Brazil and got a guy, an art director, named Marcos Flaxman and told him what we were looking for. We paid him to take a video camera and shoot it. About a week later his video came in and it was fantastic. Now we had to go. So Pato and I went. Not Leon. We had to go to Rio, from there fly to Bella Horizonte, and from there you take a car for a two-hour trip and we're *praying* it's what we hope it is. And then after this long, windy trip, we pull right into the town and there it is: the plaza. The only other time I had goose bumps like that was when I found the location for *Tempest*. It was . . . awe-inspiring. We got out of the car and Pato and I walked around the town, and with my video camera, we shot the whole movie. Then we went looking for interiors.

SW: In Ouro Preto?

PM: In Rio. Pato found a paper-clip factory and turned it into a soundstage, a studio.

SW: What did you shoot in there?

PM: All the interiors of the movie. Every single one. The only real interior in the movie is the opera house. All the exteriors were real. Hector Babenco had a company with another guy, and for fifty thousand dollars they got us the Brazilian locations. You couldn't do it any other way. So to get permission in Ouro Preto, you had to go to each building, each museum, each government building, and ask. Each one. It took a month. I thought for sure we wouldn't get it, but we got it.

SW: Had anyone shot there before?

PM: Not that I know of. There was no real movie system there.

SW: So you were making it up as you went along?

PM: Sort of. We got the Brazilian army with their tanks, swords, and horses for like a hundred thousand bucks. We used them for the parades. That was the *real* army, not extras. That was all because of John Broderick, the production manager. He wasn't just one of those guys we got from Hollywood, but someone who really knew Brazil and really knew how to get in there and make it happen.

sw: How did you keep the budget in order?

pm: The original approved budget was something like fourteen [million], but it kept going up. One day I got a call from the studio and the head of production came to my office and said that he was firing Broderick. He wanted to replace him. I said, "Why?" He said, "Look at the things he's done in Brazil." He showed me a bill for napkins, paper napkins in the nightclub scene, and it was two hundred dollars. He said, "For two hundred dollars, you could buy that club." I said, "Wait a second. You're not familiar with Brazil . . . this guy is doing a great job, I can't change in the middle." He said, "You're going to have to." I said, "Then who's going to direct your movie? I'm just curious." He said, "Are you threatening me?" And I said, "You heard what I said." And I won. It was that simple. Don't forget, when you're making a movie in Mexico, the studio is hands-on. You're practically neighbors, you're right there. But when you're making a movie in Brazil . . . you understand.

sw: When you finally shot the plaza scene, how many extras did you have? There must be thousands . . .

pm: I had six thousand paid extras in the plaza. Plus fifteen hundred who came free. There were four samba schools, and they came for the carnival. It was huge.

sw: It was epic. You've never done anything on that scale.

pm: I got four samba schools from Ouro Puerto who prepared all year for their carnival. All year. They worked on their costumes, their dancing, the whole thing. I shot it in two nights. I planned the whole thing with McAlpine.

sw: What kind of coverage did you do?

pm: Four cameras and one handheld. Five cameras total. One was at one end of the plaza, wide; one was at the other end, wide, so I had reverses; two cameras with long lenses shooting into the crowd and moving; and one handheld in the crowd as if he was one of the partiers. And that was what we did. It had tremendous energy. When I called "cut," they wouldn't stop. You had to wait for *them* to finish.

sw: How do you direct a crowd of that size?

24. Moon Over Parador *(1988) Sonia Braga and Sammy Davis, Jr.*

PM: You don't. You direct when you get closer, the specific scenes. The crowd is just dancing. And that shot with Sammy Davis, Jr. is just one of the best shots I've ever made. When he comes into the frame. It's just beautiful. McAlpine designed it. It's a great shot. [*Beat*] I realize I'm telling you a lot at the same time here, but there is a lot to go through. There's casting . . . that's Ellen Chenoweth . . . You should be asking me these questions, I know, but I'm excited to talk about it.

SW: Keep going.

PM: I got Dreyfuss right away. After *Down and Out*, I got him the script, he read it, and said yes. Sonia Braga was an inspiration and Raul I knew from *Tempest*. When Sonia came in to see me, her English was not good, but she was hot and very funny. She's a great, great woman—as great as Bette in her own way. And she's a real superstar. When we would go out in Rio, crowds of people would applaud her as we walked by. She was Sonia Braga. And she's a little gal, tiny with long hair, and totally un-afraid to do anything. So then we had to cast the rest of the movie, and I decided we were going to bring in as few people as we could to save money. So I got my friend Michael Greene to come from the States to play the special-effects guy in the movie. You know, the guy who comes back in the end and helps Dreyfuss escape?

sw: And originally, you had Judith Malina set to play the mother.

pm: Yes, she was the co-founder of The Living Theater with her husband Julian Beck. Julian's dead now, but as we speak, Judith is down in the East Village still doing The Living Theater. She's a fabulous, fabulous woman. I'll tell you what happened there in a second. First, I should tell you first that we wanted Julio Iglesias for the part that Sammy played, but we couldn't get him, so we got Sammy instead. I had to go to Vegas to see him. I told him that we were writing a song for Parador to the tune of "Besame Mucho." He said, "Okay, well, in my show tonight I'll sing 'Besame Mucho.'" That put us away. And he was not well then. He was already in bad shape. Sammy had a terrible hip problem and could hardly walk. He had a cane. So I go to see him in Vegas and I see that his hotel room is as big as my house. The guy had bowls as big as him. Some bowls were filled with Marlboros and some were filled with M&M's. He had big trunks full of stuff. One was just for cuff links, one was full of tuxedo shirts, one was full of tuxedos, one was full of CDs. He had twenty-two of them. I know because when he came to Brazil for the shoot, he brought all of them. The only place he could put them was in the lobby of the hotel because his room couldn't hold them. Let's go back to Judith Malina. [*Laughs*] God, I really am all over the joint today. I'm really excited to talk about this. Okay, so I work it out that Judith will arrive two days before her scene so we can do the wardrobe . . . I also cast the great German actor Reinhard Kolldehoff who plays [Gunther] the ex-Nazi. He had a great Nazi look. When he showed up, Albert Wolsky, who had a very wry sense of humor, came up to me looking pale and ashen. He said, [*soft and smooth*] "Paul . . . have you met Reinhard?" I said, "No, has he arrived?" "Yes, I just met him . . ." I could see something of concern in his look and I said, "What's up?" He said, "I think you should take a look at him." I said, "What is it, Al?" He said, "Well, I think he's had a stroke. He is unable to move and he can barely remember his lines." Well, my hair almost turned white. Al and I head to his room—we're at the Copacabana Hotel—and there's the guy. And I say, "Reinhard, how are you?" and sure enough, he can't lift his hand up. He said, [*weak*] "Paul, I am fine. I had a little trouble . . . just before I left . . . Berlin, but I can do the part!" "Can you learn the lines?" "I hope so!" I don't know what to do so I make a couple of calls—"Can you get me a Nazi?"—and get nothing. I couldn't do it. I'd have to delay shooting. I also had in the movie one of the greatest actors of *all time*, Fernando Rey. I worshipped him. *Worshipped*. He was on a throne to me. He was as charming and suave and tasty in real life as he is in the movies. He told me great stuff about Buñuel.

sw: Let's hear it!

pm: He was very conservative with his shooting. He'd cut it in the camera. He knew exactly what he wanted and he was completely unafraid. By the way, if you want to read a great book, read Buñuel's autobiography, *My Last Sigh*. It has a recipe for the perfect martini. Anyway, I have Dreyfuss, Raul Julia, Sonia Braga, Fernando Rey, Sammy Davis, Jr., and I have Charo. That's like a Preston Sturges cast!

sw: How did you get around Reinhard?

pm: I went to Fernando Rey and asked him what I should do. Fernando was in the scene with him. He suggested that I should shoot over Reinhard's shoulder and that I should do his lines from behind the camera. He said, "I can handle that." The problem came when I had to do Reinhard's close-up! What I had to do was shoot the scene and whenever Reinhard had a line I would shout it at him in the middle of the scene. Fernando would begin the scene with something like, "Today is a great day for a parade," and Reinhard would respond, "Yes, a great day for a . . ." and I would shout at him, "A great day for a speech!" and that's how we'd get through it.[26] Anyway, to make matters worse, two days before Judith Malina is supposed to show up, she doesn't show up. We panic. We call her agent in New York, he says, "No she's due *August* 10th, not July 10th." "What are you talking about? Are you putting me on?" "She's in Germany doing an opera." Well, we got the number where she was and get her on the phone. She starts weeping. She said it was her agent's fault. We say, "Can you get out of it for one week?" She couldn't leave. We said, "We're desperate." We offered them money, but they couldn't do it. I called Ellen Chenoweth in New York. I said, "Try to get Zoe Caldwell," but we couldn't get her. She was on vacation. Now we're down to a day and a half. I'm desperate. Suddenly I say, "I can do it." [*Laughs*] So I go to Dreyfuss and I say, "Richard, here's the situation . . ." and I tell him. Then I go to Albert Wolsky and I say, "Albert, can you get a costume for me in a day and a half?" Wolsky stops, he looks at me and says, "It will have to be basic black. With a veil. The problem is going to be the shoes. Where the hell am I going to find heels big enough?" I said, "Have them made." He said, "I'll do my best." I go back to Dreyfuss

---

26. *Moon Over Parador* was Reinhard Kolldehoff's last movie. He made over a hundred and fifty.

25. Moon Over Parador *(1988) They couldn't get Judith Malina. (Paul Mazursky with Pato Guzman and cinematographer Don McAlpine.)*

and I said, "Let's read the scene, we'll do it together, and you'll tell me if I'm out of my mind. Be honest." I did the scene and he said, "You can do it, Paul." And that was it. I played the part.

sw: And the voice. Is that your voice?

pm: Or*laaaaaaaaando*!

It is.

We heightened it a little bit in post. I never had so much fun in my life. The panty hose I liked; the shoes killed me.

sw: Did you rehearse at all for it?

pm: Very little. I just put it on and did it. My balls were killing me.

sw: What were you thinking to maintain the feminine?

pm: I thought about my mother.

sw: The credits say that the part was played by "Carlotta Gerson."

pm: Gerson was my mother's name. Jean Gerson. Oh, it was great. We were laughing our fucking asses off. I'm telling you, it was the best time of my life.

SW: I've never heard you talk about a movie this way.

PM: Well, it was like a carnival. Talk about larger than life! I got Dreyfuss's brother [Lorin Dreyfuss], who looks just like him, to play the dictator in those scenes with Richard. He would double as the dictator, but every time there was dialogue, I'd use Dreyfuss. So I have both of them in the same shot. No trick photography. I got away with it beautifully. When we did the scene in the meat locker, which Pato built, the part of the dictator is being played by Dreyfuss's brother. When Raul beats the shit out of him, he's really beating the shit out of him. I told him to do it. And Raul is brilliant in that scene. The only thing I ever told Raul was, "You're playing a South American Nazi." I had him bleach his hair blond, which I think helped a lot. The rest is all Raul.

SW: A genius. Criminally unsung.

PM: To me, Raul was one of the great treasures of the movies and the theater. No two ways about it. He never does it for the joke, even though he knows it's hilarious. He has that ability to just give a little look that will put you away. A look of ironic amusement. He was great.

SW: He can do these outbursts that are hilarious, and yet—

PM: Real. There are three things you can't give an actor: a sense of humor, talent, or the look of intelligence. Either they have it or they don't.

SW: Can you make funny funnier?

PM: I think . . . yeah, you can point out what you think is wrong. But there's no "How to be Funny." The thing about *Moon Over Parador* is this: I had never made a movie with quite that ambition in terms of physicality—

The phone rings. Paul picks it up.

Tecolote . . . Hello? [*Beat*] David! Hello, darling. [*Listens*] Good, but my blood pressure, according to Dr. Harutzi, has been too high . . . he changed my pills four times. Do you have a moment now? Okay, let me get it in front of me.

Paul reaches across the desk for a piece of paper. He turns over about five sheets before he finds the right one.

The pills did not work, so he decided that maybe it had something to do with the kidneys. He wanted me to take some dye test where they put dye in you. He said, "Of course, it's supposed to be a little dangerous for diabetics . . ." I said, "I don't want to do it. I'm going to Italy, to Spoleto, for a film festival, they're honoring me, and what if the dye does something . . ." He said, "Alright, go take the sonar test," which I did this morning. The woman who examined me asked me halfway through the thing why I was taking this test and I told her. Then she said, "Well, your kidneys are perfect." [*Listens, then reads from the paper*] Lotrel, forty milligrams, the latest one was Tekturna, there's Diovan, and then Clonidine. Right now I'm taking all four of them and I think it's too much. And the Lotrel definitely causes edema in my left leg . . . Yes? [*Listening*] He took me off the Tarka. . . . Apparently it was like one-fifty when I was sleeping . . . Anyway, I'm going to see him Monday because I don't want to keep taking four pills . . . Okay . . . But four? [*Listening*] Okay. Okay. Well, don't forget, I'm not taking the hydrochlorothiazide, so maybe one of them . . . [*Beat*] I go to the gym three times a week and I have them take my blood pressure four times every day. I start in the morning around 150 or 140. By the time I finish the exercises it's like 125 over 70 . . . I know! [*Beat*] Also, when I come back from Europe—I know this is a lot of self-denial—I am going to have to see a dietician. An M.D. I have to lose twenty pounds. . . .

The conversation finishes and Paul hangs up.

I haven't been taking the right pills. [*Beat*] I have so many, I ran out of the one I needed to lower my blood pressure and forgot about it. I just forgot. It's my fault.

sw: But you're okay?

pm: I'm very up. See, I want to see my grandchildren go to college.

Paul breathes out.

It's powerful.

He raises his eyebrows.

Molly is nine. She'll go when she's eighteen. Nine years. But Tommy is six—soon. He needs twelve years. Seventy-seven and twelve is eighty-nine. I've got to make ninety.

Quiet.

You've got to be realistic about this. You can't fuck around with it. I've had two guys die in the last month. One was eighty and one was seventy-seven. He was on dialysis. So when they told me about this kidney shit, I thought, "If they put me on dialysis, I'll take a pill. Or just jump off the fucking roof."

sw: Paul, I—

PM: It's okay! It's *okay*! Let's go on! So, we're talking about *Moon Over Parador* . . . What I'm saying was, this movie was very difficult to make, physically. And I was coming down with diabetes then. When I was in Brazil was when I got it. It was probably from all the cane sugar in the caipirinhas. Have you ever had a caipirinha?

SW: Never.

Paul laughs and wipes tears from his eyes.

You're causing me to say all these wonderful things that I forgot . . . I went to Brazil twice for this movie, and when I was leaving the first time I got a call from a guy named Bloch Adolpho. [*Spanish accent*] "Mazursky, this is Bloch Adolpho, your *meshpucha*." You know what *meshpucha* means?

SW: Family.

PM: [*Same accent, continuing*] "I want to talk to you and see you and serve you a good Yiddish meal. Call me soon at this number . . ." I thought it was an actor looking for a job, because in Brazil the actors call directly sometimes. When I get in the car on the way to the airport, I said to our production manager, "You don't know an actor named Bloch Adolpho, do you?" She said, "No, I know Adolpho Bloch. He owns *Manchette*." *Manchette* is like their *Time* magazine. "He called you?" she said. I said, "Yeah, he said he was my blood relative." She said, "What? You must call him right now!" I said, "I can't, I'm on my way to the airport!" She said, "Call him when you get back. He's the richest man in Brazil. He owns everything—museums, magazines, everything. And he's Russian. He could be your *meshpucha*." So I leave him a message and tell him that I was on my way to the airport and that I would be back in a month and I would call him then. A month later I come back, and he asks me if I can come to meet him the next day at noon for a little drink. I asked him if I could bring Pato and he said, "Bring whomever you want." So I'm wearing shorts and a T-shirt. The driver takes us to his offices, a magnificent big building, but I look messy. There are fabulous paintings everywhere. The halls on the way to the office are lined with modern art of all kinds. Pato and I get to the door, it swings open, and there's about a hundred people gathered for a luncheon in my honor. I'm wearing shorts. The guy walks over with a tray and says, in Portuguese, "Caipirinha?" and Pato and I start drinking. They're sweet, so you have no idea that you're getting out-of-your-mind drunk. Then this little old Jewish man comes up to me and says, "Mazursky! I am Adolpho Bloch!" He embraced me and held me. I said, "How are you a Mazursky?" He said, "My sister married a Mazursky. He died years ago. You look just like him." "Where is your sister from," I asked. "My sister is from Moscow," he said. I said, "Well, my grandfather is from Kiev." His sister walks over and takes one look at me and starts to cry. She starts speaking Portuguese, which I don't understand. I ask her if she speaks English, but she doesn't. *"Español?"* I ask. *"Un poco,"* she says. *"Feshtay* Yiddish?" She goes, "Yeah." So we talk in Yiddish and she tells me she was an actress, studied with Stanislavsky, worked in the Moscow Art Theater, she married a Mazursky, I look just like him, and I'm in the family. So we have this fantastic lunch. Generals, colonels, military men everywhere. When it's time to go, Adolpho puts his arms around me and says, "How much money do you need for this movie?" I said, "I have enough money." He says, "I have so much money. How much do you need?" I said, "Adolpho, Universal is paying for everything." He says, "Okay, okay. If you need anything, call me." Anyway, we reach a point in the shooting where we don't have any art for Raul Julia's character's office. I wanted it to be spectacular. He went to Harvard. Pato said, "Do you think Bloch would loan us some of these paintings?" So I call the Brazilian line producer, who said that Bloch would never loan it to us. That was the one thing that was sacred to him. He never lets it go. I said, "Well, what have I got to lose?" So I called him. I said, "Adolpho, I have a very serious request. We need two large paintings for the office in this set," and I hear a slight pause. Then he says, "Come over. Pick two. Guarantee the insurance. Have them back within twenty-four hours." That was it. He did it. No one could believe it. And those paintings are in the movie. [*Beat*] Are you hungry?

SW: I'm fine.

PM: I wanted *Moon Over Parador* to be a romantic movie. That's why I did that scene where Dreyfuss kisses Sonia Braga in front of the moon. That was Brazil to me. You know? It looks like an old Hollywood shot. I wanted to remind you of those movies. It's a fantasy. You wish it could have been like that. When I was making the movie, I listened to Brazilian music all day long. I met with half a dozen great Brazilian composers, but I ended up with Maurice Jarre. I was a huge admirer of his . . . *Doctor Zhivago . . . Lawrence of Arabia . . .* I thought I'd never get him. First, I showed the movie to Randy Newman. He turned it down.

SW: Any idea why?

PM: You don't ask them why. They turn it down, they turn it down. I don't do a pitch. So I show Maurice the movie and he cannot stop laughing.

He's a little French guy. He comes up to me and says, [*quiet, French accent*] "Paul. May I call you Paul? It's a great film. I can't wait to do the music, but tell me one thing . . ." and here we are, face-to-face, within five inches of each other. He says, "They're all brilliant, but who is the woman who plays the mother? What an actress!" I said, "Her name was Celia Gerston, a famous Argentinean actress. I was very lucky to get her." And then a moment later I go, [*as the mother*] "I'll tell you who she is, Maurice Jarre! She is *moi!*" He fell on the floor. So he did the movie and it was fantastic. Every sound I had in my fantasy, he put in the score. He got it all.

SW: Was it a David Lean fantasy?

PM: I wasn't trying to imitate him, but I wanted to make an epic, yes. It was the first time I shot war.

SW: How was that choreographed?

PM: Here's another good story: We went to the favelas, the slums, where we wanted to set the shoot-out. They were bad, but they were in paradise. Anyway, we asked this nun, who knew the area, if we could do our war scene here. We told her that we'd have fake guns and fake bullets, and she said, "No, no, no. You can't shoot here. They'll shoot back." So we couldn't shoot there, which is why Pato had to build it. So choreographing it wasn't that difficult because it was on a set we had built outside. Frankly, I don't know how I did it. I'm not bragging, I just don't remember the specifics. I remember that I talked a lot with Pato and Don McAlpine. We had no pre-production on that. We got the location a day or two before we shot the scene.

SW: In the script, we cut back to the present—the Public Theater in New York—two more times than in the film. Once, is after Jack and Madonna get together; after that, we're with Jack and his acting buddies on the street eating hot dogs. The other cut-back comes after the Dick Cavett interview. They were a bigger part of the story.

PM: I felt there were too many. It was taking me out of Parador. It was a question of energy.

SW: Then why keep them in?

PM: I wanted you to continue to be aware of the dilemma of the actor. The more he played the part, the more dangerous he became to Raul Julia. The more he got into the part, the more political he became.

SW: Politics are so prominent in your films, I'm wondering, when you were starting out as an actor, did you have any guilt that you weren't getting into a politically significant profession?

PM: No. I just wanted to be an actor. And then a director and a writer.

SW: In the movie, one of Noah's acting buddies says, "I'm trained to believe and understand."

PM: Right.

SW: It that the job?

PM: Yeah. That's what an actor does. And if I remember, Leon wrote that line. "I'm trained to believe and understand." Even if I don't, I will. That's *my* training.

SW: There's another statement about actors in the movie. Raul Julia's character says, "Actors are like children." Is that you speaking, or is that just the voice of the villain, who in this film is someone who doesn't understand actors.

PM: I hate to generalize about actors because we've heard most of them. Their profession is to play and children love to play games that amount to acting games: "You be cowboy and I'll be Indian, you be this and I'll be that," but of course, when you get down to the very serious actors, I don't know if they're playing. I don't know if Olivier was playing. Maybe he was. Maybe they are like children. I don't see that as a critique.

SW: Do you hold the studio partially responsible for *Parador*'s disappointing box office?

PM: The political satire didn't come through on the poster they approved. They wanted it to look more like a wild, romantic romp. They didn't quite get it. Getting the right advertising campaign is a work of genius when it's right. I never liked the poster for *Parador*, but I didn't have a better idea. Sometimes you're limited to who they hire. Like *An Unmarried Woman*'s poster was the result of, I think, five different companies coming up with different ideas that we combined. We took the lettering from one, the picture from another, the idea of her sitting on the ring from another, and I was involved in it. I wasn't involved with this one at all. I just didn't like it. Maybe it needed a touch of irony, not hanging from the moon like it was a science-fiction picture.

SW: Throughout these conversations, I've asked you about studio interference. I keep expecting you to tell me some awful story, but you never do. But that comes now. With *Parador*, the studio finally did cut in.

PM: Tom Pollock was the new guy at Universal. We finished *Parador*, showed it to Pollock and his wife, and they claimed to love it. And then they called for a preview in Dallas. Sam Cohn flew in from New York on the company plane. I went with them. Pollock showed up with his wife and about four other executives. I was a little nervous, but I was feeling very good. When we walk in, we see the place is only one-third full. I start asking questions. Where is everyone? Well, Dallas is playing the Lakers that night. Sam says to Pollock, "You can't preview this picture to one third of a house. It's a comedy. You need it packed." Tom says, "Yeah, but we're already here." Sam says, "I think it's wrong to do this to Paul." So they preview it. The preview's just okay. I think people were a little afraid to laugh. When you're in a big house, and the laughs begin, it's catching. It gives you permission to go nuts. If the seats around you are empty, you might feel a little crazy to laugh loud. That's why it's strange to show it to a room of six or seven executives. It's not a real audience. So after the preview, we go to dinner and Pollock's wife starts giving advice. "Maybe you should cut a half hour . . ." Things like that. I said, "I'm not going to listen to this." I didn't want tips from this woman. I was insulted and embarrassed. We all felt very tense. So we decided to have another preview at Universal's theater after I made a few tiny changes, and it did a lot better. It still didn't go through the roof, but it's a smart comedy.

sw: Was Reagan on your mind?

pm: Yes. It's all about an actor's ego. All that stuff. It's sophisticated stuff. [*Beat*] Anyway, in my opinion, Universal fucked it up. This was the final thing that happened: After we locked the picture, Betsy and I went on a vacation to Europe. I was at Wimbledon when I got a phone call from Pollock. He said he had an idea and wanted my permission to go back to the editing room. He wanted to cut the New York scenes right out of the movie and start in Parador. I said, "You can't go in the cutting room, you're not allowed to. It's against the DGA rules." He said, "I'm the head of the studio"—words to that effect. He wasn't a bad guy. I told him, "I have two cuts and two previews. If you do this, you're going to violate this and that." I said, "Here's my advice: Have a screening of the movie without the New York scenes." He said, "What about the cut to New York in the middle of the movie?" I said, "Well, close your eyes there." He didn't want to do that. Then I tried to explain to him that this was a movie about a serious theater actor and you need those scenes to show that. And then Universal didn't sell the movie the right way. Maybe out of anger. They wanted to show me that they were right.[27] And they

27. On February 19th, 1988, Pollock released an eight-page memo to Mazursky, containing, as he put it, "an extensive list of possible alterations and cuts, which addresses the issues of length and thematic focus in the current version of *Moon Over Parador*." The document goes on to outline thirty-three points for further consideration, with particular emphasis on what the studio considered to be the movie's most serious deficit: after Jack-

released it later than they said they would. The critics were mixed. You know, sometimes it takes twenty years for a movie to be appreciated. I'm not saying this will be that kind of movie, but I do think the people who didn't like it missed the ambition of it.

SW: It's an epic comedy. That's something we don't see much of anymore.

PM: I know it might sound like sour grapes in your book—maybe it is. But you've got to applaud a movie that has Sammy Davis singing "Parador, My Parador" and has Jonathan Winters in shorts. And he's a CIA man. That was a comment on the CIA, and I think we anticipated all that shit with the CIA well before it happened.

SW: What shit?

PM: The blundering, the foolishness. I thought the movie was politically very sharp. Anyway, that's my feeling . . .

SW: Was the critical and box office disappointment of this movie harder on you than the others?

PM: Yeah. I expected them to be a little hipper. Yeah.

SW: Because you had more faith in *Parador* than the others?

PM: It moved me. I liked it. It's a fantasy. Sonia Braga is Hillary Clinton, but I didn't know that then. I was disappointed, yes, but you go onto the next picture. And that was *Enemies*.

For all the political comedy in *Moon Over Parador*, it is the film's New York scenes, set at the Public Theater, that show off Mazursky's strengths. After all, *Moon Over Parador* is not about politics, but the politics of acting. Dreyfuss delivers Jack's few lines about *Death of a Salesman* (and his throwaway remark about changing agencies), with such casual intensity, Parador's fantastical surroundings seem generic by comparison. It's ironic, but hardly surprising: Mazursky's engagement with Parador is predominantly allegorical, whereas his knowledge of the actor—moreover, the New York actor—is grounded firmly in reality.

Moon over Parador contains one of the only true villains in Mazursky's

---

as-Dictator delivers his first public speech, "We [the studio] are no longer concerned with whether or not he will escape detection as an impostor." It continues: "Our involvement in Jack's adventure becomes a function of the strength of his relationship with Madonna and the extent to which we experience his growth from an actor obsessed with the execution of his latest role to a man who is changed by a relationship with a woman and with a nation." Pollock is after a more pronounced character arc here. But Mazursky isn't (see chapter on *Blume in Love*).

work. As Roberto Strausmann, Raul Julia is a delight to behold, but because he plays a corrupt and heartless tyrant, his character—like Parador itself—becomes a caricature. Mazursky never gets inside of him, perhaps because Strausmann (unlike Bob, Carol, Blume, Harry, Larry, Erica, et al.) has no capacity for joy—the very thing Mazursky understands about Parador. And it is not an allegorical understanding. In *Moon Over Parador*, Mazursky's evocation of ecstasy is very, very real. You can see it on the streets and in the close-ups. Dreyfuss, Sonia Braga, Jonathan Winters, Fernando Rey, Reinhard Kolldehoff, and Charo (oh, and Sammy Davis, Jr.) all transmit a rapturous glow. Even Raul Julia, who must stifle his humanity for Strausmann, channels manic joie de vivre. "If you are alive and even moderately aware," Paul once said, "you see around you a very insane universe. But people survive by a sense of joy."

Moon Over Parador is, like Mazursky, joyful about acting and actors. Just look at the cast! It's an adoring tribute not just to the actors that comprise the film, but to the magnanimous reach of the profession, from Hollywood to Vegas to Luis Buñuel. But in the end, Mazursky's idea of happiness is just having a good time. If he loves actors (and is one himself), it isn't only because of his love of human contact, but also because he's hell-bent on entertainment. That's *Moon Over Parador*. Like Paul Mazursky, it just wants you to enjoy yourself. And that's more than a drive to entertain; that's a life philosophy from the American cinema's expert on bliss.

Enemies, A Love Story (1989)

Tamara Broder: I'm not alive and I'm not dead.

Alicia, Paul's new assistant, is in today, and Ed Limato, one of ICM's stalwarts, is out. "They're trying to reorganize the whole agency," Paul explains. "Limato brought in a fortune with Denzel Washington, Richard Gere, Steve Martin, and Mel Gibson. They let him go because he's pissed he was no longer thought of as one of the presidents. Now they're trying to make the agency into something more like CAA, where everyone is involved in everything." Paul's been at ICM since 1967. "Maybe now someone over there will do something with *Yippee*." In a town of perpetually dissatisfied clients, Paul's forty-year alliance with ICM (in its various names and incarnations) is practically unheard of. It speaks to his good luck in business and art, and moreover, as a demonstration of mutual loyalty, it's as long as any Hollywood affiliation I know.

PM: The other night, I went to a meeting for Shoah at Laddie's house. The woman who talked is a survivor. I think she touched a few people there and maybe there will be help along the way. Boy, it was something. But after coming home from Shoah, I needed an upper so I watched *Scarface*. [*Beat*] Okay, darling. Next. I don't know what we're up to.

SW: We're up to *Enemies, A Love Story*.

PM: Ooooooooooooh. [*Whispering*] Jesus Christ. Big. Big. Well, what can I tell you?

SW: You wanted to do the book [by Isaac Bashevis Singer] since the early seventies.

PM: When the book came out, and I think it was around then,[28] I read it and my response to it was: I want to do this movie, this is a masterpiece. So I called my agent and the rights apparently were not available. I decided to send the book to Dustin Hoffman and I really got no response and I just forgot about it. From then on, between every movie I made, I tried to get the rights to the book and I couldn't get them. Finally, after *Down and Out*, I got the rights. Disney paid for it. Touchstone. I got Roger Simon to co-write it and told him, "I want to stay with

---

28. The novel debuted in Yiddish in 1966, and came out in English in 1972.

the book as much as possible, but we've got to cut." So we sat around with a few copies of the book and cut stuff and made a treatment. Roger did a wonderful job. I'm very proud of it. I mean, it should have won the Oscar. Of all the movies I've made . . . It's a pretty pure, powerful thing with a mixture of pathos and humor and darkness and light. Thank God it got a few nominations, it helped with business. But it didn't do huge business, nor would you expect it to. And I've got to give [producer] Joe Roth credit because when they had the preview at Fox, it got the worst rating you could get, like a thirty-five percent. And I said to Joe, "I think I am going to give up the business because I don't think I can do anything better than that. It's okay, there are things I can do. I'll be a shoemaker instead. It'll be okay." Joe said, "Don't change a frame. It's a master-piece. This picture's going out just as it is. We only need thirty-five percent to get our money back," and they got their money back plus some. So, in any case, it was a great, lucky, wonderful convergence of events to get a good script and then to cast it right. But I'm so proud of this one because it didn't come from me—it came from Isaac Singer. Most of my movies come from me, whether it's *Harry and Tonto* or *Down and Out in Beverly Hills*, they're really about me, but this one isn't me, in terms of having suffered the Holocaust. So I was able to put myself into another person's world and I think it really worked. [*Beat*] You know they're making an opera out of it?[29] They want me to go to New York in December after they've written the libretto so I can work with the sing-ers. The possibility of seeing Herman's three wives singing all around him . . . it's overwhelming. We'll see. Anyway, that's the story of *Ene-mies*. I think it's a great movie. It really gets me in certain places. Some-times when I'm watching it, it gets so overwhelming for me that I can't breathe.

sw: Do you remember what brought you to the book?

pm: It's a good question. I must have been a fan of Singer's. I'm sure I read a couple of the others. Later I became a bigger fan and read *Shosha*, which I tried to get. If I had the energy and the will and the determina-tion I might go after *Shosha* again, but quite frankly I'm exhausted from trying to get money for movies that I want to make. But they won't give it to me. It's disturbing. Of course, I'm not the only guy going through this. It's all changed. But back then I was a hit. [*Thinks*] Because I had

---

29. I'm not surprised only because Pauline Kael saw it coming. In her review of *Enemies, A Love Story*, she wrote, prophetically, "The plot suggests a tragicomic opera."

had such a hit with them in *Down and Out*, Touchstone gave me and Roger money to write the *Enemies* script, but when they read it, they got nervous. It looked expensive. Of course, when they read it, I had the feeling that Michael Eisner didn't realize it was about Auschwitz.

Laughing, Paul reaches for his coffee. He's laughing so hard he has to put down the mug.

Listen to this, kid. It's absolutely true. Michael said the funniest thing I have ever heard in a meeting. After they read the script, or maybe it was just the treatment, they said, "How much would it cost?" I said, "I can do it pretty low for about ten million. I need a couple of weeks in New York and then I'll do a few weeks in Canada." Michael said, "Well, can't you do it for less?" I said, "It's period. Michael, that's really hard . . ." He said, "Well, can't you update it?" I almost fainted when I heard that. I'm reminding you this is a movie about Holocaust survivors. The only way to update it would be to make it Cambodian. I would get Sun Young Fat to play the lead . . . I was doing this riff and Katzenberg didn't know what to say. Anyway, Jeffrey and Michael were very nice. I'm not saying that for the book. I mean that. They were very pleasant to work for, but I realized they'd never let me do it, so I went elsewhere and got the usual moronic turndowns. You know, they're all full of shit. [*Beat*] Basically, you've got to understand something. No matter what they say, for the most part, with some exceptions, from the later eighties on, I would say the studios stopped being interested in movies and started being only interested in money.

sw: What brought that on?

pm: The corporate takeovers changed the nature of moviemaking. [*Beat*] But then along came the great good luck to get to Jim Robinson and Joe Roth. And they got it. [*Thinks*] You asked me why I did the book and I think it's because I loved the idea of a guy who's got a wife he doesn't love, but out of guilt he's married her; a mistress he's so hot for he can hardly walk, but she's a neurotic mess and still living in the camps in her mind. And out of all this his dead wife shows up alive. *Alive.* Things were tough enough with the two, but now . . .

sw: And you and Roger bring Tamara [the "dead" wife] in much sooner than Singer does. It's a major change from the novel and one of the triumphs of the adaptation.

pm: That's right. The sooner we gave Herman the problem of three wives, the better it would be for the movie. Now he was forced to be under constant pressure. It's funny, but it's powerful, because look who you're dealing with. [*Beat*] I also invented the last scene.

sw: What was Singer's last scene?

pm: We know he's [Herman's] in Miami somewhere, suffering. I don't remember exactly.

sw: So what did you want your ending to have?

pm: At the end of the movie, I wanted you to feel, in spite of everything that happened, life would go on. They named the baby Masha, which was in Singer's book, meaning that Masha lives. That beautiful, tortured soul is now a little adorable baby. From there I cut to the Wonder Wheel, which continues to turn.

sw: Was that Singer's metaphor?

pm: There's a wheel in the book, but not like in the movie. I made it the last shot. I had that picture in my head all along and I had the picture of Jill Clayburgh carrying the painting all along. Who knows how? What I look for in a piece of material is, does it have anything at the end that's going to take me to some sublime place? If it doesn't, then I don't know if I want to do it.

sw: Is the Wonder Wheel a positive image?

pm: For me it's totally positive. Totally.

sw: Because there's the implication that it just goes around and around and around and we're stuck.

pm: No, not for me. The Jewish wheel keeps turning.

sw: You've told me that you're anti-religion.

pm: Yes. I believe religion promotes separation. I mean, I remember I would say to my mother, "I met the funniest guy," and she would say, "Is he Jewish?" I'd say, "What's the difference?" and she says, "I don't know, I'm just asking."

Paul looks up.

I'm just thinking about the music to *Enemies*.

Paul hums a few bars from the score.

God, Maurice Jarre was smart. He understood the emotion without you telling him. Oh, and his theme for Masha really pays off.

sw: What is Masha's theme?

pm: It's the down notes that come in, I think, only on the mandolin. It's ironic. It's got a double . . . [*Rethinks*] It's good-bye . . . It's the shot when she goes to the sink and you see her face in the mirror before she swallows all the pills. You see her looking at herself and at the very last moment she smiles.

sw: Yes, why does she smile?

pm: She's going to a better place. She's doing the right thing. She's saying good-bye. [*Beat*] Better to have her smile than have her cry.

sw: The scene before—"you promised we would kill ourselves!"—is played for laughs.

pm: It's supposed to be. That's why we have that cigarette in there. He smokes it like a European.

sw: Why have you made it comic?

pm: I didn't make it that way. That's the way it is. That's the way Isaac Singer sees the world. To him, it's tragicomic.[30] It's tragic in that when you talk about God you say, "I don't know of anything better right now, so I'll go along with that." And it's comic in that the situations human beings get themselves into are cosmic jokes. You'd think they'd know better after thousands of years of being human, but they can't seem to help it. And Singer has a deep understanding of the behavior of the Jews. I don't know of other people who would behave in exactly the same way.

sw: What is it about the Jewish response?

pm: You know, you ask questions sometimes that I just can't answer. I don't want to be glib, but I mean, if a Gypsy was going to kill himself— which I don't think they would—if they were talking about doing it and then the conversation went into "Well, I *did* fuck this one and that one," they would probably say, "Who cares?" In other words, Singer sees the joke in the blackness. [*Beat*] In *Shosha*, by the way, Aaron [the protagonist] has three or four girlfriends, and you'd think that's enough. He's got a communist who he likes to screw, he's got one of his friend's wives who he is screwing on the side, and he's got this actress from the Yiddish theater, but he goes to Krochmalna Street to do a little research for something he's writing and he sees it's exactly as it was ten years ago in 1926. It's still a Jewish ghetto. They're selling pickled herring on streets lined with gas lamps. When he's there, one of the old women recognizes him. It's Shosha's mother! By the way, you've begun that book with a prologue about his love for Shosha when they were young. She was an angelic blonde kid, ten years old, and they loved each other in a sweet

---

30. Roger Simon, from the production notes: "The brilliance of Singer's conception lies in his ability to reduce a terrible event to human dimensions. These people have had to incorporate the actuality of this terrible event into their lives."

way. Now she's twenty-nine years old and he looks at her and she's four foot eleven and still angelic, but simple, totally lacking in any sophistication. And what happens? Here's the cosmic joke: An arrow goes through his heart. He falls madly in love with her. *Madly.* And that's what the novel's about. *Shosha.* What is he going to do to get Shosha out of Poland before the Nazis come? So he marries her. But she's never had a man! Such wonderful problems, and all set up by Singer, who is totally unafraid of that combination. Very dark, but wonderfully light. He was very ambivalent about God. Some of those eternal questions are in the movie, which thank God they didn't ask me to cut.

SW: The scene in the kitchen between Herman and Masha.

PM: Mazursky deserves credit there because I shot it and I insisted on it.

SW: The way you describe it, Singer is Paul Mazursky's brother in literature.

PM: Except when I met him he was no longer . . . terribly sharp. He was failing. He was about eighty-two and living in Miami. I had a great emotional need to meet this great man before I made the movie, just in case he might say one word to me that would make it better.

SW: Did he?

PM: Yeah. He talked about the birds in the cage. Herman's birds. He lit up when he saw the picture of Lena Olin. He said to me, "You'll make a good movie." That's when I knew he was still horny. She had that effect on men.

SW: So what was it about the birds?

PM: I asked him if he remembered the birds. He said, "Matzele and Patzele! I loved my birds." I told Ron [Silver] about this and he became very sweet to them in the movie. Those birds were a symbol for Herman, because he himself was in a cage. His life was in a cage. He didn't know how to get out of it.

SW: You said once that Herman feels joy only when he's eating and when he's fucking.

PM: Basically right. He doesn't sit in a movie and laugh. Don't forget, he survived the war and his wife and children didn't. There's massive guilt about that.

SW: The way you handle the children in the film is very oblique. You almost forget that Herman was a father.

PM: Well, I don't want to make up things that aren't in the book. I don't want backstory with him and the kids running through the fields in Poland. I don't like the characters to tell too many stories about things that happened offstage.

sw: When you met him, did Singer say anything else revelatory?

PM: When I walked in, he was sitting around the pool, napping. I didn't want to wake him up, but Alma, his wife, went over to him to tell him I was there. I said, "I don't want to wake him up." She said, "If you don't wake him up, how are you going to talk to him?" Common sense. He looked up at me and said, "I didn't like what Barbra Streisand did with *Yentl*." He had piercing blue eyes. At one time, I remember thinking he was a lothario.

sw: Okay, the adaptation: Why not work with Leon? You did four movies in a row together, and now your writing partner is Roger L. Simon.

PM: It wasn't Leon's world. And I knew that Roger knew about *Yiddishkeit*.

sw: Why did you decide to collaborate in the first place?

PM: It's a big job. And Roger knew a lot about Jewish stuff. I don't know. I don't really remember exactly, but I feel you don't have to have the same writing partner every time. Although I *like* to have the same person every time for camera, for costume, for production design, for A.D.-ing even. I love it. It saves you all the trouble of getting to know, all over again, what this person is really like. That's the way I was with Pato, with Albert [Wolsky], with Don McAlpine, and after a certain amount of time, with Leon. My only criticism with Leon was that it would take endless amounts of time before I would see pages from him. But we changed that as we went on.

sw: And with Roger, it was his responsibility to write the first draft?

PM: For the most part, although I was there with him writing some of the dialogue. It's a way I had of working—I don't want to take anything away from these guys—they put more into the first draft than I did in terms of actually writing, but it came from endless discussions between the both of us. We would talk and talk and talk and talk about it and then Roger would go away and write. [*Beat*] You know, right now I'm writing a piece for *Vanity Fair*—so far it looks pretty good—about the table.

sw: The table?

PM: A group of five guys, maybe six, who meet every Friday for the past five years.

sw: The table.

PM: Mel Brooks, Freddie Fields, Jay Kanter, Alan Ladd, Jr., Mike Gruskoff, Gareth Wiggan and Paul Mazursky. Sometimes there are occasional visitors. Once we had Peter O'Toole, who said after his lunch at the table, "Is there any chance you'll ask me back?" The article is about how we got to meet. We were all working on the third floor of Fox in the seventies. It will be loaded with pictures of Jay's old clients, who he will never reveal anything about. They're Marilyn Monroe, Grace Kelly, and Marlon Brando. We beg him—we *beg* him to tell us, "Did Grace Kelly have a lot of affairs?" We beg him! But nothing. He won't talk. Do you know how Jay got Brando?

The phone rings. Paul goes for it.

Tecolote . . . [*Listening*] I'm going to Freddie's tomorrow. We're having the table at Freddie's. He isn't doing too well, so instead of Orso's we're going to do it at his place. [*Listening*] Who's Sidney? [*Beat*] Oh, Poitier? How nice. That guy owes me a lunch. [*Listening*] Okay, we go to The Grill—Sidney, me, and Alan Ladd, Jr. Who pays? Mazursky. Laddie can't reach for the bill, and Poitier says, "It's on me next time." Well, there was no next time. [*Laughing*] I'll see you at eleven o'clock. [*Hangs up*] So I'm writing about all that. The centerpiece of it is our emotional connection, which is very rare in Hollywood. I had it one-on-one with Federico Fellini and Raul Julia and Pato. We loved each other. That's what it's about. Okay, *Enemies.*

sw: Let's talk about your research.

pm: Well, I never lost any relatives in the Holocaust, but you can't help but know about it. It all came home to me when I went to Yad Vashem in Israel around 1976 or so. That was the first Holocaust museum. It was startling to see the records, the photos, the piles of shoes, all kinds of things. I remember I was on a tour bus and sitting next to me was a Jewish guy from the Lower East Side, a business man, a nice guy, obviously European. When I came out of the museum I said to him, "That was the most powerful thing I've ever seen. Why don't you go in and take a look?" He said, "I don't have to look, I was there." He pulled up his sleeve and there were the numbers. [*Sighs*] Ron Silver was very up on Jewish stuff, so he didn't need any kind of research. Angelica and Lena Olin are not Jewish, so I put them through the drill. I gave them a few books about the Holocaust, showed them a couple of documentaries about the camps,[31] and then I took Angelica to dinner in L.A. with

31. From a letter Paul sent to Ron Silver, dated 1/6/89: "Dear Ron, I'm enclosing *Interviews* by Magda Simon. She is a survivor of the Holocaust who I met at the Farmers Market. She is deaf and partly dumb. She's about 62 years old, very attractive and a genuine upper. Even though Herman wasn't in Auschwitz, and even though her youth was in Hungary, I think it's worth your read. I also recommend anything by Primo Levi. I'm also enclosing a tape, which *must be returned*, *De Baja Del Mundo.* It's a film made by Argentinians in

about seven or eight Holocaust survivors. She got a lot out of it. The survivors were very open about their experiences. Most of them were about sixtyish and actually had humor about their situations. But I remember one of them didn't. He was still wrecked. I asked him, "What did you do the day you were freed?" He said, "I beat the shit out of the German guard. He said he couldn't help himself and took out pictures of his children. He begged me to forgive him, and I beat him to a pulp." I took them to Jewish restaurants on the Lower East Side where a certain percentage of the waiters were survivors. That was powerful. So they absorbed, in the two-week period, a great deal. And then I had two weeks of rehearsal. I rehearsed a lot. I didn't take the scenes as far as the actual performance, but I could absolutely tell from the rehearsal that I had cast well. Every one of them.

SW: Billy Wilder didn't think so.

PM: After he saw *Bob & Carol* at a preview screening at the Crest Theater in Westwood, he said, "You made a great movie. It's very funny. Keep up the great work." And then after *Enemies* he said, "Another great movie, but it won't be a commercial success." "Why?" I asked. "Because you need a star. Ron Silver isn't a star." He had a point, but I thought it was a mistake to say that.

SW: You steeped the actors in the Holocaust and yet, in the movie you never show it.

PM: No never. No shots of the Holocaust. No shots of children being dumped into a hole. No shots of escape. The trick for me in adapting the book was to visualize the Holocaust without showing it, but in a way that didn't make it corny or melodramatic. That was the trick.

SW: How did you decide upon Margaret Sophie Stein for Yadwiga?

PM: I was sitting next to Agnieszka Holland at Le Dome for the Academy luncheon for the foreign film nominees. Agnieszka said to me, "I love your movies, what are you doing next?" I said, *"Enemies, A Love Story* by Isaac Singer." "Isaac Singer?" she said, "No you're not. I'm doing it. I'm doing it in Poland." I said, "Agnieszka, I got the script, I got the money. I'm doing it." She was shocked. She said, "Are you kidding?" I said, "No." She said, "Who's playing Yadwiga?" I said, "I don't know. I don't have anyone." "There's a Polish actress in New York named Margaret

---

Czechoslovakia. It's about the Jews in Poland living underground to hide from the Nazis. Very powerful." Mazursky sent *Interviews* to Lena Olin and Margaret Sophie Stein as well.

Sophie Stein. She's your Yadwiga. I guarantee you you'll use her if you meet her." So I went to New York and met her. She read like two or three pages for me and I got goose bumps, the biggest goose bumps I've ever had in my life. Sammy, I have nothing else to tell you. I gave her the part. My fantasy of what the part could be had come true. Often you don't get that because . . . let's say you're casting a star . . . you're not going to read the star. That almost never happens. There are exceptions. Spielberg could get stars to read for him. But most of the time, you don't know what you're going to get until you get it. That's what rehearsing is for. That's *one* of the things rehearsal is for.

sw: With such risky subject matter, you must have been a bit worried about the critics.

pm: Only a little, but after that first screening with Joe Roth, I knew I had something good. When the picture opened, I was in New York doing publicity—I was trying to do as much of that as I could—when the reviews started coming in on the fax machine in my hotel. There were about seventeen in a row. Unbelievable. That's when I knew it would be an Academy Award movie. The comment that amused me most was Stanley Kauffmann's. He said something like "Who would have thought Paul Mazursky could make a picture like this?"[32] On the one hand I wanted to shoot him, and on the other hand I wanted to kiss him. It was like that with John Simon, too. He gave me pretty lousy reviews until *An Unmarried Woman*. He raved. He loved it. Raved.

sw: In his review of *Harry and Tonto*, Simon just complains about the cat.

pm: In *Next Stop*, he hated Lenny Baker's nose. But, you know, let's not be too harsh on the critics. Put yourself in their position. Most critics have to go to the movies every day. I mean, think about it: Your head can come off after a year or two. If you're Pauline Kael, you're only writing about a few movies a week. And she only wrote half a year. She had a great arrangement. The other half was Penelope Gilliatt. How would you handle the movies you don't like, which is the majority? What I'm saying

32. Stanley Kauffmann: "Singer created the first miracle. Now his book itself creates a second: It caused—inspired—Paul Mazursky to make a good film of it. Not all who know Mazursky's earlier work (*Blume in Love*, *An Unmarried Woman*, *Down and Out in Beverly Hills*, etc.) will readily believe this. In the past he has striven to be "European," and the results have been mostly pathetic—with the pathos of a small man overreaching himself. This time there is no imitation: He works directly from what he understands and what he can see. Of course with Singer's novel in hand, he had a considerable head start over his past efforts, and he has made the multitextured most of it."

is, it's easy to be a wise guy about it. But Simon was a tough one. He liked to write about the way people looked. Did I ever tell you about when I met him in Iran? Okay, you've got to hear this. This is a great story. Well, I was flying to Iran for a film festival with *Next Stop, Greenwich Village*. On the airplane with me was Tony Ray, Otto Preminger, some other Hollywood people, and John Simon. So I'm sitting in my seat and I say to myself, "I am going to go over there and meet Otto Preminger." I had heard all those stories about what a bastard he was and I wanted to find out. Soon I see John Simon is looking over my shoulder. I was reading the play *The Tempest*, I think. He said, [*high-pitched, impish*] "Shakespeare! What are you reading that for?" I said, "Oh, I'm thinking of making a movie of it . . ." By then, I already knew that he had given me rotten reviews for *Next Stop*. I know right away that I don't like him. Okay. So I go over and sit with Otto and his son, the kid he had with Gypsy Rose Lee, and we're getting fucking drunk on vodka and eating the best caviar I ever had in my life. Well, Preminger was delightful, full of irony, and hip. That's when Simon comes by. "May I join you?" he asks. Otto says, "Well . . ." So Simon sits down and asks for some caviar, but Otto won't give it to him. Simon asks why. Otto says, "Because this is for the people who *make* the movies." Otto was kind of putting him down, but Simon sat through it. He took it. When we get off the plane, we go to the hotel. The first thing that happens is that they're giving out the rooms. "Paul Mazursky, room 416! Two beds!" I go up and get the keys. "Mr. and Mrs. Otto Preminger! A king-size bed!" Preminger stands up and points to his son and says, [*heavy German*] "Does this look like my wife? This is my son! It's Mr. and Mr. Otto Preminger! We can't sleep in the same bed!" He's outraged. It's fucking hilarious. I say, "Take my room, Otto," and he did it. From there, he was my buddy for life. So later we go down for dinner and I'm super casual as always. No tie, no jacket. Otto's got a tuxedo on. He's formal. When the maître d' sees me, he says, "You can't come in sir." Preminger says, "What do you mean he can't come in? I don't have a tie either!" And Preminger just rips off his tie and throws his jacket off and pulls me into the restaurant and starts calling out to the waiters, "Mazursky and Preminger want their dinner!" [*Thinks*] Preminger was a gutsy director and a great actor, too. He took most of his projects because he wanted to do them.

SW: Like you.

PM: I think, deep down, the reason one can do some very good work is because of a really emotional involvement with it. That's the reason I turn down scripts. If I'm not grabbed emotionally, I don't know that I could do it. It's such an enormous task to be on top of the money, the ego, the day-to-day problems—all the stuff that goes into making a movie. You've really got to believe in yourself and *it* or you're going to be crushed. But if you do—and I did with all my pictures, even the ones that weren't successful—if you have enough belief in them, maybe it's ego, nothing will stop you. Once it's over, though, I get scared again. I can't go in there and say, "I don't like the way you're distributing this. I don't like what you're doing here." But when I'm making a movie, I'm all emotion. Sometimes I would watch a scene and I would be so overwhelmed I couldn't talk. I'd go, [*throaty*] "Cut . . ." You know? Anyway, so that's that.

sw: Why did you decide to go with expositional subtitles in the movie? "Coney Island," "Central Park West," "The Bronx"—you didn't have to, but it makes New York geography a significant park of the film.

pm: Because, first of all, it guarantees that the audience will understand that he's a man who has to go all over town to function. He lives in Coney Island, he has a mistress in the Bronx, and he works in Manhattan. Later on, I pay it off with that shot in the subway station when he's running beneath that sign and doesn't know which way to go.

sw: That isn't in the book.

pm: No. In the opera I hope they do that. Secondly, I wanted the audience to know exactly where they were—and I printed the subtitles big enough to make sure of it—probably because I knew we were faking some of the locations. Some of the Bronx, for instance, was shot in Long Island.

sw: One of the effects of the subtitles is that it keeps New York—the city's specific contents—at the forefront of your mind. It makes the setting a bigger star. There's also that great establishing shot of Coney Island, the one you cut to right after Herman tells Yadwiga they're going. How did you shoot that? It looks exactly like Coney Island.

pm: Stolen. I got it from Universal. They had made shots for a movie they didn't use. Somehow we found it.

sw: So you went looking for B-roll.

pm: Yeah. I lied to a lot of people about that. I say most of my budget went into that shot. You know, Coney Island doesn't exist that way any more.

sw: Right. That's why I asked. You don't remember the movie you stole it from?

pm: Some Doris Day movie from 1951 or something. I don't remember. The scenes on the Coney Island boardwalk were shot at the real Coney Island and in Montreal.

26. Enemies, A Love Story *(1989) ext. Lower East Side—Day*

SW: Exterior locations, interior studios.

PM: The haunted ghost ride where Yadwiga tells Herman she wants to have his baby, that exterior was a real shot in Coney Island. The interior was in the studio in Montreal. The Wheel and all the rest was in Coney Island. My main objective with that was just to make it look as real as I could. That's a wonderful little montage because it begins with her mopping the floor in the house just after he's humped Masha, his mistress. He says, "Let's take a holiday."

SW: You do that throughout the movie: hard contrasts between scenes, ironic juxtapositions.

PM: We do, and so does Singer. In the book, you'd be with Masha and Herman in bed—something sexual, powerful, emotional—and then the next chapter he'd write, "Yadwiga was mopping the floor . . ." Roger and I wanted to keep a lot of that.

SW: Something that fascinates me in the rehearsal is how you work on a scene, like the one when Tamara returns, that deals with a situation so far beyond the realm of ordinary experience. In this case, it's a dead wife brought back to life.

Paul takes a Velcro sleeve out of his bag, slips it past his wrist, and continues listening.

PM: I never rehearsed that scene. I didn't want to rehearse a scene where he is shocked. I wanted to save that so that the first time he sees her *is* the first time. I did rehearse other scenes with Angelica and Ron, the scene in bed I rehearsed with them, but I didn't rehearse that one. But I don't know how, as an actor, you could find the "as if . . ." to go with that scene. Ron did it very well. He played *against*.

Paul looks down at the wristband. It has a digital gauge on it.

This is for my blood pressure, by the way.

He removes it.

One twenty-five over sixty-six.

SW: Is that good?

PM: Fantastic. Less is more with scenes like that.

SW: What did you tell Ron Silver and Lena Olin before their first sex scene?

PM: I said to Ron, "Herman does this once, maybe twice a week. Everything in his life he puts into this. All the death and all the life is right here with Masha." I said to him, "You're the luckiest man in the world to be able to kiss, suck, and caress Lena Olin. I'd give anything to play your part." She was *so* gorgeous. I said, "No dialogue. Don't add any words. There's no talking. Silent. The mother is next door and as loony as she is, we don't want her to hear anything. The minute the door closes and you enter the room, you only have one thing on your minds: you want to *fuck* each other to *death*." And that's all I told them. I staged each move, too. When to touch her, when to get her dress up, when to pick her up, take her to the bed, get into the bed, get her buttons off, lie down, get her brassiere off, and as they do it I get closer and closer with the camera and he begins to kiss her breasts and as he does, she turns to face the camera and he's sucking her nipples. [*Beat*] I just came.

SW: When you rehearse that scene, do you have them go all the way? Or is it better to save it for the take?

PM: I told them they didn't actually have to do it, but I just wanted them to get used to the moves, to the blocking. Ron's a little nervous. Okay? He's a little nervous. Lena says, [*low and heavy*] "Okay, you stand here and I stand here and—be careful when you put me down—I kiss you here." I said, "Yes, but you don't actually have to *do it*." Inside of a minute, she's scratching his bare back and Ron's facing me and he goes [*Mazursky's jaw drops, stunned*]. He doesn't know what to do! She killed him. For that scene, Lena should've gotten the distinguished sex award.

SW: At the end of that scene, you do something that occurs throughout the movie. We go from wide to close with a little push in. I've heard it called a "Mickey Rooney"—a short creep.

PM: I want to make the passion more intense and I want to avoid seeing what you should be seeing—Ron Silver from the waist down. By going in closer, you don't see it. I don't do a cut, which might have been easier.

SW: There's a lot of snow in *Enemies*. I mention it because I know you shot the film in the summer, which means all of it was manufactured. Why was it so important to you?

PM: I wanted to show the passage of seasons. And it was a pain in the ass. It's worth it alone just for the shot of Herman walking along in the snow. But snow gives you seasons.

SW: The cycle . . . the Wonder Wheel . . .

PM: That's it. [*Beat*] I'm thinking now how I don't have much fall in it . . .

SW: No, but the palette is autumnal. The browns and reds . . .

PM: For every picture I've ever done, I make up a scene-by-scene list of the seasons. What time of day is it? What is the date? That way the cameraman has it in his book.

SW: This was your first movie with cameraman Fred Murphy.

PM: When I saw John Huston's last picture, *The Dead*, I thought, "That's the guy I want to shoot *Enemies*." It had a wonderful poetry to it. I asked Angelica, who was in *The Dead*, what her father thought about Fred. She said Huston said that Murphy was the greatest D.P. he had ever worked with. Fred has often been accused of being slow, but he's not slow, he's meticulous.

SW: How did you and Murphy come up with an aesthetic?

PM: He and I and Pato talked about how we didn't want it to be a grim, dark, gray, sad looking movie. We wanted it to have sparkle—New York, Coney Island, summer. But at night, in the dark, we wanted it to be moody, powerful. Fred is a master of night.

SW: Rich, saturated colors coupled with pitch black. The diner scene with Ron and Angelica is a perfect example. Same with the Catskills at night.

PM: The Catskills in the daytime is beautiful, too. And it's funny. Those were tricky scenes for me.

SW: Why?

PM: I was being comical.[33] Would it work in this kind of movie?

---

33. Roger Simon, from the production notes: "The story's structure is based on classic farce form, as in Feydeau or Goldoni, yet it moves from hilarity to terror to despair in split seconds. Life is like that, from heaven to hell in an instant . . . "

sw: Could you talk a little bit about what you call "abstracting"?

PM: Abstracting is merely taking the essence of something, when you don't have a lot of money to do huge sets and all that, and trying to pull out of it something that tells you what it is without going to enormous lengths. Here I am doing Coney Island in 1951 and I was shooting it in 1988. The old Coney Island no longer existed, only scarred remnants of things like the Cyclone. The parachute jump was still there, but it was an empty thing, and it was broken. Many things were old and battered. Thank goodness Nathan's Hot Dogs was still there . . . But we shot all the interiors in Montreal. Pato *built* all that.

sw: Did that restrict you in any way?

PM: Well, no, because even if I shot them in New York, I probably would have built them on the set. It's much easier that way. That allowed me to make the picture rather quickly. In a real apartment, I would have had to worry about the noise, the change of light, and you can't move the walls, and all that bullshit. So Pato and I went to as many of the real places that existed in New York. We used the Tenement Museum on the Lower East Side as a guide. And then I described to him a couple of other apartments that I had lived in as a kid. Between all of that, he created these sets; Masha's, Herman's, the rabbi's—that was a house in Montreal we turned into a Riverside Drive apartment. The Catskills was an abandoned Boy Scout camp about half an hour outside of Montreal. [*Beat*] Pato was a genius. If he were around today, I would have a little more courage to do certain things. He was so matter-of-fact about his work. He wasn't like, [*Pato's Spanish accent*] "Oh no, what are we going to do?" [*Beat*] Pato . . .

sw: Throughout the picture, you're careful to give everyone a reaction shot. You go around the room or the street and check in with each character. You're very democratic with your close-ups. I think of that as a Mazurskyian touch.

PM: Well, you want, if you can, to keep them *alive*. You understand? When you're in a wide master—and I love wide masters, as you know—you want a close-up here and there. I don't think Woody does that very much, where you'll see someone just throwing a look. Think of Mr. Pesheles [Phil Leeds], for instance, when he's in the apartment. He knows something strange is going on. One of the great moments, which I never instructed them to do, was that moment when Pesheles and the yenta lady he's with walk in on Tamara and Hermann and the phone rings. Right then, for some reason, they all turned to look at the phone.

27. Enemies, A Love Story *(1989) Lena Olin and Ron Silver.*

I understood Herman turning and I understood Tamara turning, but Pesheles and the yenta? Why? I'm not sure. I never told them to, but it was wonderful. It made me realize that in those days, any phone call was an event. Who's calling late at night? [*Beat*] I've always been fond of masters, but as I began to make more films, I began to explore doing masters that moved, something that Woody does very well. But in my opinion, he cheats himself a little bit by not going in for coverage.

sw: Do you think he does that because he wants to be fast?

pm: No, no. I think it's just his style. And he's not concerned with giving you that information. The only reason to go in for a close-up is to give more information. Why are they saying that? What's going on? Oh, that's funny. Whatever it is.

sw: Did Lena Olin get Masha right away?

pm: I don't remember exactly, but I know that our rehearsal period was important to her. By the time it was over, Lena understood the Masha that I think is in that book. She had a combination of preparation, talent, and digging in for more and more and more.

sw: What's the digging in?

pm: The digging in is not being satisfied with a pleasant result.

sw: How do you know the difference?

PM: Instinct. It's just instinct. That's very hard to put into a jar and say, "This is it." You know, Kazan was famous for doing whatever he had to do to get the result he wanted, meaning he was willing to be cruel. I don't like to do that. [*Exploding*] "I don't call that acting! What are you doing? What are you *doing*? What's the matter—ACTION!" I've done stuff like that.

SW: Did Lena ever talk about Ingmar Bergman?

PM: She said one thing that pissed him off. She said once that I was the best actor's director she had ever worked with. It was in the Swedish papers and apparently Bergman took umbrage with that. But she says he's great, he's wonderful, he's brilliant, he's fantastic—and you better not be late or he'll fire you. One minute late and you're out. [*Beat*] Lena is a great actress, a trained actress, a no-nonsense actress. I haven't seen her now in years. She has no silliness about her work. She's there to do it. She's craft; she works at it. She prepares. She wanted to be her own stand-in when I shot *Enemies*. One day on the set she showed up standing in and I said, "What are you doing? The shot won't be ready for an hour." She said, "Yeah, but he's lighting *me*." I said, "Yeah, but you're going to get tired." She said, "No I won't. If I get tired I'll sit down." That's a different attitude. She has the passion. It's amazing, you know, it's a wonderful thing.

It's Masha who has the strongest effect on Paul. She's been a steady presence throughout our conversations, and even when we're not talking about her, we always seem to be evoking what she represents. Emotionally rich, conflicted, lusty, nutty—she is the extreme of life on earth, full of flesh and blood and Manischewitz, with a life force that can only come from living so close to death. Oh, and she's played by Lena Olin, which means Masha's beautiful. She evinces a human being that does to love what a prism does to light. Here are its refractions: She loves foolishly (like Bob and Carol), obsessively (like Blume), loyally (like Harry), naively (like Larry Lapinsky), sadly (like Erica Benton), terribly (like Phillip of *Tempest*), deliciously (like Madonna of *Parador*) and with the recklessness of a broken-hearted bulldozer. When he speaks of Masha, Paul trembles. Once, he cried. No one else in his movies does that to him.

Pauline Kael wrote, "Paul Mazursky has gathered a superbly balanced cast and kept the action so smooth that the viewer is carried along on a tide of mystical slyness. It's overwhelming."

Enemies, A Love Story, like Masha—like the best of Mazursky—fuses the disparate Wonder Wheels of pleasure and pain into one. The post-Holocaust pathology that motivates the film's comic mechanism renders absurdity and suffering indistinguishable. As a result, guilt, pain, and fear play like farce. The moment when Herman careens around the subway tunnels is unquestionably hilarious, but when we stop and consider what got him there, the laugh rounds out with despair. That's what happens when tragic characters are thrown into outrageous circumstances—Mazurskyian circumstances—provoked by too much love and too much freedom. In other words, people brought through hell to live in paradise.

Fred on Mazursky

Cinematographer, *Enemies, A Love Story*; *Scenes from a Mall*;
Faithful; *The Pickle*

I knew Fred Murphy was in town only because I ran into Paul and Betsy, who told me they were on their way to visit Fred and his wife Maryte at their boathouse in Venice, but had gotten lost and decided on breakfast instead. Betsy, I think, was glad not to sail, but Paul was anxious to resume the search. "Look at this day!" he kept saying to us. "This is a such a day! I want to be on that boat!" But it was getting late, and there was a game on, so the Mazurskys ducked out, I called Fred, and got lost on the way there. When I finally arrived, the sun was on its way down, so we sat in the galley. Fred drank coffee, and as it got darker, he went about the cabin turning on lights.

FRED MURPHY: Paul put a great deal of effort into finding locations for *Enemies*. That was most important to him. What it looks like, what color it is, what it says about the scene or feeling of the scene. The places we shot bear directly on how the movie feels when you see it. Planning the movie, it almost felt like one of those heist movies where all the crooks get together beforehand to figure out exactly what they're going to do at every moment. [*Edward G. Robinson voice*] "At 5:10, I'm going to walk through the door, at 5:13 you're going to open the vault . . ." We'd have a model and we'd have drawings and we'd talk through every single shot. We'd play out the whole movie.

SW: Where does Mazursky fall on the spectrum of preparedness?

FM: Very near the top, if not the very top. Ergo, we rarely shot anything that doesn't appear in the movie. Hardly anything was deleted. [*Beat*] Paul saw the movie in his head and it kind of matched the way I saw the movie in my head. I saw it as I was reading the script and I knew exactly what I was going to do.

SW: And what was that?

FM: Basically, I used a combination of two mixed colors: warm and cold. A great deal of the movie is made up of subtle variations between the two. If the light behind people is warm, the light on their face is slightly cold, or vice versa. And that was mostly gleaned by looking at a pile of old *Life* magazines. They all—partly because of age—were a little abstract: partly on the warm side, or partly on the green side. There's very little light that's really "correct," that you would call "Kodak," normal light, so to speak. That was my interpretation of the past. The past isn't white; it's a little rusty in places. [*Beat*] It gives it a slight sadness. Every scene in the movie is that way.

SW: And contrasty, too.

FM: Well, that's me. I mean, that's just a look I like that I tend to do from movie to movie. Although *Scenes from a Mall* is flatter and brighter, but even that's contrasty in its way.

SW: Is it harder to light comedy?

FM: Yes, yes . . . [*Thinks*] Actually, no. No, that's incorrect. It's *harder* to create a distinctive look in comedy, but in *Scenes from a Mall* I thought we actually did a little bit. The look of that film is actually more realistic than most comedies. I wanted a lot of sun in the mall because the mall was set in L.A., so I had to create big shafts of false sunlight, which was difficult to do because in a mall you're dealing with dozens of conflicting light sources. It took a huge amount of effort to get lights that could project that far and that clear and get them to hit the right places. [*Beat*] One of the difficult things about shooting in a mall is that there's glass everywhere, so you're always seeing the camera, the crew, and the lights reflected. So we were always trying to hide the camera. It became a little game.

SW: Do you have any memories of Woody on the set?

FM: Yeah, yeah. Woody's camera assistant, Mike Green, was the camera assistant I used on *Scenes from the Mall*, and they used to play chess in between setups while we were lighting. Woody's a very good chess player, and very funny, but not as funny as Paul. But no one's as funny as Paul.

SW: How would you characterize Mazursky's camera style?

FM: It's all very direct. He wants the camera to see what's happening in the moment. The shots are always very clear and well organized. There are only a couple of odd shots in *Enemies*. [*Beat*] Paul makes shots count. There's no excess.

SW: What keeps you collaborating with Paul?

FM: Well, Paul. [*Laughs*] Paul's certainly the most wonderfully entertaining director that I've ever worked with. Nobody has ever been as much fun, nobody as enthusiastic. He would sit in dailies and see a good shot and he would stand up and shout, "Fantastic! Marvelous! Spectacular!" and

28. Fred and Paul shooting Faithful, *August 1994.*

then he would make up words and shout them. [*Laughs*] Actually, we liked *Enemies* so much, we used to go to look at dailies early before we even started shooting. Of course, they hadn't synched the sound, so they were silent. But Paul would do all the voices! It was hysterical. And then we'd shoot and then we'd watch the dailies again at lunch with sound and then after the day's shoot, again at night. That's how much we loved *Enemies*. That's how excited we were about that movie. That hadn't happened before or since. [*Beat*] You know, directing is very stressful, but Paul never shows it. Some directors do. For them, there's a huge amount of anxiety and they show it, and it wears on the crew. That's a real gift of Paul's. He never communicates that. You know, that's an important part of directing that seems to be disappearing. The idea that the director, in a way, is throwing a big party and he has to make sure that everyone at the party is having a good time. You can't ignore that aspect of filmmaking. But you see, Paul is a producer as well as a director. And a very good producer, too.

sw: How did that manifest?

fm: He knew exactly how much time he needed, how much money he needed, and everything else the shoot needed. Because of it, you're never straining on a Mazursky set. You're never struggling. We were always comfortable and we usually finished early, like five or six o'clock. That's *early*. And he never added a million shots at the end of a day like a lot of directors do. He rarely went for those cockamamie insert ideas.

sw: No, no. There are very few inserts in Mazursky.

fm: He's not interested in that. He's interested in medium shots that play out where you're seeing people close enough to read them, but you're seeing groups of them. He likes close-ups of course, but basically he seems to like shots that develop where you see things happen. [*Beat*] I remember I got him in *Enemies* to move the camera in a little bit, that you could move in without having it follow anything. It's seemingly unmotivated, but obviously at that point you want to emphasize something that you can't see. He wasn't sure about it at first, but then he came around.

Fred Murphy has shot over seventy movies. About *Enemies* he said, "It was really one of the great experiences of my life."

Scenes from a Mall (1991)

Dr. Hans Clava: As Dr. Feingold-Fifer so brilliantly points out, the institution of marriage began when life expectancy was not even thirty years. Therefore a modern marriage has to be several marriages . . . to survive, you have to make a clean break from the past every six or seven years and remarry each other.

On Monday, July 30th, 2007, Ingmar Bergman died at the age of eighty-nine. That same day, Michelangelo Antonioni died. He was ninety-four. The next day, on my way to Mazursky's office, I picked up a copy of the *New York Times*, hoping Woody would remark on the passing of his idol—and he did. "I got the news in Oviedo," it began, "a lovely little town in the north of Spain where I am shooting a movie, that Bergman had died. A phone message from a mutual friend was relayed to me on the set. Bergman once told me he didn't want to die on a sunny day, and not having been there, I can only hope he got the flat weather all directors thrive on." "Did you hear about Bergman?" Paul asks without looking up. "Yeah," I said, "I have a feeling it ended for him more like *Cries and Whispers* than *The Seventh Seal*, but I really hope I'm wrong." "He was the greatest," Paul said. "The greatest."

SW: Did you read Woody's piece about Bergman in the *New York Times*?
PM: Yeah. It was *okay*.
SW: Just okay. I know. I was expecting more.
PM: You know, Woody didn't have too much time. It *just* happened. And Antonioni, too. On the same day.

Paul sighs and leans back against his chair.

Bergman . . . Jesus . . . You know, when you can cap it off with *Fanny and Alexander*, you're saying, "All along, if I wanted to, I could have done this too." And then he does it. And it's brilliant. It's overwhelming. It's so rich. Oh, God Almighty . . . what a wonderful, funny, charming, moving, powerful, great movie! That was the great thing about guys like Bergman and Antonioni. I really don't think they gave a shit. I was looking at *L'Avventura* the other day . . . I must have seen it five or six times already . . .

SW: How did it look?

PM: At times it's very good and at other times . . . well . . . you think you see the girl, and then you don't, and then maybe you do, and then . . . [*Paul yawns, stretching*] you start to think, "I wonder if there's any more meat-loaf in the fridge? It was pretty good last night. Better than I've had in a while. Maybe I should get some more now. I know it's only four o'clock, but I could eat." [*Beat*] I've got a doctor's appointment this afternoon and then I'm taking Tommy and Molly to dinner, so we should dot this. *Scenes from a Mall?*

SW: Yes.

PM: Okay. Well, Roger and I were hot off *Enemies*. What were we going to do next? I said, "Everyone lives in the mall. People spend their entire lives there"—don't forget, this was seventeen years ago—"So," I say to Roger, "lets do a movie and set the whole thing in a mall. And let's do our version of a Bergman movie, but a comedy." It would be like Bergman's *Scenes from a Marriage*, which I loved, and the whole thing would be very simple: We're in a house, we're in a mall. Simple. And my original head trip on it did not include Woody Allen and Bette Midler. We were not thinking *that kind* of comedy. I mean, when you know you're going to see a movie about Woody and Bette, you can't avoid going into it thinking you're going to see a comedy.

SW: It comes with baggage.

PM: Yeah, and it sounds very good commercially.

SW: Who did you want originally?

PM: I wanted Kevin Kline and Meryl Streep. Michael Eisner, when he read the script, got very excited. The rumor was out that Woody was looking for a payday. He needed some money and he knew if he acted in a movie, he would get something big.[34] And he got three and a half million, and so did Bette. So this movie that all took place in a mall, which I thought could be made for something like ten million bucks, was suddenly way, way up. When Eisner got word that Woody was interested he called Sam Cohn, one of my agents—

34. From *Woody Allen: A Biography*, by John Baxter: "Ever since *New York Stories*, Disney had been eyeing Allen as a possible addition to its company Touchstone, intended to give the studio some credibility in adult cinema by financing and releasing films outside its traditional kiddy market. Allen was interested. Orion [Woody's financier] was looking increasingly shaky, with limited capital and insufficient funds to distribute and promote its films, and he had already opened tentative negotiations with Twentieth Century Fox."

sw: And one of Woody's agents too?

PM: Yes, he was, but not anymore. Sam's getting out. He doesn't represent Woody, he doesn't represent Meryl, doesn't represent Kevin, doesn't represent Paddy Chayefsky because he's dead, doesn't represent Bob Fosse because he's dead . . . Arthur Miller died . . . Anyway, Sam called me to tell me that Eisner was going to call me and consider going for Woody. I said, "Jesus, I don't know. Woody? First of all, can he act it? There's a lot of shading in the part and a lot of emotional stuff." And Sam said, "Well, of course it's up to you, but I think he could do it. It's a big coup . . ." I said, "Has he read the script?" and he said, "No, but I could give it to him right now if you want." Then Eisner called me and told me the same thing essentially. I was getting a headache. Should I say yes? Eisner said, "If Woody agrees, I know we could get Bette Midler. What a combo!" And suddenly I must have seen dollar signs in my head. So I sent the script to Woody. Sam calls me back the next day—Woody gets right to it—and tells me that Woody loved the script. Sam says, "Woody has *a few* comments he'd like to talk to you about, but he'd like to do it." I said, "Well, what are the comments?" He said, "Well, I'll have him call you." So Woody calls me and essentially says, "I have three notes on pages thirteen, seventy-four, and eighty-six," and they were like minutiae. Little things like, "Would you mind if I didn't say *x* but say *y*?" I said, "Go ahead. As a matter of fact, say what you want. You can rewrite some of that stuff in your brilliant—" "No, no, no, no," he says, "you're the author." I said, "Would you really like to do this?" He says, "Yeah, I think it would be fun." I said, "What if I get Bette Midler?" He said, "It's your movie!"—something like that. So they get to Bette and she's worried, she's afraid of Woody in a way. She's never done a movie like this— it's only two people. I get on the phone with her and say, "Bette, don't worry. You were brilliant in *Down and Out* and you were brilliant in *The Rose*! Two completely different performances. You weren't the lady in *Down and Out* and you weren't the one in *The Rose*, so why the hell couldn't you do this one?" So she said yes. And Woody said yes. Two days later, there I was and it was no longer Kevin Kline and Meryl Streep. I had to get that vision out of my head—

sw: Now it's a whole new movie.

PM: Yes. With Kevin and Meryl it would have been deeper and sadder, more Bergmanesque, but with Mazursky's comedic undertones.

sw: Did Woody turn out to be a good enough actor?

29. Scenes from a Mall *(1991) Paul and Woody.*

PM: In my opinion, no. He's a great, great personality, a great director, and a brilliant writer. I'm glad I made the movie, I'm glad it was him, but what I'm saying is that it wasn't who I started out with. After talking to Sam Cohn and Eisner, I went with what I thought would make money. And so, my ego was pricked in a nice way. Woody Allen was going to be directed by Paul Mazursky? How could you not say yes? And Woody was very agreeable, and very pleasant, and did a very good job and I like the movie. It's just that when you make a movie and then the audience, near the end, doesn't quite go with it the way you wanted them to, it becomes . . . worrisome. Did I succeed?

SW: The trouble with the picture is, ironically, part of its charm. When you have Woody, you have certain blessings and certain limitations.

PM: It took me two months to convince him to wear a ponytail.

SW: What was that conversation?

PM: Well, he says, "What do you need a ponytail for? I'll have to put it on every day." I said, "Woody, it's nothing." He says, "Yeah, but . . ." I said, "Do me a favor. I'll shoot one test. If you hate it, I won't use it." So we shot a test and he said, "I don't love it, but I don't hate it. If that's what you want, then fine." And he wore the ponytail. I was trying to make him more L.A. Here's the guy who's known for saying that the right turn on red is the only thing we've got.[35]

SW: How were the rehearsals?

PM: The rehearsals were very, very interesting and a little scary because it's just me, Woody, Bette, and the script girl.

SW: Where did you rehearse?

PM: New York City. The props were there; I had a surfboard, which Woody could hardly pick up, [*Laughs*] their lunches were brought in, and we got to know each other very well, Woody and I. That's the best way to get to know him. He's not easy to know. It's not that he's mean-spirited or anything like that, it's that he has a lot of things on his mind. He's writing his next script, he's got a movie he's cutting, and he's starting the next. And on top of it all, I knew he was doing the movie because he's getting three and a half million bucks. But I had a good time with him. Read what he wrote up there.

Paul points to a framed picture beside his desk. It's a shot of Woody reading L.A. Weekly *in his dressing room. The inscription reads, "To Paul, pretty embarrassing when the director is funnier than the star [signed] Woody Allen."*

PM: And he means it! I'm a barrel of laughs on the set. I entertain the crew, I do impressions, and I keep everyone laughing.

SW: That's not Woody's style.

PM: Woody doesn't do that. [*Beat*] After he read the script, he called me up and told me that he couldn't cry. [*Laughs*] I had it written in there that his character cries. Woody said he couldn't do that.

SW: Was he speaking as an actor or as Woody Allen?

PM: I would say as both.

SW: You gave him more flexibility than the average star.

PM: And why would I force on Woody a persona that he can't do? You've got to use what they give you. [*Beat*] Bette was in awe of Woody. I rehearsed some of the scenes almost too much. At one point I thought, "Let's just start shooting already!"

SW: I've never heard you speak of too much rehearsal.

PM: Well, I had all this time and only two people. I couldn't rehearse every

---

35. In *Annie Hall*, Alvy says, "I don't want to move to a city where the only cultural advantage is being able to make a right turn on a red light."

scene because I really had to get them into a mall—I really wanted to get them into crowded, noisy places. One of the ideas of the movie was an extension of what I did in *An Unmarried Woman*, where I have one of the key scenes in the movie take place out on the street in public. Why didn't the guy choose to tell his wife that he was in love with another women in the privacy of their home? He couldn't do it. That's life. That I loved. That's a great choice.

sw: Both Nick Fifer [Woody Allen] and Martin Benton [Michael Murphy] do it out of left field.

pm: It's like this: You want to do it, you want to do it, you want to do it, you're dying to tell her, you don't know why, you lose your courage, now she's talking about going to the Hamptons—"we're going to do this, we're going to do that"—suddenly he loses it. "I gotta tell you this." And now suddenly they're out in public and all the truth starts coming out. I thought that was a great device, and it gave it a comic edge, which I liked. It's hard to explain the rest . . . I mean . . . Michael Eisner, when he saw the movie, said, "I really like this movie, but when they hit the Mexican restaurant, I was starting to get an itch in my pants," meaning, "I was getting a little bored." So I started thinking about shortening it a little. And I did.

sw: In the bathtub scene—I think, the best scene in the movie—Woody's character tells Bette's that he thinks it's the corniest things that have kept them together so long.

pm: Shooting them taking a bath together is one of the great moments in history [*Laughing*] because Woody's wearing a bathing suit down to his knees! Bette wears these breast things to keep them in, and I had a lot of foam for them, but every now and then a tit would pop out. It was the most hilarious—and Bette was fucking hilarious with, [*Shouting*] "How many more times do we have to do this, baby?" I said, "Bette, until we get it right." And Woody would say, "Is there any chance I could get out for a moment or two?" And he would stand up—the guy weighs about eighty pounds—dripping fucking wet . . .

sw: Did you rehearse that scene?

pm: Not really.

sw: I was surprised to learn how complicated the shoot was. It seems relatively straightforward.

pm: Here's the plan: the movie is budgeted at about twelve million. Something like that. I now get Woody Allen and Bette Midler. Then I think, wait a second, if Woody Allen and Bette Midler are going to get three and a half million each, I ain't going to work for a peanut. I probably made, for half the script, producing, and directing, three million. That's ten million dollars right there.

sw: An additional ten.

pm: With anyone else it would have been an additional seven. Six maybe, but not ten. Now, Woody will only shoot in New York. That's the caveat that I'm given. By the way, Woody said, "I don't have a driver's license." [*Laughs*] This is true! I was scared to death, but I say, "I'm willing to make the movie in New York, but I cannot do without the shots around the Beverly Center and shots driving around his house. I need a week in L.A." Woody finally agrees to do it if they will fly him on the company jet with Mia, thirty-seven kids, a couple of nannies, and put them up at the Bel-Air Hotel. And they agreed. Then I realize that if I were to shoot in a real mall, it would take me seven years to make the movie because I'd have to close it down, shoot at night, do this, do that, so I find a mall—and I'm very good at this, and with Pato by my side I was even better—I find a mall in Connecticut that looks great and can double for the interior escalator and elevator shots. And then we *built* the floor of the mall where most of it takes place. We built it at Astoria Studios.[36] There's another five million. Now the price of the movie has suddenly gone up to $18.5 million.

sw: And all because Woody was in New York.

pm: Yeah! Had we done the movie the way I wanted to do it and shot it somewhere around L.A., I could have found a mall way the hell out there and shot it. That would have saved the studio quite a bit of money, but they were willing to take this risk. They were very upset when the budget went up to $18.5 million and called me to say, "My God, what's happening?" And I'm very good with budgets. Always very tight, very precise. I said, "Look, you know my record. Every movie I made comes in on time." And then I explain to them everything I just said to you right now, that there's an additional six or seven million bucks in there. I said, "But

36. From the *Scenes from a Mall* production notes: "[Pato] Guzman was challenged to design an enormous two-story replica mall on a 26,000-square-foot stage . . . One hundred and fifty people—scenic designers, carpenters, dressers and prop people—worked for three and a half months to build and dress the huge reproduction of the Stamford Town Center." The film's aesthetic, equally involved, is also equally invisible. Director of photography Fred Murphy said, "We were trying to convey the commotion of modern life and deep emotions in the scenes. Therefore, I used 'chaotic' lighting—store window fluorescent, sunlight from atrium skylights, shadows of awnings, and reflections. All of this contributed to create a look of 'non-lighting.' "

you're welcome to come out to see what we've done." He asked me if I could shorten the floor of the mall that Pato had built. I said, "Well, then it will look like four shops." As it was, Pato had foreshortened the walkway so brilliantly that it looked like it's really long, but actually wasn't. Anyway, the guy came, he spent a week in New York, and at the end of the week he said, "Fellas, there's no way you can cut this budget. You were right." And I said, "That's it." [*Beat*] And by the way, I don't blame Woody and I don't blame Bette. When you're in the movie business and you've reached the point they had in their careers, they had every right to ask for that amount of money—and they had to get the same. When you see the salaries that people out here get now . . . I mean, I can't believe it. What happens now is that there are about twenty people who make twenty million dollars a picture. For the right person in the right circumstances, they'll work for peanuts, but basically, most of the movies you see now are burdened by twenty-five million dollars before they start. I guess the studios think it's worth it.

sw: We know that Woody likes his own productions to move quickly. Did you get a sense of his own directorial rhythm on the set?

pm: He did not like to do more than one take, if possible, but I would often do coverage. I would shoot a really good, long master with a lot of dialogue and a lot of movement, but then I'd want to cover a little on this side and on that side so I could go from one master to another in case I wanted something else from another take. Woody would say, "I'll never do it exactly alike, I can't do it again. I don't remember what I did. What if my hand was here and not there?" I said, "Let me worry about that. Just do it." And he did. In his own movies, Woody doesn't always punch in for a close-up when he should. It surprises me because Bergman, who Woody loves the most, makes epic movies about the face. You could say Bergman shows you in his characters' eyes what David Lean shows you with the desert.

sw: So when you're making your homage to Bergman, were you thinking about the importance of faces?

pm: No, I wasn't thinking about that. I was thinking about my kind of movie, where I wanted as much as possible to use the mall as the third character. The mall is a character in the movie.

sw: Yes, but the movie doesn't all take place in the mall. We open at the Fifer's house. Why not just begin as they're pulling into the Beverly Center?

PM: I wanted to know who they were first. That's all.

SW: You could've done that in the car.

PM: Yeah, I could've. In fact, if I was really short on money, I would have done that. They're both on the phone, they got two calls coming in—it would have been funny.

SW: And the kids, too. Why kids?

PM: I wanted you to know that they had children—that was very important to me.

SW: But *talking* about them isn't enough?

PM: You want to see them.

SW: Why?

PM: Because it makes the marriage sadder as it comes apart. It's more poignant and it's richer. [*Beat*] I would guess that a large percentage of the marriages that stay together stay together only for the children. You hear people say, "We were married for seventeen years, but then we got divorced when the kids grew up." They throw the line away like it's nothing. Now those kids are all in deep therapy because their parents *didn't* get divorced. My parents didn't get divorced because they couldn't afford to. That's a fact. Lower-middle-class Jewish people couldn't get divorced. If my parents had a little more money, they would have gotten divorced when I was about two. I lived in that house with my parents from 1930, when I was born, to 1950. So for twenty years they fought. The fighting was really all instigated by my mother who, I think, didn't really love my father. And I don't know whether he loved her. He was just a very simple person, very simple and kind, and he never finished high school. He was more like an animal that works hard that you want to give good water to at the end of the day and let it rest. That's all he asked for. And she attacked him every day when get got home. And it bothered me terribly. They should've gotten a divorce, but like I said, back then, that didn't happen. Now people get divorced at the drop of a yarmulke. But I don't think they loved each other. When he died, my mother called me and said, "He dropped dead on the floor." I was in L.A. acting in a television show and I got permission to go back for three days for the funeral. At the funeral, she tried to jump in the grave. Right into the hole. And I grabbed her and said, "You didn't love him." She said, "Stop it. It's none of your business. I love him now." [*Beat*] What's the point? Why are you asking me?

SW: It's all part of you.

PM: Well, the basic answer is, they loved me, but they didn't have love for each other. The arguments I saw shaped, probably, aspects of me that I don't know if I ever unearthed.

SW: What were they arguing about?

PM: Mostly they were banal. They were like, "Take your shoes off and don't get crap on the linoleum. Dinner's on the table."

SW: Sounds like a Jewish joke.

PM: Yeah, like the one I heard today. Son calls his mother and says, "Mom, how are you?" She said, "Terrible. I haven't eaten in thirty-eight days." He says, "What? Why? You have plenty of money. Why haven't you eaten in thirty-eight days?" She says, "I didn't want to have anything in my mouth in case you called me." [*Laughs*] Once, I saw my mother put a fork into his arm.

Paul's eyes widen. He leans in.

You heard me. [*Beat*] When it got that bad I would do jokes. I'd do comedy. I would be an eight-year-old stand-up doing imitations and in the middle of it all my mother would say, "Did you hear, Dave? He's so funny! He's a comedian!" I put that in *The Pickle*. The scenes with the little boy are right out of my life. The arguments between the parents, I have an argument on the Ferris wheel . . .

SW: That happened.

PM: Yeah.

SW: Did you make her laugh?

PM: Sometimes, a little bit.

SW: And your father?

PM: He tried to. She was always on the edge of the darkness. She would probably be labeled a manic-depressive today. Those pills they have now would have helped her a lot. I mean it. When I say dark, I mean *dark*. She would always tell me that I didn't love her. I would tell her that it wasn't true, but the truth was, she was right. I didn't love her. I did in a way love her, but I was afraid of her. It's complicated. It's complicated. That's all I can say. Enough.

SW: It's amazing to think that a childhood like that produced a man who has sustained a marriage of fifty-four years.

PM: It is, but I can't tell you why. I don't know. Sammy, I don't know, I don't understand. All I can tell you is that after fifty-four years of a great marriage with a wonderful woman who I love more than ever, who I'm crazy about, I have no explanation except that a miracle happened.

Somehow Betsy and I were talking about this yesterday. We said that life is divided by people who get *it* and people who don't. She has *it*.

SW: What's *it*?

PM: Irony. If you don't get *it*, you're in a sewer. Guys will tell you stories about the most gorgeous girls, but who ultimately don't get *it*. When you see them you say, "I'd like to plunder her body, I would like to do things to it that would get me into every prison in the United States, but please don't let me talk to her, please don't make me have a conversation with her on any level, I beg you please, I'd rather go to prison than have to talk to her—but let me ravage her!" So Betsy and I were talking about this yesterday. I was asking her, "Why did we get married? How did we stay together? Why did I meet this Southern girl in Greenwich Village?" and as we were talking, she told me that before she went to college, she went to something like twelve different high schools. She kept transferring out. I didn't know that. I thought, "Who is this woman I've seen every day of my life for fifty-four years? Who is she?" I loved it. I love her. Anyway, *Scenes from a Mall*.

SW: Back to rehearsals—

PM: Woody had his lunch delivered in a brown paper bag and sometimes there would be a Snickers in it. That's what he would have for lunch. He and Bette got along, but she was afraid of him a little bit. *It's Woody Allen*. A legend, a legend. She was in awe of him. What I was trying to do was get a balance out of these expert comic players so that I could find a reality. I didn't want it to be a farce, which is, I think, what his fans expected. Woody can do that kind of comedy, but I wanted something more like what he did in *Annie Hall* or *Manhattan*, and at times I think I got it. But don't forget, in this movie he plays somebody else. In this movie he plays a sports agent—

SW: A *Los Angeles* sports agent. In many ways, it's the opposite of Woody.

PM: Right. And he's not used to rehearsing, but she was.

SW: Did you ever rehearse outside, in the real world?

PM: Yes, I did take them to a real mall so we could walk around together and they could do the scene without me even watching. Woody wasn't really for it, but he did it.

SW: How could they be incognito?

PM: It was difficult. They often weren't spotted for like fifteen or twenty minutes. My son-in-law, Steve, who worked with me on the picture, was responsible for going up and down the elevator with them.

SW: What for?

PM: Woody's afraid of elevators.

SW: So what did Steve do?

PM: He would be lying down in the elevator out of the shot in case Woody got scared or nervous.

SW: I heard—maybe you can confirm this for me—that Woody had never been in a mall before.

PM: He told me that he had never been in a mall before. That's true. But I think that's changed now that Su—Soon—whatever her name is, because he's now making movies in England and Paris and Spain. He's traveling all over with her. I think something's happened with him.

SW: You make it sound like a good thing, but the fact is, he hasn't made a great movie since he stopped working with Mia.

PM: When was that?

SW: Well, *Husbands and Wives* was their last. That was 1992, a year after *Scenes from a Mall*. There were several good Woody Allen movies after that, but the overall trend has been down. Way down. *Hollywood Ending*? Do you think he reads the reviews?

PM: He doesn't read reviews. The people who are close to him tell you not to bother him with that stuff. I don't know how he is today, but that's how he was then. [*Beat*] I thought that *Husbands and Wives* was *very* successful. It is one of his best movies. I was very jealous that Sydney [Pollock] got that part, but he was brilliant in it. If Woody thinks I'm so funny, why doesn't he use me? You can put *that* in the book!

Paul stands up and throws his hands in the air.

I'm available!

Paul dances up to the desk and leans into the recorder.

Woody! Woody! If you're reading this, call me!

SW: How was Woody with notes? Could he execute them?

PM: Whatever I asked of him, he would basically do. But I never asked him to do things that I didn't think he could do. I would just ask him to change the staging a little or to shift the board to the other hand or to maybe take another two steps and end up over here so I could frame the shot better—

SW: Technical stuff.

PM: Yeah, and he was totally cooperative.

SW: So directing Woody is different.

PM: Well, yes, I would say . . . I'd say I directed with gloves on. A little bit. I know that I'd always be thinking a little bit to myself, "No one's ever directed this guy really. What do you tell him?" I wasn't going to use Methody things, you know, stuff like that. There were times when I would sort of *show him* how I wanted him to do it. That's when he said to me, "You know, you're a lot funnier than I am, you should play the lead in all of your movies." [*Beat*] Bette was terrified of him. I really think she was.

SW: There's a great deal of performance going on in the mall. The mime, the hip-hop group, the magician—it amounts to a kind of Greek chorus.

PM: I've always felt that mimes in malls, though amusing, can be a giant pain in your ass, particularly if you're in the midst of some kind of dialogue with your mate. They get on your nerves. Bill Irwin is a brilliant, brilliant mime and he made up all that stuff in rehearsal with Woody and Bette. None of that was scripted. I just had ideas for him. The question was, how do I keep the movie from being a total bore? So I added all those guys. They're very important extras. Getting them in New York was easy, because in New York, the extras are really actors, they're not afraid to do extra work. Whereas in L.A., you recognize the extras—you know all of them. It would ruin a movie for me. "There's the dress extra, there's the guy who has his own tuxedo . . ." In L.A., they all think it's beneath them, but in New York, it's a real art.

SW: There are so many adulterous men in your movies. What is it that continues to draw you back to this material?

PM: Well it's a question of who I'm making movies about. I'm not dealing with royalty, I'm not dealing with gangsters, I'm not making Westerns where you know the guys are screwing every hooker in town—adultery was commonplace—and in the gangster movies, they're always fucking their girlfriends behind the wives' backs. But I'm dealing with the middle class and upper middle class. If we were to take surveys, I would suspect, based on those around me, that people have all been married two or three times, and most have had affairs which have led to the breakup of their marriages. Now it's a fact of life. In the case of *Scenes from a Mall*, I just figured it would be more interesting and funnier if we found out that not just one of them did it, but so did the other. [*Thinks*] In the old days, people didn't seem to be as *needy*. You know, they were happy to go to work and go home and turn on the radio—

SW: If they were as needy, they certainly weren't as vocal about it.

PM: It didn't seem so to me. But not anymore. Especially in the cities. Now people you think would never get a divorce or have an affair, you found out they're splitting after nine years. [*Beat*] It's what Fellini and Truffaut and Antonioni made movies about. I guess that inspired me too. But it's hard to get it out of your mind. It's rich. Maybe doing these movies has kept me from running around. My fantasy life is always engaged.

SW: Woody's the same way. Adultery is all over his movies.

PM: Yes, but he *does it*. But I think he was faithful to Mia for a long time. It's only when the girl, Su—or Soon—it's only when she came into it that things got . . .

SW: And she came into it around the time of *Scenes from a Mall*.

PM: She's in it.

SW: Where?

PM: She's at the yogurt counter. She serves him yogurt.

SW: Right before he tells his wife that he's been having an affair?

PM: Yeah. Woody asked me to give her the job. But I should tell you I had no idea about any of that stuff, though I knew that he and Mia were having a hard time. She came to Connecticut for the week we were shooting [in the Stamford Mall] and they had a hotel and everything, but he'd go back to New York every night. He didn't stay.

SW: That's chilling.

PM: Why?

SW: I read that Mia Farrow suspected that the Soon-Yi affair began on those rides to and from the set of *Scenes from a Mall*.[37]

PM: That's a—wow. [*Beat*] There you go. [*Beat*] Mia was in Connecticut and Woody would say to me, "I've got to get back, I want to see the Knicks game, and I want to take a bath in my bubbly . . ." Something like that. He liked his baths. [*Laughs*] Soon-Yi was on the set a lot. Mia was there was the little kids, we set up a play area for them, and I got to know her. Later, I was cast as her husband in *Miami Rhapsody*, which was a real bit of irony.

SW: Why?

PM: Because I saw the trouble between them on the set of my movie. I didn't know there was anything with the girl [Soon-Yi], but I knew something was *off* with them. I could just sense the awkwardness of the way they were when they were together. Woody always wanted to get into the car and get back home . . . But here he is, years later—we're

---

37. "She [Mia Farrow] later surmised that . . . his [Woody Allen's] intimacy with Soon-Yi, if not their actual affair, began during long limo rides to and from Astoria . . ." (John Baxter, *Woody Allen: A Biography*.)

talking about seventeen years later—and it's lasted. And they have two daughters . . .

Paul stops.

SW: What's wrong?

PM: I'm just going over it in my head . . . I'm trying to remember it, but it's not easy . . . There we are in the hall of the hotel, it's me, Betsy, Woody, Mia, and the kids, a nanny . . .

Paul stops again. He gives up on the puzzle.

PM: I want Woody to direct me in a movie. It would be a crowning achievement in my career.

SW: Call him.

PM: I can't call him.

SW: Why?

PM: I just can't.

SW: Have Sam Cohn call him.

PM: I'll tell you what I'll do. I'll try to find a way to drop him a note. Me. No agent. "Woody, I really enjoyed so-and-so, and here I am looking at the picture of you in my office and you wrote on it that I'm the funniest guy whatever, when am I going to be in one of your movies? I come cheap. Best wishes, Mazursky."

If you cast Woody Allen, you're going to get Woody Allen. That's why you cast him. If you cast Meryl Streep, Kevin Kline, Lena Olin, or Art Carney, you'll get any number of characters in any number of novel combinations, but what you certainly won't get is Woody Allen. For that, you've got to get Woody. What he does, nobody can do better, but he wasn't up to *Scenes from a Mall*. What should be his big emotional scenes—when he tells his wife about the affair and then again when she tells him about hers—are lost to jokes. There is a fine line between human comedy, full of chiaroscuro, and tonal confusion, where the darks and lights fade into dim. Lesson learned.

And yet Eisner had a point: Woody and Bette make sense together. More than that, sometimes they're perfect. Vincent Canby wrote, "By no leap of the imagination do Woody Allen and Bette Midler seem to have been made for each other. He is a passionate skeptic, an observer. She is someone who participates with her entire being. They are pastrami on rye and a double-dip strawberry ice cream soda. Yet by the end of *Scenes from a Mall*, one of

Paul Mazursky's madder and more reckless comedies, these two remarkable acting personalities appear to be a perfect match, made in Southern California if not in heaven." Canby goes on to describe the kind of chemistry Erland Josephson and Liv Ullmann had in *Scenes from a Marriage*.

The net result is somewhere in between. Woody is wonderfully, woefully Woody, and Mazursky's movie surfs the wave of his irregular charms.

Albert on Mazursky

Costume Designer, *Harry and Tonto*; *Next Stop, Greenwich Village*;
An Unmarried Woman; *Willie & Phil*; *Tempest*; *Moscow on the Hudson*;
Down and Out in Beverly Hills; *Moon Over Parador*; *Enemies, A Love Story*; *Scenes from a Mall*; *The Pickle*

On the phone.

SW: Looking over your credits, I see you've worked with Paul more than you've worked with any other director.

ALBERT WOLSKY: Oh, by far, by far. It was a relationship of about eighteen years. The beauty of it was, he's totally collaborative and yet he has his own ideas. And he's very knowledgeable, especially about my field, which a lot of directors are not. Paul always involved me very early, even before pre-production, before, if you will, being put on salary. I didn't care about that, I cared about trying to figure out what is this movie going to be like. By the time we started, I would know what I was doing. We weren't talking about the costumes—that would come much later— we just talked about the movie and what attracted him to it and who he might be casting. He was very inclusive that way. It's very smart because he gives you such an edge. Finally, you're there for the director's vision, and if you have an edge on that, it helps you a great deal.

SW: What is your sense of the vision?

AW: Every movie has its own vision, but if I were to speak generally, I would say that it's about character. It's about the people. It isn't that he doesn't care what it looks like, he cares very deeply, but that's not where it starts. It's not, finally, what it's about.

SW: Would you spend much time on set?

AW: Yes. With Paul, I'm always on the set. At least for the beginning, as the movie is establishing itself. I like to start off every shooting day on the set, but I don't need to be there for all of it.

SW: What are you looking at when you're on set?

AW: Basically, I'm in a waiting mode. Once a scene gets moving, I'm done. I have no function there. But sometimes things change at the last minute and I'm needed. But Paul runs a very exciting set. He's funny, he makes everybody very comfortable, he tries to make everyone have a good time,

30. *Paul and Albert on location in Ouro Preto, shooting* Moon Over Parador, *1987.*

but he's also very serious, and very disciplined and he likes to work fast. Most sets are not fun.

sw: What does Paul want out of a costume?

aw: You mentioned, in your chapter, about the cape in *An Unmarried Woman* . . . What caught my eye in your paragraph there was that he liked it, and then he asked Jill if she liked it, if she was comfortable. And she said of course she was. That, you see, is the key. It is very important for Paul that the actors feel right in their costumes.

sw: But anything else seems counterintuitive. How else could you get a good performance?

aw: That's true, but he's just *checking*. He's just asking so that she knows he's asking. Paul knew what the answer would be.

sw: How do you know that?

aw: Because I do all that in the fittings. I will not send out an actor if he or she is uncomfortable.

sw: I don't want to speak for you, but if it's the job of the designers to tell the story—

AW: That *is* my job. It is my job to help visually tell the story. That's the *only* job.

SW: Well, that must be an incredible challenge when you're working with a filmmaker who values the invisible.

AW: It is, it is. You can do certain things, and control certain things, and just hope that nobody will get caught.

SW: Something that I've found with Paul is that he's reluctant to talk about the composition of his movies. I'm wondering how he communicates that to his designers.

AW: I don't know if we ever sat down and said, "Okay, we want to do it like a Renoir painting," or "Let's make everything green." I don't think I've ever worked that way with him. [*Beat*] We talk about light. We talk about—it's hard to explain—who knows what makes you go where you go? The thing about working with Paul for so long is that when you really know someone like that, things come more quickly. You can get to more places.

SW: What was your experience working with Sven Nykvist on *Willie & Phil*?

AW: Sven was fascinating to me. I remember Nykvist's screen tests were the funniest I've ever scene. To light it, he used a bare lightbulb! I asked him why and he said, "I'm making it as ugly as I possibly can so that I know what I'm up against." And he was right. It taught him what he could do and what he couldn't. That I liked.

SW: *Willie & Phil* is has a very organized look, both in set and costume.

AW: I remember one scene in that movie when I pushed a little too hard. It was the picnic scene. I did it all white, trying slightly to make it look old-fashioned. I tried to make it an homage to *Jules and Jim*. I also pushed a little bit too hard in *Tempest*, too. Everything I did was a little bigger. I was still using real clothes, but there was a definite *control* there. I tried to make New York brittle and rich and then go to Greece and make it colorful and loose. Cassavetes wears a kimono on the island. It's a real kimono, actually called a *yukata*,[38] and I used a little trick with it. I gave him bigger sleeves. You'd never know that, but somehow it changes his movements and it also changes the image. And in that respect, it's a stylization. No one's going to say to me, "Look what you did with those *yukata* sleeves!"

38. In Japan, the *yukata* is traditionally worn after bathing, making it appropriate for Phillip's beachy lifestyle. The garment also seems to serve the very functional function of covering Cassavetes's stomach, which had grown irregularly from his cirrhosis.

sw: What does that do to the character?

AW: It helped to give him more breadth of movement. In a way I thought it went back to Shakespeare's play. It made him majestic. And yet I didn't feel I should do a non-real kimono. [*Beat*] Real is important to Paul. But still, there are serious aesthetic decisions being made. At the end of *An Unmarried Woman*, when Jill's carrying the painting, I made her totally white because I felt the only color in the shot should be the painting she's carrying. No one's going say, "Look what Wolsky did with white and color," but it's how I work.

sw: What about the underwear?

AW: You've got to give Paul credit for the socks. I thought he was insane. I thought she was overdressed there, but it was wonderful. It made things go a little askew, but it was terrific.

sw: In *Enemies*, Angelica Huston's first scene seems a great marriage of makeup and costume.

AW: Oh, yes. Wonderful. She's *terrific* to dress because she really understood the character. She wanted to look almost grotesque in that scene. She knew what she was doing. You know she *got* me to that dress. It's not always me and the director—actors contribute a great deal. But with Angelica, I wouldn't have gotten there myself. She wanted this pinky-red and I thought, "Why?" And then I began to investigate it and I actually found a real authentic piece.[39] It's not something I would have given her to wear in that scene because my instinct would be to ask, "Where did that dress come from? How did she get it?" Realistically, she would have probably had a blouse and skirt.

sw: And Lena Olin?

AW: Lena Olin. As *Enemies* goes on, she gets lighter.

sw: I realize there are hundreds of actors I could ask about specifically. But Shelley Winters tops the list.

AW: She was a combination of smart and partly totally crazy, and yet I adored her. I adored her. Her neuroses were never from vanity, only from character. I would try something on her and say, "Shelley, it really doesn't fit. We can't even *close* it." [*Laughs*] She'd say, "Can't you let it out?" I'd turn it inside out and see that there was maybe an eighteenth of an inch on each seam, so I'd say to her, "No." "Well, can't we add

39. After reading this, Paul added, "She wanted that dress. It wasn't my choice. You know why? This is a guess: She wanted to look *hot*. She wanted to look sexy and alive because she had come back from the dead."

pieces? Can't we . . ." She'd put you through that. But that's the way she got to character. Paul probably wouldn't want her to behave any other way.

Albert Wolsky was born in Paris in 1930. Talking to him on the phone, you can almost hear the sound of good taste in his voice.

The Pickle (1993)/Faithful (1996)

Yetta: And never forget it, Harold. That's what a human being can make you feel.

"Okay, read it back to me."

Alicia clears her throat. "Dear Woody," she reads, "I imagine you are somewhere in Europe, Canada, or New York. Hope you are all well. Somehow the urge to appear in a Woody Allen film has entered my brain. I'm available. Happy days, Paul Mazursky."

Paul leans back in his chair. "Good," he says, "Send it, darling." She exits as Jeff Kanew enters. "The boys are here," he says, sitting. "I consider this like the neighborhood candy store—Doc's. Just drop by Doc's and see who's hangin' out." Kanew twists open a bottle of Arrowhead and puts his feet up on the coffee table. He has a gentle face and a white beard, putting him somewhere between rabbi and cherub. Suddenly, Kanew's dog appears out of nowhere and jumps onto his lap. It barks and Mazursky turns away from his e-mail.

PM: I haven't had a pet in so many years because the bitch I'm married to is allergic. We used to have dogs and cats and all kinds of pets and then one day she got really allergic and went to an allergist who told her, "You have to get rid of your dog." She came home and told me and I said, "What do you mean, 'get rid of it'?" She said, "We've got to get rid of it." I said, "But I love the dog." She said, "Do you love me or do you love the dog?" There was a long, long, Jack Benny pause. So Jill came in and I said to her, "Jill, honey, mom wants us to get rid of Bogie." Jill says, "Well, if you get rid of her, I'll kill myself. I'll run out in the street and jump in front of the car." She was thirteen. Back then, Betsy had been seeing a psychologist named Murray, so I said, "Let's go see Murray." I didn't know what to do. I wanted to get rid of the dog because I love my wife, but I didn't want Jill to kill herself. [*Laughs*] So we go to see Murray. Fine. A hundred and twenty-five dollars an hour. Three of us in therapy. Murray tells us, "Tell me what's going on." Betsy says, "It's very simple: I went to the allergist and I'm dead if they don't get rid of the dog." Jill says, "It's very simple: I'll kill myself if they get rid of the dog." Murray says to me, "What about you, Mr. Mazursky?" I said, "I don't want either of them to die. I want them to live." [*Laughs*] He said, "But what do you want to do about the dog?" I said, "I'm confused. I love Jill, I love Betsy . . . and I *really* love Bogie." He asked us where we slept and we told him that Jill sleeps upstairs and the dog sleeps with us downstairs. Murray says, "I don't know if it will work, but just to start—take it easy now—change rooms with Jill. Paul and Betsy go to Jill's room and Jill, you go down to where your parents and the dog stay." Meanwhile, I'm thinking to myself about how the bedroom upstairs has a tiny fucking bathroom. Betsy says, "I don't feel like walking up a flight of stairs, but I'm going to try it. And if that doesn't work, I'm going to kill *myself*." Murray says, "Alright." So we try it—and it's a tiny bit better, but not much. A week later, the dog fell into the pool, Betsy took him to the vet on Melrose and Robertson, and he never came home.

JEFF KANEW: Betsy killed the dog?

PM: Well . . .

SW: What did Jill do?

PM: Despair and crying. [*Beat*] So I started thinking last night, if Betsy passed, I could finally get a dog and a cat. Maybe two dogs. Because I'm telling you it's awful. Last night I saw a commercial for dog food and I almost starting crying. If my wife dies, it will be a small sadness compared to the great joy I will have with my new pets. Okay, what are we up to?

Paul gets up and joins Kanew and me on the couch. He lifts the dog onto his lap.

SW: *The Pickle.*

PM: Oy.

KANEW: [*Standing*] See you guys later.

PM: Stay. You can stay.

KANEW: I want you all to myself or not at all.

PM: Wait, are you the guy I met at Rage last night?

KANEW: Yeah. In the back room. That was me.

PM: [*Laughing*] Alright, buddy. Come over for dinner tonight if you like. Don McAlpine's in town. He'll be there.

Kanew gets up and the dog leaps out of Paul's arms to follow.

PM: You want to leave the dog here?

KANEW: No, you'll kill him.

Kanew walks out. The dog follows.

PM: Did I tell you about *Shadows on the Hudson?*

SW: No. What?

PM: Okay, Michael Gruskoff called me up—he's one of the guys from the table—he said he's got a script based on an Isaac Singer novel. It's called *Shadows on the Hudson.* It's Singer's last novel, I read it years ago. And it's a wonderful script. Anyway, they've offered it to me, but they have no money. So I sent the script out yesterday to Daniel Day-Lewis. If he wants to do it, we have a good shot at getting the money. It's a fantastic part for him. But let me tell you, it's very, very, very hard to get made. It's Singer at his craziest. Hertz—the Daniel Day-Lewis character—is married and has two children. He's forty-six. He was a child prodigy in Europe, a chess genius and a math genius. Now he's in America and he has very little regard for the kids. And his cock never stops. Two mistresses: One's a younger woman, one's older, both very hot. He's a little crazy, like Herman from *Enemies.* [*Beat*] God, I want to do this movie . . . I can't get crazy yet, but we'll see . . . Okay, go ahead.

SW: Okay, *The Pickle.* This is the first film since *Willie & Phil* that you wrote alone.

PM: What would happen, I wondered, if I had to take the worst job in the fucking world, the kind of movies that open big on Friday? That's how the idea for *The Pickle* came about. And then Preston Sturges got into my head. I wanted to try to do it in that style, with lots of scenes of overlapping dialogue and confusions. I wanted to show how this director, played by Danny Aiello, goes from suicide to joy. That's what moviemakers are—we're manic-depressives.

SW: You cast Danny Aiello. A very good actor, but he didn't convey that quality.

PM: Danny is a great actor. He was great in *The Purple Rose of Cairo* and *Do the Right Thing.* But I never really thought he was perfect for *The Pickle.* The part required a more worldly guy. And that's not Danny. Danny's real New York. When I cast it, I tried to get them to let me use Donald Sutherland, but they wouldn't go for him.

SW: Sutherland makes sense. In several ways, Harry Stone is a continuation of Alex Morrison.

PM: Yes, in some ways. *Alex* twenty years later.

SW: Who else did you consider?

PM: I went for Elliott Gould, but they wouldn't go for that either. Then I said to Frank Price [at Columbia], who had green-lit the movie in thirty seconds, I said, "Frank, let me play the part. Even Woody Allen thinks I should play the lead in my own movies." He said no.

sw: Did you fight him on it?

pm: A little bit, but I didn't make it an ultimatum. If there is a sadness in my career, it's that I never had an opportunity to play a big part in one of my own movies. One day I said to Frank, "You know, Frank, we *could* save a million dollars. I'll do it for nothing. And you know I can do it. I'm good." He said, "We need a name." So we got Danny Aiello, who was hot at that time, and we paid him a million. And Danny is *good* in the movie . . . the only thing is . . . it's like . . . he's not naturally convincing as that person.

sw: At what point did you realize this?

pm: Early on. Early on. But I tried to wipe it out of my head and *feed him* as much juice as I could about what was there. I would discuss what it was like to live in Europe. Danny had been to those places, but he had never *lived* there. [*Thinks*] The most difficult thing in the whole movie was trying to come up with a script for the movie within the movie, the one about the pickle. Frank Price was not one hundred percent pleased with that part of it, so I kept writing it and rewriting it. That stuff doesn't totally work.

sw: Do you still have the fears that Harry Stone has?

pm: No, I really don't. I'm content in my life. I'm not worried about it. The last few years for me, as for many filmmakers who I know at this point in their life, have been difficult. To go around with [unmade scripts] *Pictures of Fidelman*, *An Honest Man*, and *Nirvana*, and get very close with some of them and then not see it happen—that's hard. I don't want to pretend that I don't care, that it doesn't mean anything. It's a pain in the ass, but you've got to have a sense of humor about it or you'll go crazy. You really will.

sw: To what extent did the reaction to *Scenes from a Mall* lead into ideas for *The Pickle*?

pm: It's a good question. *Scenes from a Mall* was an American box-office failure. So after the movie came out, I walked around town with a scarlet letter on my chest. You did something bad. You went and made a very expensive, twenty-million-dollar movie with Woody Allen and Bette Midler and nobody went. You should be castrated. Maybe you should just be put to sleep. After you bomb, the studios should put you away and give you a little injection—like Bogie the dog. There was something of this going on in my head, which might have led me to *The Pickle*. I whipped out the script pretty fast. The only thing I was having trouble with, like I said, was writing the movie within the movie. I probably should have gotten a science fiction guy to help me write that part. So I came up with what I thought was funny stuff . . .

SW: But it's supposed to be a piece of shit movie?

PM: No, it's more than that. It's a fantasy about what a better world can be. That's what it's about.

SW: How did you come to cast Clotilde Courau?[40]

PM: [*Sighs*] I went with the casting director to Paris to cast the part. The casting director had set up appointments with me for about twenty French actresses at a gorgeous hotel. The concierge began to think either that I was a sex maniac or a pimp because the best pussy in Paris came up to my room beginning at 10:30 in the morning. Some would drink wine with their breakfast. One of the girls I saw was Sophie Marceau, who is, I think, the most beautiful woman I have ever seen. Gorgeous beyond belief. Anyway, I had many, many choices and the girl I chose was in many ways the least attractive, but she had a fearless attitude that I liked. But I told her, "When we get to the bed scenes, we're going to have nudity." She said, "Fine." And when I got to the bed scenes she wouldn't do it. So both she and Danny Aiello were uncomfortable with the lovemaking stuff. Danny was uncomfortable just taking his shirt off! They were both inhibited and I was trying to have wildness in there.

SW: What could you do to help them around that? Was there anything?

PM: I tried to get her to do it with her bra on, but it wasn't the same. I don't think I did the best job of directing. I think I probably should have screamed at them or done a Kazan-like thing. I didn't do it.

SW: It's ironic because you excel at creating an atmosphere where actors who play lovers can really let themselves feel free enough to make the wildness seem realistic.

PM: It was difficult. You know, I hate to talk about anything I've done in a negative way. I like *The Pickle*. There's a lot about it I like. But when you make the kinds of movies I make, which are movies about humans, acting becomes the biggest factor, and when you cast wrong—this I've told you many times—you're in big, big trouble. I've always thought the

40. Clotilde Courau became the Princess of Venice in 2003 when she married Prince Emanuele Filiberto, the grandson of Umberto II, the last King of Italy.

least profound emotion you can have is self-pity. It doesn't do you any good. It takes you down a road that leads you to therapy and more therapy, then you change therapists, then your therapist dies, then you have more self-pity, then you find another therapist and by now you're forty-eight years old and you're wondering, [*singing, as Peggy Lee*] "Is that all there is?" Self-pity gets you nowhere. So you say to yourself, "I've got to make the fucking movie." You wake up in the morning and you realize there are a certain number of shots you have to make and you've got to stop saying to yourself, "How would it be with somebody else?" You've got to make do with what you have.

SW: And you even had Michael Caine at one point.

PM: Michael Caine would have done it. I met with him. He said, "I like the script very much—move it to England and I'll do it. I can't do an American accent." I could have done it and Michael Caine would have been . . . Jesus Christ . . . *really good*. What can I say? I wanted to do it in Brooklyn and that was it. Look, I don't want it to seem like I think Danny Aiello and Clotilde failed me. They did pretty good, but . . . I wanted a Lexus and I got a Mercury. They needed a little more sexual daring.

SW: They verbalize it, but you don't see it.

PM: Right, right.

SW: Let's talk about Shelley then. This was your third and final collaboration with her. Did she show you a new side of herself?

PM: We were like old friends by then. And we were real friends. In fact, I walked into her bedroom and saw her naked. [*Laughs*] I ran out. I was scared, Sammy, I'm telling you it was frightening. Anyway, her back was bothering her when we were going to shoot that scene out on the boardwalk. Her back, and her knees—everything. So she didn't want to have to walk up and down that thing ten times for ten takes. I offered to put her in some kind of a car to drive her down, but she agreed that the scene would be much better if we were walking. And she did it.

SW: In pain?

PM: Yes, and she did it. Five or six times. She always scores for me. Look, you want to talk about *Faithful* today too?

SW: Yeah.

PM: Okay, but my only problem is, I don't know whether to go into all that . . . *shit*.

SW: What shit?

PM: The Bob De Niro shit. It's all garbage. It's so distasteful. It might . . . I don't know . . .

31. The Pickle *(1993) Danny Aiello and Shelley Winters, Coney Island.*

sw: Let's start and see where we go.

pm: Okay. What would you like to know?

sw: This was the first script you directed that you didn't write. How did you come to accept?

pm: I thought the script was a very clever black comedy about jealousy and I liked the idea of making a movie that was mostly in a house. How could I make it move? I met with Bob [De Niro] and Jane [Rosenthal]. Their company, Tribeca, was producing the film. They were delighted to have me. And we went to Cher.

sw: Right away?

pm: Right away. And she said yes. We had a very good meeting with her. The only question was who was going to play the husband. And I came up with Ryan O'Neal. Bob loved the idea, predicated on meeting him, you know, to see if he was okay, because there were a lot of stories. Cocaine. Whatever. Whatever. We met at the Bel-Air Hotel where Bob had a wonderful suite. And it was all great. Ryan was great, De Niro was great, I was great, Cher was great, and we were off and running. The first snag came in the making of the budget. They said they wanted to make the movie for about four million, but I wasn't going to agree to a number until I had a budget made. So I had a budget made and it came to about ten million. That's when Jane Rosenthal called to have a meeting with me. "This is ridiculous," she said. "We can't do this movie at ten million dollars. Who *made* this budget?" I went over the budget very carefully with her, explaining in detail every element—I'm very good at this. She couldn't believe it and told me she was going to make her own budget. There was tension there. But budgets often cause tension. So she got a lady who specialized in low-budget films and her budget came out to $10.2 million.

sw: Great.

pm: That was very funny. When you're making movies, you're constantly in wonderland craziness. Anyway, Jane Rosenthal agreed to the $10.2 and everything was going great. I got Fred Murphy for camera, I got a great Steadicam guy, I got Ellen Chenoweth to cast it, I got Jeffrey Wright— that wonderful actor from *Angels in America* . . .

sw: Allison Janney . . .

pm: The best people. We had a great deal of difficulty finding this house, but eventually we found it in Purchase, New York. An extraordinary house. Completely empty.

sw: Are all the interiors shot in the house?

pm: All of it. We put the furniture in. We decorated; we did everything. No soundstage.

sw: Why was it so hard to find the house?

pm: I was looking for sight lines that I felt would lend themselves to great shots. Once I found the house, I pre-shot the whole movie on video. I mean, *basic* scenes. Figuring out how I go from room to room, up the stairs, down the stairs, angles, outside . . . I storyboarded it on video. Rehearsals went well and the movie went very well. We were all on cloud nine. I'd get calls once a week or so from De Niro. "Fabulous," he said, "great work."

sw: What is De Niro like as a producer?

pm: All he did in this movie was approve Ryan. He came around to the house maybe once during the entire shoot. And he saw the dailies. When it was over I thought we had a small masterpiece, a treasure. Everybody was excited, everybody was on board, and the picture was cutting like velvet. I found the music—some of my favorites—Dinah Washington and Sarah Vaughn, and we were ready to test it. That's when I started hearing a rumor that *Cher is cutting her set of dailies*. Wow. They had given her an editor.

SW: Had Tribeca seen what she was doing?

PM: De Niro saw it and he didn't say anything to me afterward. I don't think he liked it. The editor, Nick Smith, had flown up to San Francisco to show it to Bob and his girlfriend. Nick said he didn't smile once. He didn't laugh. I said, "I guess he hated it." Nick said, "I don't know." That's when I knew there was going to be trouble. I was kind of insulted that no one had called me to give me their reaction. So we tested it in New York and it got like an eighty or something. I don't know the exact chronology of what happened after that, but the next thing I know, I'm meeting with De Niro and Cher in Bob's house here in L.A., and she's saying that she wants to fully recut the movie and I tell her absolutely not, out of the question. "You're not allowed to touch my movie," I tell her, "you're an actress." And I say to Bob, "Would you want her to recut *Godfather* for you?" I remember all this vividly: De Niro kept making me very good cups of espresso with a lot of sugar. I said, "Cher, what happened?" I felt betrayed. She wrote me a letter saying, "I know you think I don't like it because of the way I look. Well, it's not because of the way I look." So she's had work done! So what? I thought it was very good for the movie. She's playing a fifty-year-old alcoholic suicidal! So what happened was, she and I got into a very big argument because I found out she was cutting the movie behind my back and I threatened to go to the *New York Times*.

SW: Aren't there guild rules against actors recutting the movie? Don't you have that in your contract?

PM: Of course. They're not allowed to do that.

SW: Did you go to the Directors Guild?

PM: The DGA, in my opinion, was weak. They said, "Wait, wait, wait before you go to the *New York Times*, because once you go to The *New York Times* it's a *fait accompli*." It was crap. They were scared. They should have come down on my side immediately.

SW: Isn't that their job? Isn't that they're supposed to do?

PM: That's what I thought. [*Beat*] Then came something else. The Weinsteins, who had Miramax, offered me a hundred thousand dollars in cash for my version in Europe. They would distribute Mazursky's cut over there and over here, in America, they would see Cher's.

sw: Did you ever see Cher's version?

pm: Yeah, on video. It was ridiculous.

sw: How so?

pm: No point in me going into it, you've just got to take my word for it. It got a lower mark in the tests. The big argument was she refused to do publicity for my version of the movie. That's when Bob said to me, "What do you care? Let her have her way. It's no big deal." I said, "Bob, you can't do that." And we got into an argument at my house that was pretty bad. I actually asked him to leave. The next day he called me to apologize. I said, "I accept your apology." He said, "No, I want to come over to your house and apologize to you." I said, "You don't have to." Betsy was waving to me, "No, no, no." Then De Niro says, "I'm parked in a limo across the street." I said, "Okay, come in." So he came in and put his arms around me and kissed me on both cheeks, and unless I'm crazy, he kissed me on the mouth too, which is the kiss of death. [Laughs] The Godfather gave me the kiss of death. Young Vito Corleone. He said, "I'm really sorry, Paul." I said, "It's okay." And in a matter of about five or six minutes, he slowly got back to where we started with all the trouble, and I said, "Bob, don't go there!" And that was the end of it.

sw: But Cher still had her cut. How did your version get released?

pm: Okay. Norman Jewison, an important figure in the Directors Guild, had gotten word of what was going on. Norman came to my aid. I don't know why, except that he's a wonderful man. He called me from Canada and told me that he had heard from Nick, the editor, what had happened. And Norman decided to send a telegram to twenty-five famous directors, describing what De Niro's company had done. All twenty-five of them signed it. When Tribeca got copies of the telegram, they backed down and reinstated my cut.

sw: So Jewison saved the movie.

pm: Yes. It all ended okay because they released my version. I saw some of it on TV the other night and I thought parts of it were very interesting. I kind of liked it. I wouldn't say it was a typical Mazursky movie, but it is filled with a lot of funny, wry stuff. It's fun. Had the studio sold it right, I have to believe they could have had a better experience with it at the box office.

sw: So this goes down as the single worst experience of your career?

pm: Yes. The disappointment for me is that I was very proud of the picture, and I thought it was nice that I made a movie that I didn't write, that I did it for Bob De Niro, that I did it for a New York company, and it ended with a bad taste. That was not a nice feeling. That's all. Life goes on.

The Pickle doesn't work. What happened? We never get inside Harry Stone. Mazursky is revisiting the vast career behind him, but rather than deliver it up with new insight, he just replays the oldies, now paler by comparison. We're looking at copies. Compare, for instance, the Brooklyn of *The Pickle* with the Brooklyn of *Next Stop, Greenwich Village*. Compare the performances of Shelley Winters. Compare the portraits of the artists.

Mazursky works best on a micro, not macro scale (his micro is macro), but in *The Pickle*, his thematic reach (art, death, divorce, lust, fatherhood, childhood, Hollywood) overwhelms his attention to the moment. *Faithful*, on the other hand, has its share of well-attended-to moments. Ironically, most of them are Cher's. Her handle on lonely housewife depression is so convincingly rendered—glassy distant eyes that say, "I'm not here"—it's easy to glimpse the person beneath the face tuck, and she crackles with glib wit.

But outside of Cher, *Faithful* struggles to pull its madness back to earth. When the banter comes this quickly, an actor needs something stronger to stand on than a witty riposte—he needs a soul. Palminteri is too wound up in his familiar persona to reach for specifics, and Ryan O'Neal is almost not there. Like Raul Julia in *Moon over Parador*, they play bad guys—not Mazursky's true line of interest.

Mazursky knows nothing will stay as it is for long. His best films prove that in the daily spin-cycle of life, funny and tragic alternate so rapidly they can appear interchangeable. But in *Faithful*, they alternate so rapidly, they lose genre. By the end of the film, we've surfaced in a drama that bears a stronger resemblance to *Sleuth* than *An Unmarried Woman*, making *Faithful* the only Paul Mazursky film to feature a plot more complex than its characters. And without a lick of love in sight, what's Paul doing there in the first place?

Winchell (1998)/Coast to Coast (2003)

Barnaby Pierce: Open comedy and secret anger. Never quite centered. Make any sense?

Paul's decked out in vintage Mazursky: a T-shirt with *The Godfather* logo worn under a silk Chinese vest, topped off with a panama hat. "Okay, buddy," he declares, "after what you wrote about *The Pickle*, I'm going to take you on today." He smiles. "By the way, I got a letter from Woody. It was very sweet. Very sweet. He said I'll be in his next movie in the States—if possible. Right now he's making a movie in Europe because that's where he's getting his funding." A few moments later, Paul gets a phone call. Daniel Day-Lewis has turned down *Shadows on the Hudson*. A few moments after that, he's moving on.

PM: There's just something about me that doesn't quite get depressed. I say, "Fuck 'em."

SW: But you've been depressed. After *Alex in Wonderland*, right?

PM: Yes, it was the bad reviews. That hurt. That was my depression. But I came out of it with renewed vigor and with the realization that I was an American and couldn't live as an expatriate. Wait, now I gotta call Gruskoff. [*To Alicia*] Darling, could you get me Mike Gruskoff please? [*To me*] Watch how I handle this.

We wait for Alicia's cue.

ALICIA: Okay, Paul. Mike Gruskoff for you.

Paul picks up the phone.

PM: Okay, that was Gene Parseggian. Daniel Day-Lewis passed. He said, "*Shadows on the Hudson* is not for Daniel Day-Lewis," I didn't ask him why—there's no point—he wished me luck with it, and that was the end. Next. [*Listening*] We'll talk later about whether we should go to someone else or if we should just let [Jeff] Berg go out with it. [*Beat*] No one expected Daniel Day-Lewis to do it. Marty had to chase him for almost a year to get him into *Gangs of New York*. He is always a long shot. Don't forget, we also have Bob Downey, Viggo, Liev Schreiber, Alec Baldwin ... Let's think about it. I'll talk to you later. Bye-bye.

He hangs up.

Next. *Next.* It's like meeting a woman: Either she wants you or she doesn't. There's no use trying to talk her into it. If she doesn't see it, you don't want her. And that's it. It doesn't have to depress you. [*Beat*] But I'd be lying if I told you I've been thrilled for the last decade. No one who has been turned down the way I have will be running and twirling and leaping for joy. By the same token, I've got such a wonderful life, such a wonderful family, and so many interests, *and* I see the cosmic joke, that to take it too seriously would be to take it into nonsense. Who's turning us down? Is it the lord of the world? No! It's some agent or some publisher or some financier . . . So what does it mean? When you've had the kind of successes I've had, you know it's a mixture. But you, when you haven't had any, you might say to yourself, "I'm wasting my time. Maybe I don't have it. Maybe I should listen to them." Anyway, that's it . . . Let's talk *Winchell. Winchell* was written by Scott Abbott.

SW: How did you get the script?

PM: A young agent at ICM called me and said, "I don't represent you, but I read this script and I think it's perfect for you. May I send it?" He didn't even tell Jeff Berg, who was his boss. So I said to him, "Send it." I read it and when I finished the last page, I called the kid back and said I wanted to do it. He said, "I'll call Jeff." From there, the deal was consummated very quickly. It was clear to me that they were going to spend money. The budget was ten million.

SW: Was Tucci your first choice for Winchell?

PM: The first person we went to was Alec Baldwin. He read it and called me and said that he wanted to work with me but didn't think the part was right for him. But I liked the fact that *he* called me, not his agent. I don't remember who it was who thought of Stanley Tucci, but Tucci said yes. And when Paul Giamatti read, I was thrilled. I told him I wanted him on the spot. He was unknown then. Now he's a star.

SW: For whatever reason, Stanley Tucci is evocative of the thirties and forties. Any idea about why that is?

PM: He has tremendous energy. After about a week's rehearsal, he shows up one day with laryngitis. He and I have had conversations on the phone, everything was great, but he shows up [*mouthing*] and he can't talk. So he takes out a pad of paper and writes out, "Let's rehearse. I can't talk, but I'll just move my lips." Now I'm nervous. I've not yet heard the voice of Walter Winchell. Stanley had been working with the best

32. Winchell *(1998)* *Stanley Tucci as* *Walter Winchell.*

voice coach in New York, he had been studying the recordings of Winchell, but I had no idea if he could actually do it. Three, four days go by. The doctors told him not to shoot. The day of shooting comes. Tucci walks in, sits down in front of the microphone, and [*as Winchell*] "Good evening Mr. and Mrs. America, this is Walter Winchell . . ." It was beyond perfect. I almost kissed him. It was thrilling to watch him work. *Thrilling.* The thing is, unless you hire Jack Nicholson, you never really know what you're going to get until you get it. And there I was thinking, "Am I going to get it?" But I got it. I got it. [*Beat*] Stanley's a big-time actor. He's got what I call "the chops"—Richard Dreyfuss has it too—it's energy, intelligence, and passion. They can stoke the fires. With them, you don't just get a good performance, you get the inner life of the character.

SW: It's a terrific ensemble. All the way down to Christopher Plummer as Roosevelt.

PM: Brilliant. Brilliant. He was brilliant. Of course, I was in awe of him. There was one moment when he was moving his wheelchair around the room and he stopped the chair to make a really important point and he stopped it right where the key light was *every time*. He knew how to do that. I didn't tell him. What a brilliant actor and what a nice man. What a modest man. "Is that alright?" he would say, "Can I do anything else for you?" He was just spectacular. He's a prize.

SW: What appealed to you about *Winchell*?

PM: First of all, I liked the script. Secondly, I really like the idea of doing a movie about this son of a bitch, Walter Winchell. Nobody came to his funeral but his daughter. Nobody. And he screwed around constantly, he was miserable to his wife and kids, and he was, in a way, the most powerful man in America. Roosevelt valued him.

SW: *Winchell* has a tempo that's different from any of your other movies. It's always moving, always rushing ahead, where a picture like *An Unmarried Woman* really took its time.

PM: I wanted it to be like *Winchell*. I wanted it to have that staccato feeling of his broadcasts.

SW: Your long scenes of the 1970s have become peppy scenes of the 1990s. That's the main reason why I have a hard time finding Mazursky in this movie.

PM: Well, I didn't write it, it's not about me, and I didn't impose my sensibility on it. I may have imposed it in terms of the way I work with actors, where I'm always looking for those intimate, small moments that define what people are like, but what movies don't often show you because they're in such a hurry. But there are moments like that in *Winchell*. We have moments like that—just a look, a glance. But it's not about me.

SW: How was working for HBO?

PM: Great. It's an excellent company. They help you get the best. The reason they can be as good as they are is because it *doesn't* go to theaters. They don't have to cater to any of that shit.

SW: More like the seventies?

PM: Yeah.

SW: Does knowing that you're shooting for TV change the way you're shooting?

PM: Not much. For most people, when they're making movies for the tube, the tendency is to use more close-ups, which I'm pretty sure I did. I think I covered it a lot more than I normally did.

SW: You did. You're cutting more in *Winchell* than in any other of your films.

PM: That's for energy.

SW: Did Herman Kurfeld, the man who Giamatti played, ever see the film?

PM: He loved it. He was on the set a lot, weeping. He *loved* it. He thought Giamatti caught it perfectly, he thought Stanley caught it, he thought I caught it.

SW: Okay, let's talk *Coast to Coast*, written by Frederic Raphael. It's a lot like *Two for the Road*, also a Raphael script.

PM: When I got *Coast to Coast*, I saw it as a strange version of that movie, but thirty years later. They're now no longer thirty and twenty-eight and they've been married a long time. They've got problems with one kid, a daughter who is tough to deal with, and shortly before they leave, Judy Davis's character announces, "I don't want to live with you anymore. I want a divorce. I'm not in love with you." That's what the movie's about. It's not hard to figure out that along the way he's going to try to make a move, there'll be arguments, there'll be accusations, and you'll meet their children.

SW: A cross-country movie and none of it shot in the U.S.?

PM: I shot the whole thing in Toronto, which is no mean feat. Believe me.

SW: Not a single day in America?

PM: Nothing. Not a day. That was a challenge, but don't forget, I also had Richard Dreyfuss and Judy Davis—both pros, *pros*. They made everything easy. [*Beat*] There was only one problem with Judy. I wouldn't even call it a problem. There was a scene in what was supposed to be a fishing village in the Ozarks and I got them drunk, not really drunk, but drunk in the scene. I had a set for their hotel room because the place was impossibly noisy and I wanted control. And here came my big problem. Dreyfuss's character reaches a point when he grabs her and kisses her and they end up making love. She said to me, [*Australian accent*] "I'm not going to make love to him after all he's done to me in this marriage. It's out of the question." I said, "Then I have no movie. What do you want me to do?" She said, "That's your problem." The producer sees me going out of my mind and he says, "What are you going to do? *You're* the director." And I got a little pissed at him. I said, "Why don't you direct it? You tell her what to do!" Schmuck. It was a problem. I had to think about it. I called lunch so I could think. I thought for about twenty or thirty minutes and then I had a brainstorm. I went over to Judy and I said, "Look, it's a mercy fuck. You've been with him for thirty years, he's a little drunk, it ain't going to kill you, get it over with. And during the mercyness of it, you get a little turned on." I didn't use all those exact words, but it was like that. And she said, "Mercy fuck . . . Mercy fuck . . . *that* I can do." And that was it.

sw: I don't understand. How was Judy Davis shocked when she had read the script and knew exactly what was coming?

pm: Doesn't make a difference. Many actors, when it gets to the point of actually doing the scene, suddenly realize that they're incapable of finding justification. Most actors wouldn't do what Judy did, they would fake it. She doesn't work that way. She works from rock-bottom truth. The persona is one of pure intelligence, like Bette Davis. It says, "Don't fuck with me." She could play anything. She has a truth button. It's got to be true or she can't do it. She thinks, "If it's not true, I'll do bad acting, and if I do bad acting, the gods will come down and kill me." It's that kind of mentality. Every actor—including Paul Mazursky—has been given the direction to push more, to have more energy, to do it faster. There's a way to do that very slick so it looks good, but really, it doesn't go deep. I don't want that in my movies. So it takes time. It takes time to get there. The actor needs time to figure it out and so do I as the director. On *Coast to Coast*, I only had thirty-three days. That's tough. At a certain point, about two weeks before we finished, I called Showtime and I said, "I need two more days. You know how I work, but I cannot do this in time unless I rush, rush, rush, and I don't want to do that." About a week before, their line producer showed up and said, "You got your two days" like it was a fucking favor. And I begged them to let me shoot in L.A. I said, "Let me shoot in L.A. and I'll give you a spectacular ending." But I knew we had to end back in Connecticut, so I talked myself out of it.

sw: I know one of the ways you communicate with your cinematographers is by showing them paintings that you want to emulate for the look of your film. Did you show [cinematographer] Jean Lapine the work of any artist for *Coast to Coast*?

pm: Balthus. I showed him Balthus. I don't know why I did, but I was desperate to try to get a look for the movie. Sometimes when Balthus shows places—farmland or countryside—less the human figure, there's an odd and wonderful feeling to it. It's larger than life. So when I show the car driving through the hills, I wanted some of that in there. Jean

Lapine told me it helped him a little bit. [*Beat*] In my home, I have a Balthus print. Mike Nichols, I think, has a real one.

SW: There's a lot of Steadicam in *Coast to Coast*. More than in any other Mazursky picture.

PM: We didn't have a lot of time and we had to move quickly. With Steadicam, you don't have to lay track. And by the way, I don't like the nervous camera. All that handheld. I've used it before the Steadicam, but only because we didn't have anything else. It kept the picture from being stiff. And I don't like to overuse close-ups. But you know that already. They're pushing me toward . . . *feeling something*, whereas I'd rather make up—

The phone rings. Paul takes it.

Tecolote. [*Beat*] Jeff Berg! [*Listens*] You do? Okay . . . Well, Daniel Day-Lewis has passed, but we don't need him. [*Beat*] Okay. [*Beat*] I'm very excited, Jeff. It could be a great movie. Thank you for reading it . . . Okay . . . Okay . . . I would say twenty [million].

Paul's silent, intent, and then his voice drops.

We could probably do it for that, but I think we should start at twenty. Mike [Gruskoff] and I don't expect to make a fortune. [*Beat*] Okay, bye-bye.

He hangs up.

I had the same burn in me when I made *Enemies* . . .

SW: What did Berg say?

PM: He said, "I read it, I loved it, I'm selling it. We're going to get this made."

Paul leaps out of his chair.

Waaaaahoooo! Here we *go*!

Winchell moves at the pace of its subject, racing ahead like an overcaffeinated copy-editor. It stops at nothing, pursues story at all costs, and hits every major biopic plot point along the way. Most of the time you see them coming—the rise, the fall, the scandal, the sex—but when they come you aren't disappointed. "If there is justice in Hollywood," went *Variety*, "then HBO's bracing, flamboyant biopic *Winchell* will be remembered as the vehicle that made full-on stars of Stanley Tucci and Paul Giamatti"—and indeed it is. As Walter Winchell, Stanley Tucci is flashy and magnetic, without losing Winchell to caricature. Paul Giamatti is warm and smart—as compelling a screen nebbish as there ever was—and everyone else keeps apace nicely. But the narrative momentum is so strong, it seems to prevent the actors from getting the most out of their moments. With a little more time there might have been a few more opportunities, or accidents for the actors to enjoy. After all, story in Mazursky isn't reported, it's felt. It isn't what's happening, but what's sensed.

One moment in particular may help us to understand what we're missing. Playing the role of Winchell's father, Mazursky himself begins a scene with a bit of ad-libbed dialogue, something about baseball. The remark is a throwaway, perhaps the least important piece of information in the entire movie—and for that very reason, the most naturalistic and the most compelling. During that brief, seemingly accidental aside, *Winchell*'s narrative train goes off its well-oiled rails into immediate, human terrain. That's when *Winchell* looks most like a Mazursky movie.

You might pitch *Coast to Coast* as *Harry and Tonto* meets *Scenes from a Mall*. But in performance style and dialogue (script, of course, by Frederick Raphael), it represents a marked shift away from the uninhibited emotionalism of Mazursky's best, in a favor of a cooler, quieter, more refined approach to domestic disruption (is it because we're no longer dealing with Jews?). Dreyfuss and Davis don't convey the volatility of the Blumes, the comfort of the Bentons (*An Unmarried Woman*), or the whimsy of the Fifers (*Scenes from a Mall*), but their buried reserve of mutual affection resonates throughout. When they're onscreen together, they're aces. Richard Dreyfuss gives a performance devoid of pandering and smoldering with unrest; and Judy Davis, master of cranky insight, keeps the movie from getting too safe. There's no better drinker in the movies. To watch Judy Davis with a glass of wine is to know her character's mind, and thankfully, in *Coast to Coast*, Mazursky is wise to let her off with a DUI.

Yippee A Journey to Jewish Joy (2006)

David Miretsky: Reb Nachman's approach to Torah is very emotional. It's through the heart. To pray to God, you can only make your voice heard if you do it in happiness and joy.

It's the day after Thanksgiving. Paul's on the phone with his younger daughter, Jill. Their conversation, like most conversations over the past month, is about the WGA strike that began on November 5th. I know that last Friday, after his nine o'clock gathering at the Farmers Market, Paul and some of the others went up to CBS to picket. As the former site of *The Danny Kaye Show*, Mazursky's first steady writing gig in Hollywood, CBS was more than just conveniently located (up the street from the market), it was personal. And for me, there is something appropriate about ending my conversations with Mazursky as two of his favorite causes—Hollywood and revolution—erupt outside his window. Paul says good-bye to Jill, and in a single sweep, hangs up the phone and picks up *Variety*. There is no greeting today, only headlines.

PM: Okay, they're going to try to negotiate again on Monday. [*Reading from* Variety] "The big question: Is the agreement to meet largely a PR move in response to the rising tide of pressure from outside parties affected adversely by the shutdown of so many TV skeins and some previously green-lit pics?" [*Flips the page*] "The writers strike claimed two more casualties Monday. Warner Bros. called off a February production start on *Shantaram*, the Mira Nair-directed adaptation of the Gregory David Roberts novel that was to star Johnny Depp. The Weinstein Co., meanwhile, postponed *Nine*, the Rob Marshall-directed musical that was slated to start production in March with Javier Bardem, Penelope Cruz, Sophia Loren and Marion Cotillard starring. Delays were caused because the scripts weren't ready. Sony previously delayed the Ron Howard-directed *Angels & Demons*, and United Artists halted the Oliver Stone-directed *Pinkville*, citing the same reason." [*Beat*] Wow.

Paul puts down the paper and removes his glasses.

In order for the writers to make their point, which as far as I know has a lot to do with Internet and DVDs, they have to do this. But then the producers will respond with, "Then we'll do more reality shows" and all that. But this strike needs to happen. They've got to raise the number on the DVDs. It's terribly low. [*Beat*] Look, have you ever been to the Writers Guild Theater on Doheny?

SW: Yes. It's tiny.

PM: It's the home base of the Guild, it's the symbol of the writers in this town, and it's like a tiny little living room theater in a town where the DGA has like a masterpiece palace and the Academy on Wilshire is like a shrine. But the Writers Guild Theater has like an old curtain and shitty seats and if a guy with a big head sits in front of you, you don't see. You know what I mean?

SW: Yes, of course.

PM: I'm all for the strike. You see, the problem is, this should have happened years ago. They took the worst deal in the history of mankind, because they weren't yet knowledgeable about the potential of DVD. Their deal was unbearable! [*Really agitated*] There's no television show, there's no movie without a writer. There's *nothing*. Period! There's a blank page—that's it. Without the writer, they got shit. And if they think they can write it themselves, they should get rid of the fucking guilds and see what happens. It's an insult to the craft. It really is. [*Sighs*] Let's not talk about this any more. It's only going to get me worked up. What are we on to today?

SW: *Yippee.*

PM: *Yippee* already? Jesus. We're almost done. What do you want to know?

SW: You've been traveling your whole life, why bring a camera now?

PM: I got tired of not making a movie. I had had so many turndowns—with *An Honest Man* and *Pictures of Fidelman*—that finally I just said to myself, "How much would it cost to shoot this movie about following David Miretsky to Uman?" And I figured out a budget that was something like under fifty thousand dollars. And then I did it.

SW: How long did it take to shoot?

PM: A week.

SW: How much did you know about what you were going to see there?

PM: I had seen pictures of the dancing that was done at Uman, but not much else. I thought it would be an adventure. The worst thing that would happen would be that I would lose some money. So that's what happened. And I fell into all kinds of wonderful pieces of luck.

SW: Like in Munich.

PM: We were laid over in Munich so we went to the Oktoberfest and we saw the Germans singing. I said, "We're doing this! Shoot this! Shoot that! Shoot me here on the train station!" For me it was powerful, because I knew Dachau was ten minutes away. I felt like I was there for Hitler celebration day. Here I am on my way to see the Hassidic Jews praying to a dead rabbi, but first I'm going to shoot the Nazis having a jolly good time.

SW: Had you ever begun a movie with this feeling of not knowing what's going to happen?

PM: No. In most movies that I made, probably all, I'm so into the script that my deepest worries would be a combination of the usual suspects in the anxiety catalogue. I'm talking about, "Did I cast right? Because if I didn't I'm screwed." "Do I know how to make a movie even though I've already made seven, eight, twelve?" It's always the same thing. The night before you start, you're saying to yourself, "I don't know how to do this. Why am I bothering to do this? I don't know how to make a movie! All I can do is say, 'Action!'" And the third concern is, I'm wondering how good the movie is going to be. After all, I don't have that much objectivity. People will see it as a faux pas, as a mistake. But having felt that way so many times, I also know that after a day or two I'll start to feel cocky. [*Laughs*]

SW: So after forty years of moviemaking, you have the same apprehensions.

PM: Always. But, with the documentary, it was worse because it could have led to nothing. Look, we shot the interviews here and they were okay. But what does that mean? I got a series of three interviews shot over a series of a couple of visits, but do I have a movie?

SW: You picked three very different Orthodox Jews to follow through Uman.

PM: Yes, there was David, who read Philip Roth and who made eyeglasses, there was Shmuel Levy, who sang rock and roll and smoked grass—a Hassid without the curls—like a hipster from the old days in the Village, and then finally to meet Reb Tauber, who said that going to Uman for Rosh Hashanah was a life-changing experience. Hard to believe, but they all said it. So I went to see if I would believe it.

SW: Do you believe it?

PM: From their point of view, I do. From my point of view, I don't have to go back. I might some day—I might do a *Yippee* follow-up—but I pretty much got it. What was powerful to see was this celebratory joyousness that I hadn't experienced anywhere else. And it wasn't about God, which I liked. This was rock and roll! They were dancing as they were praying!

SW: When did you know you had a movie?

33. Yippee (2006) The joy of Mazursky.

PM: I started to get excited when I saw the terrible room where we were going to be staying. I knew that I could do funny riffs and talk about the wallpaper and the thing for my neck and the guy snoring—all that stuff was funny. I decided then I could do it with a sense of humor, that I could be a secular Jew. The fact that they welcomed that approach shocked me. And they let me shoot on Shabbat, which I couldn't believe.

SW: Would you say this was the scariest thing in filmmaking you have ever done?

PM: Yes! Throughout the shoot I was worried that I wasn't going to have an ending. I knew I had some good stuff, but I didn't know if I was going to have an ending that would leave you feeling anything. Only after I saw it cut together did I know that I would end the movie shooting myself watching the movie here in the office and end with the joke, Schwartz meets Coen in the garment district.

SW: You have fascinating exchange with Julian Unger toward the end of the movie. When you were shooting that, did you know where it was going to go? In other words, you're thinking as a performer, a director, and interviewer—and all at once—does it take you out of the experience?

PM: Not me. He said this stuff about dancing on the graves of martyrs and I felt like weeping. It took everything I had not to fall apart there because it's so sad, it's so unbearably sad what happened to the Jews, and there's so much of it. That's when I thought I was making something very, very worthwhile, and that it might help explain in some odd way to people who didn't really know how profound this persecution of the Jews was and how the memory of it was still going on in this real way.

SW: It's very revealing that you have this as your penultimate scene. It contains the combination of joy and intense sorrow that we see in so many of your movies, which is actually the Jewish cosmic joke.

PM: Maybe. I don't think Uman changed me. I'm still absolutely one hundred percent secular, I don't believe in a God—when it's over, it's over—but I meant it when I said I gained respect for the Orthodox people, a people who I never understood, a people who looked so ridiculous to me in their coats and hats and hair. But they're not. They could say to me, "Yeah, but did you ever wear a zoot suit?"

SW: A movie that is ostensibly about worship, in the end, becomes about you loving the people around you. That, to me, is an intense statement about the humanitarian instinct in your work.

PM: Sammy, I don't know. I know for this whole book you've been trying to get me to tell you what I think about my life and my work, but the fact is, when I sit down and think about it, I'm afraid it's going to freeze my mind in a way that makes me think that I can't do something because it "isn't me"—whatever that means. I don't even know what me is.

SW: But you have a very striking sense of who you are in relation to your secularism. That's what I'm saying. You've changed in many ways, but in that way, you've always been the same Paul Mazursky.

PM: No, you're right.

SW: And yet, you're putting yourself in a position to reconsider it. It's a very tall order.

PM: It was thrilling to me, but I didn't think of it as about God. When all the Jews are standing around chanting and all that business, my personal feeling was, they weren't thinking about God—this holy enormous unknown—but about Rabbi Nachman, a real man, a human being.

SW: Yes.

PM: Yes. And if *Yippee* were my last film, that would be okay. I wouldn't die from it. It's better than leaving an episode of CSI. Think of the epitaph: PAUL MAZURSKY: HE DID TWO CSI'S.

If being Jewish means feeling joy, then Paul Mazursky is as Orthodox as they come. He nearly says as much in the final moments of *Yippee*: "You're probably wondering, 'What happened to Mazursky?' Was I zapped at the lake? Did I have a religious conversion? Did I find the answers? I'm still not religious. I'm still secular. I'm still the wise guy from Brooklyn. But something did happen to me. I learned a kind of tolerance, and maybe love, affection for David and Shmuel and Rabbi Tauber and Julian Unger and

Aram and all of those guys I was telling jokes to." Mazursky had a wonderful time because he was surrounded by wonderful people. Whether he is making a movie, travelling with his family, or hanging out at the Farmers Market, that's what it all amounts to—the people. It always has. Ask Paul what he recalls of *King Kong*—the first movie he really remembers—and he'll tell you not about the gorilla, but about Carl Hut throwing up on his leg.

Tzadik

Minetta Lane, Fall 2007

PM: Oh boy, what a life!

He leans back in his chair and clasps his hands behind his head.

Betsy and I were in New York this last weekend, as you know, and after waiting and waiting in the freezing cold, we finally got a cab—very hard to get. It's thirty degrees, maybe thirty-five. Cold. *Cold.* We pick up my granddaughters, Kate, who's twenty, and Carly, who's twenty-three, who's off to take a term in Paris—a life that I didn't start leading until I was forty-five. [*Laughs*] In any case, the girls took us to a restaurant on Minetta Lane called La Bella Vitae—the good life. Fan*tas*tic food. Cauliflower pan-roasted with raisins and pine nuts—a magnificent taste. Figs wrapped in prosciutto. Great pasta, great pork, we all shared everything with the whole family there, reaching over each other for the food on the other one's plate and talking and laughing. And seeing Minetta Lane, I have to admit both Betsy and I were moved to tears. It may be that as we get older we're crying a lot, but seeing the Village again, driving past 16 East 11th, where we used to live, seeing the Arch where I picked her up in the park, driving by another apartment on Sullivan Street that she lived in, and then around the corner there was Minetta Lane right around the corner from the Little Red School House. We suddenly felt all those years of stuff we had seen in the Village in that seven or eight years we were there, when the park was safe, when you could leave the door to your apartment open at one o'clock in the morning, when Louie's bar in Sheridan Square would give you two beers for a quarter, where the Italian bartenders were very protective of the college girls and if a wise guy came in to cause trouble with them, a baseball bat would come out from behind the bar—[*Italian accent*] "You lookin' for somethin' buddy?"—and the riffraff would leave. [*Looks away*] Betsy and I realized, as much as we love it, we're really not New Yorkers anymore. We're ex-New Yorkers. It's not that we don't love it, we *do* love it, we always go back, but the city has changed. First of all, most of the people we know are dead. Jules Olitski, Jerry Rapkin, people I knew well . . . We're basically down to Sam Cohn, our friends Will and Dionne, our friend Joanne Jacobson, a great,

34. Betsy and Paul.

great woman, who changes apartments every two years—she just bought a dog for three thousand dollars that doesn't listen to anything she says. And Manhattan is noisier than ever. It's metal and noise. It's *Blade Runner.* Nonstop cursing in Portuguese, Spanish, you name it, but walking through the streets is like playing bumper cars. And Betsy uses a cane now. But we made it everywhere. Oh, and we went to all the museums, to the Met, to MoMA, to the Morgan, but of all of them, the Frick is my favorite. It's unbelievably great. [*Rapturous*] You just walk around half a dozen paintings you've seen many times, and then you sit, you take your coat off, and you listen to the organ music and you look. You just look.

sw: Do you feel like an exile in New York?

pm: I feel older. I can't walk the streets with the energy I used to have. I used to really run through the streets—*run*. And Betsy walks so slow, I have to stop the traffic with one hand so we can cross the street together.

sw: What about Brooklyn? Do you ever go back?

PM: No. I have nothing there.

Mazursky sweeps the air around him.

This is my home now. I love my house. I love my pool. I love my place at the beach. I love the fact that at any given moment I can take a drive to the desert. I love having my grandchildren right nearby, except for the older ones who are grown up now. And when Tommy and Molly, the little ones, get to be grown up, Betsy and I will adopt two kids. We want them to be frisky, wild kids, running around with dogs, so we can race with them in our wheelchairs.

The Films of Paul Mazursky

I Love You, Alice B. Toklas! Warner Brothers, 1968

Director: Hy Averback; **Writers**: Paul Mazursky and Larry Tucker; **Producer**: Charles H. Maguire; **Starring**: Peter Sellers (Harold Fine), Jo Van Fleet (Mrs. Fine), Leigh Taylor-Young (Nancy), Joyce Van Patten (Joyce Miller), David Arkin (Herbie Fine), Herbert Edelman (Murray), Salem Ludwig (Mr. Fine); **Music**: Elmer Bernstein; **Cinematographer**: Philip Lathrop; **Editor**: Robert C. Jones; **Production Designer**: Pato Guzman; **Costumes**: Theadora Van Runkle.

Bob & Carol & Ted & Alice Columbia Pictures, 1969

Director: Paul Mazursky; **Writers**: Paul Mazursky and Larry Tucker; **Producer**: M. J. Frankovich; **Starring**: Natalie Wood (Carol Sanders), Robert Culp (Bob Sanders), Elliott Gould (Ted Henderson), Dyan Cannon (Alice Henderson), Horst Ebersberg (Horst), Lee Bergere (Emilio), Donald F. Muhich (Psychiatrist); **Music**: Quincy Jones; **Cinematographer**: Charles F. Lang; **Editor**: Stuart H. Pappe; **Art Director**: Pato Guzman; **Costumes**: Moss Mabry.

Alex in Wonderland MGM, 1970

Director: Paul Mazursky; **Writers**: Paul Mazursky and Larry Tucker; **Producer**: Larry Tucker; **Starring**: Donald Sutherland (Alex Morrison), Ellen Burstyn (Beth Morrison), Meg Mazursky (Amy Morrison), Glenna Sargent (Nancy), Viola Spolin (Mother), Andre Philippe (Andre), Michael Lerner (Leo), Paul Mazursky (Hal Stern), Federico Fellini (Himself), Jeanne Moreau (Herself); **Music**: Tom O'Horgan; **Cinematographer**: Laszlo Kovacs; **Editor**: Stuart H. Pappe; **Production Designer**: Pato Guzman; **Costumes**: Moss Mabry.

Blume in Love Warner Brothers, 1973

Director: Paul Mazursky; **Writer**: Paul Mazursky; **Producer**: Paul Mazursky; **Associate Producer**: Anthony Ray; **Starring**: George Segal (Stephen Blume), Susan Anspach (Nina Blume), Kris Kristofferson (Elmo Cole), Marsha Mason (Arlene), Shelley Winters (Mrs. Cramer), Donald F. Muhich (Analyst), Paul Mazursky (Hellman); **Music**: Bill Conti; **Cinematographer**: Bruce Surtees; **Editor**: Donn Cambern; **Production Designer**: Pato Guzman; **Costumes**: Joel Schumacher; **Casting**: Nessa Hyams.

Harry and Tonto Twentieth Century Fox, 1974

Director: Paul Mazursky; **Writers**: Josh Greenfeld and Paul Mazursky; **Producer**: Paul Mazursky; **Starring**: Art Carney (Harry Coombes), Herbert Berhghof (Jacob Rivetowski), Avon Long (Leroy), Rashel Novikoff (Mrs. Rothman), Phil Bruns (Burt Coombes), Cliff De Young (Burt Coombes Jr.), Joshua Mostel (Norman Coombes), Dolly Jonah (Elaine Coombes), Melanie Mayron (Ginger), Geraldine Fitzgerald (Jessie Stone), Chief Dan George (Sam Two Feathers), Larry Hagman (Eddie Coombes), Andre Philippe (Chess Player), Sally Marr (Celia), Paul Mazursky (Gay Hustler); **Music**: Bill Conti; **Cinematographer**: Michael C. Butler; **Editor**: Richard Halsey; **Production Designer**: Ted Haworth; **Costumes**: Albert Wolsky; **Casting**: Marion Dougherty.

Next Stop, Greenwich Village Twentieth Century Fox, 1976

Director: Paul Mazursky; **Writer**: Paul Mazursky; **Producers**: Paul Mazursky and Tony Ray; **Starring**: Lenny Baker (Larry Lapinsky), Shelley Winters (Fay Lapinsky), Ellen Greene (Sarah), Lois Smith (Anita), Chris Walken (Robert), Dori Brenner (Connie), Antonio Fargas (Bernstein), Lou Jacobi (Herb), Mike Kellin (Ben Lapinsky), Michael Egan (Herbert), Rashel Novikoff (Mrs. Tupperman), John Ford Noonan (Barney), Jeff Goldblum (Clyde Baxter), Paul Mazursky (Film Director); **Music**: Bill Conti; **Cinematographer**: Arthur Ornitz; **Editor**: Richard Halsey; **Production Designer**: Philip Rosenberg; **Costumes**: Albert Wolsky; **Casting**: Juliet Taylor.

An Unmarried Woman Twentieth Century Fox, 1978

Director: Paul Mazursky; **Writer**: Paul Mazursky; **Producers**: Paul Mazursky and Tony Ray; **Starring**: Jill Clayburgh (Erica Benton), Alan Bates (Saul Kaplan), Michael Murphy (Michael Benton), Lisa Lucas (Patti Benton), Cliff Gorman (Charlie), Pat Quinn (Sue), Kelly Bishop (Elaine), Linda Miller (Jeanette), Andrew Duncan (Bob), Daniel Seltzer (Dr. Jacobs), Matthew Arkin (Phil), Penelope Russianoff (Tanya), Paul Mazursky (Hal); **Music**: Bill Conti; **Cinematographer**: Arthur Ornitz; **Editor**: Stuart H. Pappe; **Production Designer**: Pato Guzman; **Costumes**: Albert Wolsky.

Willie & Phil Twentieth Century Fox, 1980

Director: Paul Mazursky; **Writer**: Paul Mazursky; **Producers**: Paul Mazursky and Tony Ray; **Starring**: Michael Ontkean (Willie Kaufman), Ray Sharkey (Phil D'Amico), Margot Kidder (Jeanette Sutherland), Jan Miner (Maria Kaufman), Tom Brennan (Sal Kaufman), Julie Bovasso (Mrs. D'Amico), Louis Guss (Mr. D'Amico), Kathleen Maguire (Mrs. Sutherland), Kaki Hunter (Patti Sutherland),

Jerry Hall (Karen), Donald F. Muhich (Psychiatrist #1), Laurence Fishburne III (Wilson), Natalie Wood (Herself); **Music**: Claude Bolling and Georges Delerue; **Cinematographer**: Sven Nykvist; **Editor**: Donn Cambern; **Production Designer**: Pato Guzman; **Costumes**: Albert Wolsky; **Casting**: Juliet Taylor.

Tempest Columbia Pictures, 1982

Director: Paul Mazursky; **Writers**: Leon Capetanos and Paul Mazursky; **Producer**: Paul Mazursky; **Starring**: John Cassavetes (Phillip Dimitrius), Gena Rowlands (Antonia Dimitrius), Molly Ringwald (Miranda Dimitrius), Raul Julia (Kalibanos), Susan Sarandon (Aretha Tomalin), Vittorio Gassman (Alonzo), Sam Robards (Freddy), Paul Stewart (Philip's Father), Jackie Gayle (Trinc), Anthony Holland (Sebastian), Jerry Hardin (Harry Gondorf), Lucianna Buchanan (Dolores), Betsy Mazursky (Mrs. Bloomfield), Paul Mazursky (Mr. Bloomfield); **Music**: Stomu Yamashta; **Cinematographer**: Don McAlpine; **Editor**: Donn Cambern; **Production Designers**: Pato Guzman and Gianni Quaranta; **Costumes**: Albert Wolsky; **Casting**: Juliet Taylor.

Moscow on the Hudson Columbia Pictures, 1984

Director: Paul Mazursky; **Writers**: Leon Capetanos and Paul Mazursky; **Producer**: Paul Mazursky; **Co-producer**: Pato Guzman; **Associate Producer**; Geoffrey Taylor; **Starring**: Robin Williams (Vladimir Ivanoff), Maria Conchita Alonso (Lucia Lombardo), Cleavant Derricks (Lionel Witherspoon), Alejandro Rey (Orlando Ramirez), Savely Kramarov (Boris), Elya Baskin (Anatoly Cherkasov), Udo Kier (Gay man on street), Betsy Mazursky (Bloomingdale's manager), Paul Mazursky (Dave); **Music**: David McHugh; **Cinematographer**: Don McAlpine; **Editor**: Richard Halsey; **Production Designer**: Pato Guzman; **Costumes**: Albert Wolsky; **Casting**: Joy Todd.

Down and Out in Beverly Hills Touchstone Pictures, 1986

Director: Paul Mazursky; **Writers**: Leon Capetanos and Paul Mazursky, based on the play "Boudu sauvé des eaux" by Rene Fauchois; **Producer**: Paul Mazursky; **Co-producer**: Pato Guzman; **Associate Producer**; Geoffrey Taylor; **Starring**: Nick Nolte (Jerry Baskin), Richard Dreyfuss (Dave Whiteman), Bette Midler (Barbara Whiteman), Little Richard (Orvis Goodnight), Tracy Nelson (Jenny Whiteman), Elizabeth Pena (Carmen), Evan Richards (Max Whiteman), Donald F. Muhich (Doctor von Zimmer), Valerie Curtin (Pearl Waxman), Paul Mazursky (Sidney Waxman); **Music**: Andy Summers; **Cinematographer**: Don McAlpine; **Editor**: Richard Halsey; **Production Designer**: Pato Guzman; **Costumes**: Albert Wolsky; **Casting**: Ellen Chenoweth.

Moon Over Parador Touchstone Pictures, 1988

Director: Paul Mazursky; **Writers**: Leon Capetanos and Paul Mazursky, based on a story by Charles G. Booth; **Producer**: Paul Mazursky; **Associate Producer**; Gary Shusett; **Starring**: Richard Dreyfuss (Jack Noah/President Alphonse Simms), Raul Julia (Roberto Strausmann), Sonia Braga (Madonna Mendez), Jonathan Winters (Ralph), Fernando Rey (Alejandro), Charo (Madame Loop), Marianna Sägebrecht (Magda), Reinhard Kolldehoff (Gunther), Dana Delany (Jenny), Michael Greene (Clint), Sammy Davis Jr., Dick Cavett, Ike Pappas, Ed Asner (Themselves), Paul Mazursky as "Carlotta Gerson" (Momma); **Music**: Maurice Jarre; **Cinematographer**: Don McAlpine; **Editor**: Stuart H Pappe; **Production Designer**: Pato Guzman; **Costumes**: Albert Wolsky; **Casting**: Ellen Chenoweth and Flavio R. Tambellini.

Enemies, A Love Story Twentieth Century Fox, 1989

Director: Paul Mazursky; **Writers**: Roger L. Simon and Paul Mazursky, based on the novel by Isaac Bashevis Singer; **Producer**: Paul Mazursky; **Co-Producers**: Pato Guzman and Irby Smith; **Executive Producers**: James G. Robinson and Joe Roth; **Associate Producer**; Elizabeth Sayre; **Starring**: Ron Silver (Herman Broder), Lena Olin (Masha), Angelica Huston (Tamara Broder), Margaret Sophie Stein (Yadwiga Broder), Alan King (Rabbi Lembeck), Judith Malina (Masha's Mother), Rita Karin (Mrs. Schreier), Phil Leeds (Pesheles), Elya Baskin (Yasha Kobik), Paul Mazursky (Leon Tortshiner); **Music**: Maurice Jarre; **Cinematographer**: Fred Murphy; **Editor**: Stuart H. Pappe; **Production Designer**: Pato Guzman; **Costumes**: Albert Wolsky; **Casting**: Ellen Chenoweth and Rosina Bucci.

Scenes from a Mall Touchstone Pictures, 1991

Director: Paul Mazursky; **Writers**: Roger L. Simon and Paul Mazursky; **Producer**: Paul Mazursky; **Co-Producers**: Pato Guzman and Patrick McCormick; **Associate Producer**; Stuart Pappe; **Starring**: Bette Midler (Deborah Fifer), Woody Allen (Nick Fifer), Bill Irwin (Mime), Daren Firestone (Sam), Rebecca Nickles (Jennifer), Paul Mazursky (Doctor Hans Clava); **Music**: Marc Shaiman; **Cinematographer**: Fred Murphy; **Editor**: Stuart H. Pappe; **Production Designer**: Pato Guzman; **Costumes**: Albert Wolsky; **Casting**: Joy Todd.

The Pickle Columbia Pictures, 1993

Director: Paul Mazursky; **Writer**: Paul Mazursky; **Producer**: Paul Mazursky; **Co-Producer**: Stuart Pappe; **Executive Producer**: Patrick McCormick; **Starring**: Danny Aiello (Harry Stone), Dyan Cannon (Ellen Stone), Clotilde Courau (Françoise), Shelley Winters (Yetta), Barry Miller (Ronnie Liebowitz), Jerry Stiller

(Phil Hirsch), Chris Penn (Gregory Stone), Little Richard (President), Rebecca Miller (Carrie), Stephen Tobolowsky (Mike Krakower), Caroline Aaron (Nancy Osborne), Ally Sheedy (Molly Girl/Herself), Spalding Gray (Doctor), Griffin Dunne (Actor/Himself), Paul Mazursky (Butch Levine); **Music**: Michel Legrand; **Cinematographer**: Fred Murphy; **Editor**: Stuart H. Pappe; **Production Designer**: James Bissell; **Costumes**: Albert Wolsky; **Casting**: Carrie Frazier and Shani Ginsberg.

Faithful New Line Cinema, 1996

Director: Paul Mazursky; **Writer**: Chazz Palminteri, based on his play; **Producers**: Robert De Niro and Jane Rosenthal; **Co-Producer**: Geoffrey Taylor; **Associate Producer**; Henry Bronchtein; **Executive Producer**: Dan Lauria and Peter Gatien; **Starring**: Cher (Margaret Connor), Chazz Palminteri (Tony), Ryan O'Neal (Jack Connor), Paul Mazursky (Dr. Susskind), Stephen Spinella (Young Man at Rolls), Jeffrey Wright (Young Man at Rolls); **Music**: Phillip Johnston; **Cinematographer**: Fred Murphy (Conrad Hall uncredited); **Editor**: Nicholas C. Smith; **Production Designer**: Jeffrey Townsend; **Costumes**: Hope Hanafin; **Casting**: Ellen Chenoweth.

Winchell HBO, 1998

Director: Paul Mazursky; **Writer**: Scott Abbott, based on *Walter Winchell: His Life and Times* by Herman Klurfeld; **Producer**: Stan Wlodkowski; **Executive Producer**: Rob Fried; **Co-Executive Producer**: Richard Zinman; **Starring**: Stanley Tucci (Walter Winchell), Paul Giamatti (Herman Klurfeld), Glenne Headly (Dallas Wayne), Christopher Plummer (Franklin D. Roosevelt), Xander Berkeley (Gavreau), Kevin Tighe (William Randolph Hearst), Paul Mazursky (Winchell's Father); **Music**: Bill Conti; **Cinematographer**: Robbie Greenberg; **Editor**: Stuart Pappe; **Production Designer**: Marcia Hinds-Johnson; **Costumes**: Hope Hanafin; **Casting**: Juel Bestrop.

Coast to Coast Showtime, 2003

Director: Paul Mazursky; **Writer**: Frederic Raphael, based on his novel; **Producer**: Michael Levine; **Executive Producers**: Jerry Leider and Richard Waltzer; **Starring**: Richard Dreyfuss (Barnaby Pierce), Judy Davis (Maxine Pierce), Maximilian Schell (Casimir), Selma Blair (Stacey Pierce), Fred Ward (Hal Kressler), Saul Rubinek (Gary Pereira), David Julian Hirsh (Benjamin Pierce), Paul Mazursky (Stanly Tarto); **Music**: Bill Conti; **Cinematographer**: Jean Lapine; **Editor**: Richard Halsey; **Production Designer**: Tamara Deverell; **Costumes**: Anne Dixon; **Casting**: Robin D. Cook.

Yippee: A Journey to Jewish Joy Tecolote Productions, 2006

Director: Paul Mazursky; **Producers**: Milton Kim and Paul Mazursky; **Co-Producers**: Jeff Kanew, Bill Megalos, and Steve Cody; **With**: Paul Mazursky, David Miretsky, Shmuel Levy, Ezriel Tauber, Dr. Julian Unger; **Music**: Walter Wezowa; **Cinematographer**: Bill Megalos; **Editor**: Jeff Kanew.

Index

Entries in bold are films directed by Paul Mazursky.

A SERIES FROM WESLEYAN UNIVERSITY PRESS

Edited by Lisa Dombrowski and Scott Higgins

ORIGINATING EDITOR: Jeanine Basinger

SAM WASSON is the *New York Times* bestselling author of *Fifth Avenue, 5 A.M.: Audrey Hepburn, Breakfast at Tiffany's, and the Dawn of the Modern Woman* and *A Splurch in the Kisser: The Movies of Blake Edwards.* Currently, he's working on a biography of Bob Fosse. He lives in Los Angeles.

Library of Congress Cataloging-in-Publication Data

Mazursky, Paul.

Paul on Mazursky / Sam Wasson [interviewer].

    p. cm. — (Wesleyan film)

Includes index.

Includes filmography.

ISBN 978-0-8195-7143-4 (cloth : alk. paper)

1. Mazursky, Paul—Interviews. 2. Motion picture producers and

directors—United States—Interviews.

I. Wasson, Sam. II. Title.

PN1998.3.M339A3 2011

791.4302'33092—dc22

[B]   2010052094